FAITH AND THE FRAGILITY OF JUSTICE

FAITH AND THE FRAGILITY OF JUSTICE

Responses to Gender-Based Violence in South Africa

MEREDITH WHITNAH

RUTGERS UNIVERSITY PRESS
New Brunswick, Camden, and Newark, New Jersey
London and Oxford

Rutgers University Press is a department of Rutgers, The State University of New Jersey, one of the leading public research universities in the nation. By publishing worldwide, it furthers the University's mission of dedication to excellence in teaching, scholarship, research, and clinical care.

Library of Congress Cataloging-in-Publication Data

Names: Whitnah, Meredith Chase, author.
Title: Faith and the fragility of justice : responses to gender-based violence in South Africa / Meredith Whitnah.
Description: New Brunswick : Rutgers University Press, 2025. | Includes bibliographical references and index.
Identifiers: LCCN 2024040400 | ISBN 9781978838635 (paperback) | ISBN 9781978838642 (hardcover) | ISBN 9781978838659 (epub) | ISBN 9781978838666 (pdf)
Subjects: LCSH: Gender-based violence—South Africa—Religious aspects. | Women—Violence against—South Africa—Religious aspects. | Anti-apartheid movements—South Africa—Religious aspects. | Christianity and justice—South Africa.
Classification: LCC HV6250.3.S6 W45 2025 | DDC 362.880968—dc23/eng/20240829
LC record available at https://lccn.loc.gov/2024040400

A British Cataloging-in-Publication record for this book is available from the British Library.

Copyright © 2025 by Meredith Whitnah
All rights reserved

No part of this book may be reproduced or utilized in any form or by any means, electronic or mechanical, or by any information storage and retrieval system, without written permission from the publisher. Please contact Rutgers University Press, 106 Somerset Street, New Brunswick, NJ 08901. The only exception to this prohibition is "fair use" as defined by U.S. copyright law.

References to internet websites (URLs) were accurate at the time of writing. Neither the author nor Rutgers University Press is responsible for URLs that may have expired or changed since the manuscript was prepared.

♾ The paper used in this publication meets the requirements of the American National Standard for Information Sciences—Permanence of Paper for Printed Library Materials, ANSI Z39.48-1992.

rutgersuniversitypress.org

For John and Nina Whitnah, who cultivated
my commitment to love, truth, and justice.
And in loving memory of Mary Ellen Konieczny,
who inspires me, still, to dream bigger.

CONTENTS

	Introduction	1
	PART I: THE FORMATION AND REPRODUCTION OF THEOLOGICAL CULTURES	
1	Racial Positioning and Theological Cultures in the Fight against Apartheid	19
2	Continuity of Theological Cultures in an Emerging Democracy	49
	PART II: THE POWER OF THEOLOGICAL CULTURES FOR GENDER-BASED VIOLENCE AND GENDER JUSTICE	
3	Theological Cultures and Gender-Based Violence	77
4	Theological Cultures and the Fragility of Gender Justice	104
5	Implications for Actions	133
	Conclusion	149
	Appendix A: Key Features of the Theological Cultures	155
	Appendix B: Sources, Case Selection, and Standpoint	156
	Acknowledgments	161
	Notes	165
	References	193
	Index	207

FAITH AND THE FRAGILITY OF JUSTICE

INTRODUCTION

> This is what healing demands. Behavior that is hurtful, shameful, abusive, or demeaning must be brought into the fierce light of truth, and truth can be brutal... But if we want real forgiveness and real healing, we must face the real injury.
> —Desmond Tutu and Mpho Tutu

Anglican archbishop Desmond Tutu and his daughter Reverend Mpho Tutu wrote these words in a 2014 book on the power of forgiveness. Desmond Tutu was an important leader in the anti-apartheid movement, winning the Nobel Peace Prize for his efforts in 1984. He continued to be a prominent religious figure in the post-apartheid democracy, from the time he convened the Truth and Reconciliation Commission (TRC) after the end of apartheid to his public appearances at events and publication of multiple books on themes of justice, reconciliation, and forgiveness.[1] Indeed, his support for a broad range of justice issues has made him one of the most important prophetic Christian voices of the late twentieth and early twenty-first centuries.

And yet, the difficult truth is that Tutu and other prominent South African religious leaders who have been adamant that the Christian faith requires its adherents to pursue justice and enact love have not always attended to all forms of hurtful and abusive behavior, especially regarding gender. In June 1985, a few months after Tutu left his post as general secretary of the South African Council of Churches (SACC) to become bishop of Johannesburg, the SACC convened for its annual National Conference. The conference was intended to focus on women, with the theme "Women, a Power for Change." But, given the escalating political violence at the time, the conference newsletter reported that they pivoted from the original theme, as "events from outside overruled, and the agenda was radically changed to deal with life and death issues."[2]

From our historical vantage point, this separation between the 1985 conference's intended focus on women and "life and death issues" is significant. South Africa has repeatedly made international headlines with accounts of gender-based violence (GBV). Reported rates of rape and intimate partner homicide are among the highest in the world.[3] After the country was dubbed "the rape capital of the world" by a variety of news sources in the 1990s, the issue has continued to saturate media accounts, receive government attention, and spark controversy.[4] For instance, in March 2012 a group of young men gang-raped a seventeen-year-old girl who was reported to have the mental capabilities of a five-year-old. A video recording of this incident was widely circulated on the internet a month later, garnering international outrage.

That was five days before I first traveled to South Africa to conduct research on how religious organizations that had resisted apartheid have also addressed GBV. Religion's involvement in supporting or mitigating violence is a central concern in our contemporary global context. We know that the same religious beliefs and traditions can motivate social engagement for violence or for peace. We also know that institutions and organizations play a key role in producing conceptions of violence that sustain racial, gendered, and other dimensions of social inequality. Yet, the role that religious institutions play in contributing to or challenging race-based violence, GBV, and inequality remains under-addressed.

Faith and the Fragility of Justice fills this gap through a historical, qualitative, and comparative study of three Protestant Christian nongovernmental organizations (NGOs) in South Africa that resisted the racial injustice and violence of apartheid but have varied in their perceptions of and practical responses to GBV. The book addresses three questions: What factors explain the connections and disconnections between religious challenges to racial injustice and efforts to address gender injustice? Why do organizations vary in their recognition of racialized and gendered violence? And how, then, do their different perceptions of such violence impact their practical attempts to address it?

The central argument of the book is that the organizations' theological convictions intersect with their posture toward various social groups to shape their actions. I use the term "theological cultures" to refer to the patterns of intersecting beliefs and social positioning that shape the organizations' responses to social issues. I show that the pursuit of justice is dependent not only upon their racial, gendered, and structural characteristics (such as their financial resources and relation to the government), as we might expect. Their actions are also dependent upon their particular theological claims. In making this argument, *Faith and the Fragility of Justice* demonstrates that religious beliefs are a central dimension of institutional processes that sustain or challenge social inequality and violence. The book shows that enacting justice is a fragile endeavor, as it demonstrates how the religious recognition of racial inequality and violence can both facilitate and constrain responses to gender inequality and violence.

At the same time, the theological convictions that motivate religious organizations' actions are not produced in an institutional vacuum but are conditioned by various social factors. This is not a new sociological claim. Indeed, an extensive body of research on religion and social inequality illuminates the ways that the social structures of race, class, and gender impact religious institutions. But I also add a different dimension to our understanding of the role of social contexts in religious responses to social issues. I demonstrate that the organizations focus on, have varying access to, and sometimes identify with, particular social groups in their discourse. This includes groups that are formed on the basis of race, gender, and economic status, such that the organizations focus in distinct ways on blacks and whites, men and women, and the rich and the poor. They are also oriented to the state in different ways. I refer to these postures toward different social groups as a "web of social positioning." This positioning intersects with the organizations' theological beliefs to shape their actions.

What I am describing here is not a static, deterministic structure, but a dynamic, contingent process that unfolds over time and across various social problems. Throughout the chapters that follow, I show that there is a particular path that the organizations follow as they cultivate theological cultures that are transposed from race to gender. This path is shaped by various factors, including their financial stability, composition of their staff, and relation to their constituencies. In the midst of these complicated social dynamics, the theological cultures forge distinct paths across time and from racial to gendered violence.

The path a theological culture follows can result in a partial response to GBV. The SACC's theological convictions centered on the belief that a liberating God took the side of the poor, and the church was to enter into suffering solidarity with the oppressed. These theological convictions were powerfully applied to their solidarity with the majority black population struggling for freedom from apartheid. But, as the vignette above implies, these beliefs intersected with a posture toward women that was ambivalent about whether they, too, were a marginalized group. And yet, women in the organization also drew on the SACC's theological convictions to argue for their equal dignity and challenge sexism. These internal tensions over women's liberation result in a partial practical response to GBV.

A theological culture can also facilitate a strong response to GBV. The Pietermaritzburg Agency for Christian Social Awareness (PACSA), the second organization profiled in the book, centered their theological justification for fighting apartheid in the belief that God's redemptive work involved Christians working to transform unjust social systems into just ones.[5] These theological convictions intersect with a posture of empathy toward the suffering black population and critique of white people who are complicit in that suffering, calling on them instead to seek out the marginalized and enter into concrete actions of solidarity. For PACSA, there is also a theological mandate to transform the unjust system of patriarchy in order to attend to suffering women. Part of that process must include men recognizing and seeking to change their role in the problem. PACSA develops a robust practical response to GBV.

Finally, a theological culture can also prevent a strong response to GBV. African Enterprise (AE), the third organization profiled in the book, suggests that justice is achieved through reconciliation. For AE, God ordains a particular order for social life that is centered on right relationships, both with God and with other people. Relational alienation is a violation of God's way, which can be healed through both spiritual and social reconciliation. While the reconciliation theological culture facilitated AE's explicit condemnation of racial injustice, it does not translate to gender. I show that their focus on God's order for society also includes the belief that gender roles are God-ordained. These theological convictions intersect with a posture toward women that recognizes the brokenness of their lives but does not critique sexism. AE does not develop any programs to address GBV.

This argument about the power of theological convictions that intertwine with organizations' social positioning to shape their actions is both anti-reductionistic and anti-deterministic. On the first point, I mean that while religious convictions are formed within particular social environments, we also cannot reduce them to underlying social factors. On the second point, I mean that while a particular path is forged, such that once the particular religious convictions are formed they are remarkably powerful, the path could also have gone differently. Throughout the book, I highlight the ways that these organizations' religious convictions intersect with their social positioning in ways that shape their actions. I also point out the contingencies that were at work in this process. In so doing, *Faith and the Fragility of Justice* elucidates the complex intersection of race, gender, and religion within institutions that play an important role in either resisting or supporting social inequality and violence.

INSTITUTIONS AND INTERSECTIONALITY

Today, the term "intersectionality" is commonly used to refer to the way that people navigate their lives in different ways based on their race, gender, sexual orientation, and other features of their individual identities.[6] But the thinkers who first developed the concept posited that intersectionality also happens institutionally. As they did so, they contended that violence maintains intersectional oppression. For instance, legal scholar Kimberlé Crenshaw's articulation of the concept originated in her observations that legal institutions failed to account for the ways that black women's experiences of violence were shaped by the ways that racism and sexism function together, not separately.[7] And sociologist Patricia Hill Collins contends both that violence is a mechanism that supports intersecting systems of oppression, and that social institutions and organizations are an essential part of this process because they produce and reproduce our very definitions of what constitutes violence.[8]

Intersectionality is, thus, a helpful analytic lens for sharpening our ability to see the role of institutions in reinforcing racist and patriarchal systems that use violence to maintain power. It is also helpful for illuminating how these processes work with respect both to those who are most vulnerable in these systems and those who benefit from them. Indeed, as racism and sexism intersect with one another, whiteness and maleness are often considered to be the norm or the default, from which the "other" categories diverge. Hae Yeon Choo and Myra Marx Ferree thus point out that we need to attend both to "unmarked categories" (e.g., white, male, rich, etc.) and to "marked categories" (e.g., black, female, poor, etc.) in systems of intersecting axes of power.[9] Naming these patterns is important for recognizing and reckoning with the workings of power in complex social systems.

Implied in much of this work is the understanding that organizations and institutions position themselves in different ways to different social groups, in ways that have practical consequences. This book makes that insight more explicit. I illuminate the way organizations cultivate a web of positioning that shapes their actions. That is, the groups have different postures toward various social groups, including blacks and whites, men and women, and the rich and the poor. Particular patterns of both focusing on and identifying with these groups are forged in their public discourse. These patterns have implications for their practical attention to GBV.

THE FRAGILITY OF INTERSECTIONAL JUSTICE

In making this argument, I build on the work of numerous scholars who have illuminated the ways that tensions often emerge around the incorporation of different groups and their particular concerns *within* the very communities and movements that are working to address unjust social relations. Sometimes racial and gender inequalities are reified within the very groups that are seeking to promote broader social change. In the United States, for instance, the first-wave feminist movement emerged, at least in part, in response to women's experience of marginalization within the abolitionist movement.[10] We also know that many white women in the suffrage movement capitalized on their racial privilege to secure the vote, excluding black women from these processes.[11] In the U.S. civil rights movement, tensions emerged over the incorporation of women's concerns with sexual and reproductive justice.[12] And black women within the civil rights movement were often marginalized within the ranks of the civil rights organizations that were most prominent.[13]

Similar patterns emerge in contexts beyond the United States. Studies of women's participation in liberation movements, for instance, have found that women have often experienced social and cultural constraints as they participate in broader movements for social change, as their participation may challenge existing norms around women's place in society. But sometimes their status, especially as wives and mothers, also works to their advantage as they deploy these identities to support the broader movements of which they are a part. Indeed, sometimes women deploy explicitly feminist claims about women's equal dignity to men's to argue for social change, while other times they rely on gender essentialist norms about their capacities as mothers.[14] Thus, tensions sometimes exist between a specific focus on women's experiences of oppression because of sexism and their contributions to social change.

The stakes of these tensions are particularly high when we consider GBV. Reflecting the central insight of intersectional theory that violence plays a crucial role in maintaining intersecting systems of oppression, oftentimes gendered violence has been deployed as a strategy to maintain both racial and gendered power. From the U.S. context, we know that rape was used as an instrument of control of enslaved black populations, and that the trope of a black man raping a white woman was often used as a pretext for racial terrorism in the form of lynching.[15] In contexts of war and racial or ethnic conflict, rape is often used against both men and women.[16]

Throughout the world, people have mobilized over the last few decades both to call attention to the reality of GBV and to work against it.[17] But even in recent instances of conflict, a clear pattern has emerged: these are not typically the first stories we hear.[18] A tendency to minimize or fail to recognize the way that GBV operates as a dimension of interlocking systems of power continues in our contemporary context. There are many reasons for this, but one of them is undoubtedly the role of important social institutions in masking our attention to the realities of this form of violence. This book focuses on one such institution: religion.

As Patricia Hill Collins observed in her early analysis of the role of violence in maintaining intersecting systems of power, "Definitions of violence lie not in acts themselves but in how groups controlling positions of authority conceptualize such acts."[19] She goes on to state, "Violence sanctioned by individuals controlling authoritative social institutions, typically the government, religion or just plain old tradition, becomes legitimated."[20] Collins perceives that religion plays a crucial role in upholding intersecting systems of power through its capacity as a legitimating institution. But she and many other intersectional theorists and thinkers have tended not to spell out the reasons why. That is, what are the specific features of religion that give it this kind of power? My contention is that we must recognize, and reckon with, the ways in which religion plays a distinct role in these processes, as it produces and reproduces theological convictions that are mobilized to buttress—but sometimes also to challenge—the violence that sustains the workings of power.

RELIGION AS A DIMENSION OF INTERSECTIONALITY

The lack of significant attention to the role of religion in sustaining intersecting systems of power is surprising, given the extensive body of empirical work that demonstrates the important role religious institutions play in producing and reproducing beliefs that shape people's actions in the world. Put simply, work in ethnic and gender studies that focuses on intersectionality has tended not to develop a robust account of religion's role. At the same time, work in the sociology of religion that attends to social inequality has tended not to develop a robust account of intersectionality. But a growing body of interdisciplinary scholarship has illuminated that theological convictions are institutionally formed in ways that reflect and reinforce racial and gender systems.[21]

Sociologist Melissa Wilde has recently coined the term "complex religion" to refer to the ways religion intertwines with other social constructs.[22] In her own work on denominations' positions on contraception in the United States, Wilde argues that, while some theological convictions matter, social structural factors of race and class provide the key explanatory power.[23] I extend the complex religion approach by showing how the inverse can also be true. That is, in the cases I study, theological beliefs have a distinct power of their own to shape the organizations' responses to GBV, even as they also intertwine with the organizations' social positioning.

This insight about the role of religion in supporting systems of inequality, and the violence that sustains them, needs to be tempered by the recognition that religion is not only in the service of the powerful. In fact, as one of the founders of sociology, Max Weber, contended, religion has a capacity both to be shaped by and to shape other social spheres.[24] This insight is particularly important when we look at the role of religion in violence and peace-making. A significant body of empirical evidence suggests that, as historian Scott Appleby puts it, religion actually has ambivalent tendencies.[25] That is, the same religious tradition can motivate actions for violence or for peace. Religion can certainly be used to justify violence. This has been true historically, but has held particular resonance recently, as violent acts against civilians that have been motivated by religious convictions have received significant public attention.[26] But religion can also provide significant resources for active resistance to unjust social systems.[27] And it can be a resource for peace-making.[28] Religious activism can encompass a range of material and symbolic factors, from religious buildings generally being safe spaces for groups of people to gather to the cultivation of norms and values that motivate involvement in social life against unjust social structures.[29]

What has tended not to be taken into account in this work is the ways that religious traditions that are cultivated to respond to one form of injustice and violence may both facilitate and constrain efforts to respond to other forms of injustice and violence. Indeed, recent groundbreaking work on religion's intersections with the systems of race and gender has foregrounded attention to one or the other—not fully investigating the ways that religion's intersection with race may also matter for its intersection with gender, and vice versa.[30] In this book, I interrogate the connections and disconnections among these social constructs, as I examine how significant attention to one of these social realities does not necessarily translate into attention to the other.

MECHANISMS OF INTERCONNECTIONS

What are the mechanisms that shape these patterns of connection and disconnection? And how does it happen that religious institutions' theological convictions intersect with their social positioning to shape their actions? As I stated above, what I describe in this book is not a static or fixed pattern, but a dynamic and contingent process. Indeed, the process that is at work here is akin to what Jason Kaufman describes as "endogenous cultural change."[31] That is, the social power of the organizations' theological cultures is seen as we examine how their discourse and actions concerning the apartheid system shapes their subsequent discourse and actions around GBV.

This remarkable continuity is due to the fact that the theological cultures forge a specific path within each organization. The term "path dependency" is sometimes used by sociologists and other scholars to describe the ways that events create a chain reaction that determines what follows.[32] This concept can help to illuminate the ways the theological cultures follow a distinct path that shapes their responses to different social issues across time. There are powerful mechanisms at work in the interplay between the cultural production of theological convictions and the organizations' particular postures to different social groups. Once formed, the theological cultures prove remarkably durable across time and across social issues.

But there is a danger in using the concept of path dependency in overly deterministic ways.[33] For the organizations I study, it is clear that things could have happened differently. The theological cultures adapt, are malleable, and their practical expressions are shaped by various contingencies, including the organizations' economic resources and relation to the state. Attending to this tension between durability and malleability is important if we are to fully understand and reckon with the role of religious institutions in challenging and upholding intersecting systems of power.

RACE, GENDER, AND RELIGION IN SOUTH AFRICA

South Africa is an interesting and important place to examine the ways that theological convictions intersect with organizations' social positioning to shape their actions. Both historically and today, religion has played a significant role in both supporting and challenging racial and gendered inequality and violence. Historically, Christianity was intertwined with the processes of colonization and their resultant political systems.[34] Yet, tensions existed within missionaries' ideology and their accompanying practices. In fact, as historian Richard Elphick has documented, institutional and ideological support for equality existed within the missionary context, but it was ultimately subordinated to the push for "separate development" that garnered religious ideological support and paved the way for apartheid as a system.[35]

Indeed, religious beliefs were a crucial part of the design and implementation of apartheid, a system of legal segregation based on racial categories that was in place from 1948 to 1994.[36] A particular interpretation of Calvinist doctrine was deployed to buttress the creation and implementation of apartheid policies.[37] And multiple leaders in the various iterations of the apartheid regime had ties to the Dutch Reformed Church and its theologies. This included D. F. Malan, who became prime minister in 1948 and was a former Dutch Reformed clergyman.[38] Andries Treurnicht, who was a key architect of educational programs that led to uprisings in the townships in the late 1970s, had also served as a Dutch Reformed clergyman.[39]

But religious actors also occupied a prominent position of resistance to apartheid, both nationally and internationally.[40] Leaders publicly denounced apartheid and organized peaceful protests, which sometimes resulted in their detainment and torture.[41] Religious organizations that already existed made the dismantling of apartheid a central part of their mission.[42] Debates about the appropriateness of religiously motivated engagement against the unjust structures of apartheid resulted in conflicts within religious denominations, including in the Dutch Reformed Churches.[43] These conflicts had partly to do with contentions that religious congregations and authorities were turning a blind eye to the unjust situation, but they also entailed the recognition that religious beliefs were clearly intertwined with the apartheid ideology and Afrikaner nationalist identity.[44] Some argued that a particular stream of Calvinist belief was so central to the apartheid system that only an equally powerful theological remedy could undo its impact.[45]

There is thus a clear pattern in South Africa of religious beliefs playing a crucial role in both mobilizing resistance and supporting a social and political system that entailed devastating inequality and violence. We can clearly see contrasts and patterns in South Africa that also exist across the globe regarding the ways in which religious beliefs can spark resistance to or reinforce social inequality and oppression.

These patterns are also true for gender. While the intersections of gender and religion in the apartheid era in South Africa have historically received comparatively little attention, gender was a very salient dynamic of the anti-apartheid movement.[46] Apartheid was a gendered system, seen especially in the realm of domestic work as well as the government's policies of forced removals to enforce segregation and build up a migrant labor system.[47] And women were involved in overturning apartheid in a variety of ways, sometimes with an explicit feminist ideology underpinning their actions, but often not.[48] Women participated in the African National Congress, the major political party of the liberation movement, and they mobilized to assert their rights in the democratic transition. Their activism contributed to a vibrant, if tumultuous, conversation about the need to recognize women's contributions to the struggle against apartheid.[49]

Women's involvement in the struggle and the development of concern for women's rights in South Africa mirrors a trend that has been established in recent years by scholars of women's movements, particularly in majority world countries.[50] We know from these studies that women are involved in liberation movements in a variety of ways, and that there are often tensions that exist between such movements and the explicitly stated needs and demands of women.[51] These studies have pointed out the importance of understanding women's multidimensional participation in the civil sphere, even as they also highlight the ways that patriarchal factors constrain women's freedom and contributions.

What has been far less documented is the way in which religion has had comparable significance for gender with respect to these movements to overturn unjust structures.[52] Within the South African context, we know that religion has been and continues to be an important site for the production and cultivation of beliefs that can validate or confront gendered injustice, including GBV.[53] We also know that gender emerged as a concern for some of these religious groups with the development of feminist contextual theology, and especially in the democratic era with the rise of HIV/AIDS.[54] But there has also been a tendency in the broader scholarship on religion's role in pursuing justice in South Africa to treat gender as an issue that emerged in the early democracy.[55] The historical evidence I present in this book challenges such a presumption, especially with the case of the SACC.

The stakes of both scholarly and practical attention to religious organizations' inclusion and exclusion of gender are particularly high when we consider the case of GBV. As I noted earlier, South Africa has one of the highest rates of GBV in the world. Public awareness of and attention to the problem mirrors a global pattern of growing concern in the late 1970s and 1980s.[56] South Africa's Rape Crisis Center was founded in 1976, which coincided with a period of renewed anti-apartheid protests.[57] The prevalence of GBV has also increased since the democratic transition, as has the attention it receives.[58] While the role of religion in the problem remains understudied, some empirical work has demonstrated that religious leaders, churches, and faith-based organizations have sometimes emerged as key actors who offer both spiritual and practical support to try to address the problem. But these efforts are complicated by the ways that these religious entities can also perpetuate the subordination of women through their teaching and practices.[59]

Several studies on gender and GBV in South Africa have also pointed out that there has been a tendency to downplay or minimize the severity of GBV, both within the liberation movement and in the post-apartheid context. Political scientist Shireen Hassim notes that when accounts of domestic violence emerged in women's community groups during apartheid, the response from the wider political leadership was "contradictory"—that is, they wanted to facilitate women's participation in the liberation movement but did not necessarily see GBV as part of the problems that the movement needed to address.[60] Others have pointed to the lack of adequate attention to the realities of sexual violence in the testimonies that were given to the TRC in the post-apartheid context. These analyses highlight how the process itself was not conducive to women narrating either their experiences of such violence or of the broader implications of such violence, nor did it make space for men who had experienced sexual violence to recount their experiences.[61]

But these accounts of a failure to attend to GBV both during the struggle against apartheid and in attempts to promote healing from its trauma have not attended to the role of religion in shaping these processes of inattention to the gendered dimensions of GBV. This lack of attention to religion is surprising, given the well-established importance of religious actors and organizations both to the anti-apartheid struggle and to the workings of the TRC.[62] This book thus fills a critical gap in our knowledge. Existing scholarship on South Africa has tended either to attend to the ways that religious convictions motivate engagement against racial injustice without focusing on gender, or to attend to the complexities involved in mobilization against gendered injustice without examining religion. I call our attention to the *fragility* of justice by examining how the religious convictions that were deployed to challenge racial injustice and violence shape organizations' discourse and actions about gender injustice and violence.

THE ORGANIZATIONS

Case Selection and Data

I selected the SACC, AE, and PACSA because they share some important characteristics. As I describe in more detail in appendix B, there has been a proliferation of NGOs in South Africa, and many groups are doing important work to address GBV. Thus, I originally thought I might include a combination of organizations that were founded pre- and post-apartheid, and introduce that important variation as a possible part of the story of what makes for effective responses to GBV. But as I encountered these three organizations, I realized that the more interesting puzzle was this: These multiracial, Protestant Christian, ecumenical organizations had agreed that apartheid was wrong, and that Christians needed to take actions to challenge it. But they seemed to have very different responses to GBV. I wanted to know why.

Thus, I limited my case selection to groups that were established well before the end of apartheid and continued on into the democracy. The time period I study spans from the late 1970s, when PACSA was founded, the latest of the three organizations, through 2004. The book thus covers the emergence of a third and final wave of protest against the apartheid regime, beginning in the late 1970s and continuing through the 1980s, through the transition to democracy in 1990, and about a decade following the democratic elections of 1994. Examining these critical years allows us to trace the production and reproduction of theological cultures across time and across social issues.

I also limited the analysis to Protestant Christian groups that were not connected to a particular denomination but rather were explicitly ecumenical. All three have emphasized the importance of bringing churches together across denominational barriers. In general, they have not been connected to the African Initiated Churches (AICs), though the SACC in particular made attempts to bridge from the mainline denominations to the AICs. Instead, all have been more connected to the mainline missionary churches. They have each increasingly incorporated strands of Pentecostalism as the religious landscape has changed over time. They have also each been multiracial. And they all have an international dimension, especially in terms of their funding sources.

There are also some important patterns of variation, in terms of the degree to which the organizations are embedded in a local community (PACSA) versus occupying a higher national and international profile (SACC and AE). Their internal organizational structures, constituencies, and relation to the political sphere are also different, as I describe in more detail below. These differences all have consequences for how the organizations address GBV. However, as I shall show, their different responses to GBV cannot be reduced to these organizational characteristics. The intersection of their theological convictions with their social positioning has explanatory power beyond these structural factors.

To investigate the ways the organizations' theological cultures are publicly expressed and institutionally concretized, I gathered and analyzed over five thousand pages of archival materials. In South Africa, I collected archival data from PACSA and AE's repositories, the Alan Paton Centre at the University of KwaZulu Natal in Pietermaritzburg, and the Historical Papers Library at the University of the Witwatersrand in Johannesburg. I later realized that there were some holes in the archival materials from the SACC and AE, in particular, so I collected and analyzed additional archival material from Yale University, Wheaton College, and an online repository of some of the SACC's materials to address these gaps. The data include public statements, sermon texts, newsletters, annual reports, and correspondence. For context and background, I also read and analyzed the published works of several of the leaders of the organizations, as well as published histories and essays about the organizations.

South African Council of Churches

The SACC was established in 1968 and their headquarters are in Johannesburg. They emerged from another organization, the Christian Council of South Africa, based on discussions about the need to have an independent entity that represented the churches of South Africa.[63] People within the SACC participated in conferences of the World Council of Churches, of which they are a member. The SACC was originally headed by white Christian leaders, but beginning in the 1970s there was a transition to black church leadership. This trend of black leaders has continued, with the exception of Afrikaner clergyman Beyers Naudé, to the present. White people have been involved in the organization, and leaders advocated for a nonracial state to emerge in the democracy. Men have tended to occupy the SACC's primary leadership positions, but their leadership has also included some women in various programs, as vice presidents and, in the democracy, as general secretaries.

In terms of their organizational structure, the SACC has thirty member churches, mostly mainline Protestant "missionary" churches, but also Pentecostal and Catholic entities.[64] There is a distinction between "members" and "observers" (e.g., the Catholic Bishops Conference was an observer church for most of the struggle against apartheid), and member churches are specific denominations or para-church groups that have a national dimension. There are eight provincial offices that are governed by representatives of churches in their respective provinces. I focus on the national organization. It is governed by a National Conference, which includes a National Executive Committee (a president, vice president(s), and the general secretary). A Central Committee then carries out policies and programs. An Executive Committee adopts the annual budget and consists of the president and vice president(s), general secretary and deputy general secretary, plus others elected by the Central Committee. The general secretary is responsible for managing the organization's everyday functioning.[65] Within the national office, there have been various iterations of programs, desks, and initiatives.

African Enterprise

AE was formed in 1962 with the intention of "evangelizing the cities of Africa in word and deed in partnership with the church."[66] They have offices in multiple locations, including elsewhere in Africa, as well as organizational bases in the United States, Australia, Canada, and parts of Europe. I focus on the South African office, which is located in the hills of Pietermaritzburg, outside the city itself. AE was established by Michael Cassidy, a white South African who studied in the United Kingdom, then at Fuller Seminary in the United States, and was influenced by Billy Graham's style of evangelism. The primary leadership of AE South Africa has remained consistently white. Black people have served as evangelists and in certain leadership positions, and at one point a mixed-race (what is described as "coloured" in South Africa) man was the South African "Team Leader." But by and large the primary leadership ranks have remained closed to nonwhites. AE has had at least one woman chairperson of their board, but otherwise women have not been represented in their top leadership.

People who work at AE represent a range of denominations. Cassidy is Anglican, but the staff has ranged from Pentecostal to mainline Protestant. Structurally, the organization is headed by a team leader, who is responsible to a board of trustees. Historically, there was a relatively small group of evangelists, as well as people hired to help with the everyday functioning of the organization. There is also an international team leader who oversees the functioning of all the national offices of AE. As with the SACC, throughout the organization's history there have been different programmatic efforts housed under different desks or offices. From the early days of coordinating particular "missions," activities have routinized to a certain degree into particular organizational positions.

Pietermaritzburg Agency for Christian Social Awareness

PACSA was started in 1979 by a group of white Christians who wanted to "conscientize" fellow white Christians about the evils of apartheid.[67] They aimed to expose information about the treatment of black people by the apartheid regime, and over time a number of nonwhites have participated in their work. Their top leadership has mostly been white, though over time they have hired multiple black and coloured staff. Both men and women have served as directors and staff members. Like AE, PACSA is also located in Pietermaritzburg, but is in the city center. It has been the most locally embedded of the three organizations, with a particular focus on Pietermaritzburg and the surrounding area in the province of KwaZulu Natal.

PACSA was started by people who participated in mainline Protestant churches, though it, too, has incorporated people who attend Pentecostal denominations over time. Its organizational structure is somewhat different from the other two. Their first leader, Peter Kerchhoff, originally had the title of "Coordinator," but later leaders were referred to as "Director." Over time it has taken a variety of organizational forms. In the early days, PACSA was run by a coordinator and a tiny number of staff. Over time they have established particular programs, and their staff has grown. These desks have produced research and programs in particular areas, ranging from economic justice to gender.

OVERVIEW OF THE BOOK

The story of the role of theological cultures in shaping these religious organizations' discourse and actions develops in two parts. Part I considers the development of the theological cultures to challenge apartheid, as well as how they adapt in the democratic transition and first decade of the democracy. Chapter 1 examines how the organizations' theological cultures shape their advocacy for Christian social engagement against apartheid. It analyzes both the distinct theological convictions that motivate their mission and actions and how these convictions intersect with their posture toward different racial groups. Chapter 2 then analyzes whether and how the theological cultures change during the transition to and early years of the democracy. I demonstrate that even as new concerns emerge, the organizations' theological cultures are continuous with the past. Indeed, the theological cultures follow a distinct path from their anti-apartheid theological convictions and social positioning to their discourse and actions in the transition and early years of the democracy. In the democracy, theological convictions intersect with their posture toward social groups in different ways, especially in terms of race, economics, and their orientation to the state, to shape their actions.

Part II examines the ways the theological cultures shape attention to GBV and gender justice. Chapter 3 analyzes each organization's discourse about GBV. I demonstrate how the organizations' theological convictions intersect with their posture toward women victims of violence. Here an interesting and important puzzle emerges. The organizations' responses to GBV are clearly shaped by their theological cultures, but they vary significantly in whether or not they understand GBV to be an issue of gender and power. Chapter 4 tells us why this difference exists. This chapter examines how the organizations' theological convictions intersect with their postures toward women and men, demonstrating the fragility of possibilities and efforts to cultivate a conception of gender justice. Chapter 5 then examines the practical implications of the organizations' theological cultures for their actions concerning GBV. On one level, this chapter simply documents patterns of practical attention and inattention to GBV, showing how the organizations' theological convictions intersect with their posture toward women to shape their actions. But on another level, it also brings together the threads of this section of the book as it analyzes how these patterns are rooted in the organizations' capacities to cultivate gender justice, more broadly. Throughout, I explain how other factors matter, even as I also show that they are ultimately not the determinative explanation for the organizations' varying discursive and practical attention to GBV. Distinct theological convictions intersect with a dynamic web of social positioning to shape the organizations' actions. The conclusion reflects on the implications of this argument both for our understanding of religion's role in challenging and supporting intersectional injustice and for our practical pursuit of a more just and loving world.

PART 1 THE FORMATION AND REPRODUCTION OF THEOLOGICAL CULTURES

1 · RACIAL POSITIONING AND THEOLOGICAL CULTURES IN THE FIGHT AGAINST APARTHEID

> The time has come. The moment of truth has arrived. South Africa has been plunged into a crisis that is shaking the foundations and there is every indication that the crisis has only just begun and that it will deepen and become even more threatening in the months to come. It is the KAIROS or moment of truth not only for apartheid but also for the Church and all other faiths and religions.
> —*The Kairos Document*

In June 1985, black theologians in South Africa met in the township of Soweto to discuss the need for a public and practical Christian response to the escalating social and political crisis in the country. With the intensification of state repression and violence against a burgeoning mass democratic movement protesting the apartheid regime, these religious leaders were concerned that the churches in South Africa not sit on the sidelines. In September of that year, the Institute for Contextual Theology published *The Kairos Document*. The document declared that it was time for the churches in South Africa to give up any attempts to hold a neutral stance in the crisis, and to align themselves with the oppressed black majority population that was calling for the overturning of the apartheid regime and for establishing full democratic rights. Not only this, but *The Kairos Document* also denounced both "State Theology" (the apartheid state's use of theology to justify apartheid) and "Church Theology" (theology that was being promoted by church leaders in ways that did not adequately condemn the unjust and violent regime). Instead, the statement called for the church to develop "Prophetic Theology," a public theology that would address "the particular circumstances of this crisis, a response that does not give the impression of sitting on the fence but is clearly and unambiguously taking a stand."[1]

This use of theological language both to condemn the oppressive system and to call for churches to enter into practical solidarity with the liberation movement both diagnosed and prompted a crisis moment for the church in South Africa. Unsurprisingly, it prompted a range of responses. A number of black evangelicals were inspired to form a group called Concerned Evangelicals, and they wrote their own statement, "Evangelical Witness in South Africa," which they published in 1986.[2] Yet many white evangelicals expressed concern at the politicization of the church, if not outright hostility to the statements.[3] A conservative Christian news media source, *Signposts*, condemned the statement as a sign of Marxist infiltration into the churches, and others heralded it as a "false prophecy."[4] Bishop Desmond Tutu, one of the most iconic black religious figures in the anti-apartheid movement, did not sign *The Kairos Document* for a different reason: while he supported it, he was also concerned that it did not recognize fully the contributions of white Christians to the movement.[5] The statement also reflected and intensified debates about whether churches and everyday Christians should support the use of violent tactics against the state.[6]

The Kairos Document and the range of responses to it highlight the social significance of religion in supporting or challenging systems of oppression. Indeed, they provide further evidence of a long-standing sociological insight about the power of religion to enact social change or to maintain the status quo.[7] At the same time, this particular episode in South African political and religious life also illuminates the fact that religious challenges to such systems can take multiple forms. That is, the efforts to publish *The Kairos Document* and the varying responses to it are not only the story of those who opposed and those who supported apartheid. This is also a story of varying—even conflicting—modes of calling for religious resistance. What social factors influence these multiple ways of challenging injustice? The central contention of this chapter is that race and religion intersect with each other to shape different forms of social engagement.

To explain the social processes through which this intersection happens, the chapter draws on three key sociological insights. First, we know that religion does not function wholly independently in social life, but is fundamentally shaped by other social realities, including race.[8] Second, at the same time, a long-standing tradition of sociological understanding has emphasized that religious claims do hold distinct power in social life and should not be reduced to other social realities.[9] Third, as race is formed and re-formed through dynamic processes, these processes involve both oppression and resistance.[10] Anti-racist projects—that is, discursive and practical efforts that link ideas and beliefs to policies and structures—can develop as critical dimensions of resistance.[11] This chapter brings these ideas together to argue that theological convictions intersect with organizations' posture toward different racial groups to shape their actions.

As I explained in the introduction, I refer to these institutionally embedded religious belief systems as "theological cultures." One key component of a theological culture is the distinct theological claims that the organizations make.

Indeed, the SACC, AE, and PACSA ground their identity and actions in specific theological convictions that have their own social power. The SACC stresses God's liberating power; AE, God's reconciling power; and PACSA, God's transforming power for challenging injustice (see the table in appendix A for key features of the theological cultures). The SACC and PACSA both contend that the church must engage in solidarity with the marginalized, while AE suggests that the church is to model how spiritual reconciliation with God also involves social reconciliation.

At the same time, these theological convictions are not produced in an institutional vacuum. The second key component of a theological culture is the posture the organizations take toward different social groups. In this chapter, I focus on the ways the organizations both focus on and identify with different racial groups. The SACC focuses on and identifies with the oppressed black experience, and authors speak from the perspective and position of those who are proximate to the suffering they describe, sometimes even experiencing it themselves. AE, by contrast, focuses on and identifies with the experience of white people, describing cross-racial encounters that center on the white experience. PACSA also focuses on and identifies with the experience of white people, but they emphasize the need for whites to enter into proximity to black suffering and to forgo complicity in the system.

These theological cultures shape the organizations' different modes of social engagement. The SACC and PACSA share some similarities in their theological convictions, particularly around God's solidarity with the marginalized. But their different posture toward racial groups shapes the enactment of this theological conviction. The SACC's leaders speak and take action from the position of the suffering black population with whom God is in solidarity. PACSA's leaders speak and take action from the position of white people who occupy a relative distance from black suffering that needs to be breached. AE and PACSA have a similar social positioning with respect to racial groups. But their different theological convictions shape the ways that this posture is manifested. As AE emphasizes reconciliation, they invite cross-racial encounter in racially neutral spaces, while PACSA's emphasis on transformation invites whites to leave their places of comfort and privilege, entering into solidarity with black suffering.

The following analysis of these three organizations' public discourse spans the emergence of a third and final wave of protest against the apartheid regime in the late 1970s to the beginning of the transition to democracy in 1990.[12] I take each organization in turn, demonstrating how their theological convictions intersect with their social positioning to shape their actions. By examining the ways in which distinct theologies intersect with race, we can better understand the different possibilities for religious organizations' discourse and actions to promote social change in the midst of injustice and violence.

SOUTH AFRICAN COUNCIL OF CHURCHES

Identity and Actions

As I described in the introduction, the SACC was founded in 1968 as an ecumenical, representative body of churches in South Africa.[13] During the third wave of protest against apartheid that this chapter analyzes, the previously white-led organization transitioned to having black church leaders as its general secretaries and making up the Executive Committee. These leaders interacted with black and liberation theologies from the United States and Latin America to develop what was termed "contextual theology" in order to critique apartheid.[14] They also articulated ideas that resonated with those in the broader liberation struggle in South Africa at the time, including both those in the Black Consciousness Movement of the 1970s, which emphasized black dignity and empowerment, and those in the multiracial United Democratic Front in the 1980s, which advocated for nonracial democracy.[15]

The theological culture of the SACC focuses on liberation. Leaders argued that in order to achieve a truly just society, liberation from the oppressive social, political, and economic system of apartheid was necessary. A just society would be known by its people of all races being liberated to be fully human, given equal standing, reconciled to one another, and living in harmony. And this quest for liberation necessitated close identification with those who suffered.

As with the other organizations, the SACC's focus on liberation was shaped by their organizational characteristics and identity. Of the three organizations, the SACC was the most prominent in the anti-apartheid struggle. Their structure differs from the other two because they are a representative body of churches in South Africa—the majority of which are black. The SACC's role as a representative body means that sometimes they focused on how particular denominations were either supporting or challenging apartheid, and highlighted varying responses among their member churches.[16] There were also sometimes tensions between the executive leadership team and leaders of member churches concerning the SACC's role in challenging the state.[17]

The SACC's theological culture of liberation had practical implications for their efforts to challenge the injustice and violence of the apartheid regime. After transitioning to being a black-led organization in the 1970s and being designated a black organization by the state in 1972 when the majority of the leadership was black, their alignment with the broader liberation movement increased during the 1980s.[18] At this time, the SACC was led by such charismatic church leaders as Desmond Tutu, Beyers Naudé, and Frank Chikane. Tutu, a black Anglican bishop, won the Nobel Peace Prize in 1984, giving him and the SACC greater international status.[19] Naudé was an Afrikaner clergyman who had resigned his ministerial position with the white Dutch Reformed Church because of his involvement in the Christian Institute, a theology group aimed at developing contextual theology and condemning apartheid.[20] Frank Chikane was a black Pentecostal minister whose denomination revoked his ministerial license because of his political actions. Prior to becoming the general secretary, he was detained and tortured by the police.[21] These charismatic leaders sometimes ran afoul of the SACC's church membership because of their political activism and confrontation with the state, but they also served as important, public theological voices that represented the SACC's concerns in the public square.[22]

In the early 1970s, the SACC's Inter-Church Aid Division devoted practical attention to community and development projects and emergency-aid situations. An economist also conducted a study of the impact of migratory labor on the family. Over time, the SACC's efforts increasingly focused on providing both legal and financial support to political detainees, and providing care for dependents of political prisoners.[23] These actions brought scrutiny and pressure from the state, and in 1981 the apartheid government formed the Eloff Commission, ostensibly to investigate the financial situation of the SACC and their international donors. But it was also clearly an attempt to discredit the SACC for their connections with the liberation movement.[24]

As SACC leaders argued that there was a theological mandate for providing support for the cause of liberation, they also increased their public and political stances against the state throughout the 1980s. In response, the state engaged in repressive tactics. This included, for instance, the 1988 bombing of Khotso House, the SACC's headquarters in Johannesburg, and poisoning Frank Chikane when he was general secretary.[25] By the late 1980s, the SACC had become a major channel for international financial support to the liberation movement, and most of this money was spent on supporting victims of apartheid.[26] This period of the late 1970s until the transition to democracy was thus marked by the SACC's increased radicalization and practical identification with the liberation movement.

In the analysis below, I demonstrate how the SACC's distinct theological emphasis on liberation intersected with their posture toward different racial groups to shape these actions. Their theological convictions center on God's liberating power for the oppressed and the church's requirement to be in solidarity with the marginalized. They articulate this belief system from the posture of those who are aligned with this suffering and marginalization. This intersection of theological conviction and social positioning meant that they took concrete actions of political solidarity with the oppressed black majority.

Theological Convictions: A God of Liberation, a Suffering Church in Solidarity with the Marginalized

The SACC's theological culture centers on liberation. Drawing on liberation theologies and developing a distinctly South African contextual theology, leaders at the SACC articulated connections between various theological principles and the social oppression that characterized South African society. For instance, General Secretary Desmond Tutu links the theological principles of conversion and liberation to one another in his report to the National Conference in 1976: "Never before have I been so convinced there has been the need shown for a deep and meaningful conversion to Jesus Christ as Lord and Savior, which is the only means of liberating people . . . into the fullness of what it means to be a son or daughter of God."[27] This message of conversion-as-liberation includes freedom from anything that keeps people from experiencing their God-given dignity. Tutu goes on to assert, "In Christ we are all equal. Conversion means being brought into that company of the committed which is prepared to take up its cross and follow Christ, to lay down its life for others, to see in the face of every man [sic] the face of Christ and to want to serve Him, to see the possibility to serve free from ideological, racial, denominational or other restrictions."[28] For the SACC, religious conversion itself is premised upon equality as a theological principle, and fully enacting one's conversion means living free from all social restrictions.

The SACC's theological discourse contains particular attention to God's solidarity with the marginalized. For instance, Tutu contended that "it is part of God's mission and purpose for His world to bring about wholeness, justice, righteousness, peace and harmony and reconciliation. God was a liberator, God who took the side of the poor, the weak, the oppressed, the widow, the orphan and the alien."[29] This idea that God's mission of justice is intertwined with God's solidarity with the poor is central for the SACC. Indeed, such theological concepts as "reconciliation" are directly tied to liberation and God's solidarity with the oppressed.

The SACC's theological emphasis on God's identification with the poor is interwoven with reflections about the particular model that Jesus's life, death, and resurrection offers for Christians. In these accounts, Jesus's own marginality is highlighted. For instance, in one of a series of reflections on the biblical text of Jesus's entry into Jerusalem ahead of his crucifixion in Luke 19, Gerrie Lubbe, a religious studies professor and Afrikaner clergyman who led the South African chapter of an interfaith peace activist group, writes, "Jesus was not caught up in the centre between the right and the left wings of the society of His day. Neither was He caught up between the centre and the margin, between the haves and the have-nots, the powerful and the powerless. He was on the side of the marginal ones of society. . . . Jesus became a marginal man himself. . . . It was not in the city of peace but outside (Hebrews 13:12) where He paid the price for peace."[30] The SACC makes the theological assertion that Jesus is not neutral or central or between political positions, but actively took a position of marginality. This depiction of Jesus fuels their convictions about the need for the church to stand in solidarity with the marginalized, as well.

For the SACC, if God is on the side of the poor and Jesus's suffering and death model the importance of entering into solidarity with the marginalized, then the church has particular responsibilities. In one sermon, Tutu notes,

> The Church must be the church of the poor—blessed are the poor in spirit for theirs is the kingdom of heaven—it must be the voice of the voiceless, it must be

concerned about exploitation, about detention without trial and arbitrary banning orders. It must wash the disciples' feet. If it is such a serving church then it must be a suffering church as well. Suffering is of the essence of Christianity because Christ said "unless you take up your cross and follow me, you cannot be my disciple." An affluent comfortable church cannot be the Church of Christ—an affluent church which uses its wealth for itself.[31]

One of the main contentions of the SACC is that theological principles have practical consequences, particularly for the church's decisions and actions. Here, service is not mere charity, but is actively linked to God's identification with the poor. And service that actively takes up the plight of the poor will also involve suffering. The issues at play in this text range from justice and critique of the state's policies of detention and banning to economic positioning. Comfort and affluence are not characteristics of the church that aligns itself with God, who is in solidarity with the poor.

These calls for the church to enter into solidarity with the poor also involve direct calls for the church to align itself with the liberation struggle. Just as Jesus was marginal and suffered, the church is called to be on the side of those who struggle against the injustice of apartheid. Beyers Naudé made this appeal directly in his National Conference address as general secretary in 1987: "The church should make it unmistakably clear, in so far as it has not done so, that it fully supports the striving for justice and liberation of the oppressed people of this country."[32] Further, this cannot only be verbal affirmation: "It will require a much clearer identification with the goals of liberation which the oppressed people of South Africa have set themselves and of concrete proof that the churches are willing not only to make verbal pronouncements but to give concrete support in every possible form to the achievement of this goal."[33] Recognizing the church's failure to act in solidarity with the liberation movement, Naudé calls for direct and concrete proof of their support in this particularly tumultuous time.

Indeed, leaders of the SACC sometimes reflect on the ways that the church can enact a vision of society that would not be characterized by racial division and oppression. Tutu contends that the church must "speak up" and promote a vision of a different way of living together:

I believe that the Church must speak up for God, speak up for justice, peace, compassion and reconciliation against evil, injustice, oppression and exploitation. It must wake up South Africans to the realities of our situation.... And the church must hold before all South Africans the vision of this new society of which we in the church are a first fruit, that it can happen, has happened here in South Africa that people of different races, colours, cultures and sexes have come together to a fellowship that transcends all differences, where diversity[,] far from making for separation and division[,] has enriched a splendid unity.[34]

This vision of unity out of difference flows from convictions about the church's obligation and opportunity to enter into solidarity with the oppressed. As the church speaks up and wakes up the rest of the country, so it also can serve as a microcosm of what's possible in South Africa.

This passage also reflects a tension in the SACC's discourse. On the one hand, leaders insist on the theological principle of God's solidarity with the oppressed and the need for the church to identify with and transform the situation of the oppressed. On the other hand, they draw on and help to cultivate the idea that a society characterized by unity out of diversity is possible. As I show next, this tension, far from constraining their action, allows the SACC both to focus on and sometimes to identify with the experience of the oppressed, even as they hold out a vision of a different social order, one that is marked by freedom from oppression.

Social Positioning: Focus on and Identification with the Oppressed Black Population

The SACC's theological convictions about God's solidarity with the oppressed, Jesus's own modeling of marginality, and the need for the church to enter into suffering solidarity intersect with their direct focus on and identification with the black oppressed population and the liberation struggle in South Africa.[35] As I show in more detail below, this is a contrast to both AE and PACSA, whose posture focuses on and identifies with a collective white experience, though this happens in different ways because of differences in their theological convictions. The SACC's discourse focuses on the experience of those who are oppressed and aligns the church with the liberation struggle in concrete and practical terms.

For instance, Frank Chikane makes the simple declaration that "the Church of God in South Africa has already been detained, imprisoned, teargassed, water-cannoned."[36] This direct identification with the oppressed is also seen in Desmond Tutu's report to the SACC's Executive Committee in 1984, when he writes, "We are invited to share in the sufferings of Christ for only so can we share in the glory of the resurrection."[37] He goes on to say, "In our own situation in South Africa, to be this, means standing with God on the side of the poor and voiceless, the oppressed and the exploited, the uprooted and those being made aliens in their own motherland."[38] There is a specific connection here between the theological principle of solidarity and its manifestation for black experience in South Africa, seen in the allusion to "those being made aliens in their own motherland," a phrase that refers to the apartheid government's creation of new "homelands" and the forced removals of black people.[39]

Likewise, Tutu's defense of the SACC's work to the Eloff Commission includes a theological contention that God's own attention is on the experience of the oppressed in the apartheid regime: "Our God cares that children starve in resettlement camps.... The God we worship does care that people die mysteriously in detention. He is concerned that people are condemned to a twilight existence as non-persons by an arbitrary bureaucratic act of banning them without giving them the opportunity to reply to charges brought against them."[40] Making the theological principle of God's solidarity with the oppressed concrete, Tutu specifies that God's solidarity with the poor applies to people who are suffering through the policies of forced removal, detention without trial, and banning without due process. That is, this theological conviction is manifested in the particular South African experience of those who are struggling for liberation.

As they connect the lived experience of the oppressed to God's own care for and solidarity with this experience, the SACC also identifies the church with the movement for liberation. The relevance of the Gospel for blacks, in particular, is seen to be a matter of theological urgency as much as sociopolitical urgency. In an anonymous reflection on "Jesus Christ, the Life of the World: A Black South African Perspective," the author expresses the vast chasm between what Jesus promises and the reality of black life under apartheid. The author posits, "Is it not the case that the divine life which Christ promises is in fact mutually exclusive with the Black life that is devoid of dignity, freedom and social justice?"[41] The author goes on to assert that this contrast between God's intention of equality and the realities of oppression for blacks requires resisting the structures that dehumanize black people:

> To affirm that Jesus Christ is the life of Blacks is tantamount to repudiating the existing economic, socio-political arrangements in our society. It is to affirm that Jesus Christ who is the true life is not the author of socio-political structures that have sentenced Blacks to a life of poverty, underpayment, to the overcrowded and crime-ridden townships with the humiliating life in single hostels and similar legalized dehumanisations. Rather this cruel and oppressive world which denies Black people a full and meaningful life has been made by sinful people.[42]

Both giving specific examples of the plight of blacks in the apartheid regime and making the theological claim that such a system cannot have been authored by God but, rather, by "sinful people," this text focuses on the experience of blacks under apartheid to challenge the possibility that apartheid could be acceptable for Christians. In fact, if "Jesus Christ is the life of Blacks," then the apartheid system must be repudiated; the way that society is arranged is incompatible with the Gospel. The SACC's theological convictions intersect with a particular focus on black experience.

Indeed, this same author goes on to express the necessity of channeling this theological conviction into political action: "If God's atoning work in the life, death and resurrection of Jesus Christ means anything at all, it must mean that God is able together with those who remain faithful to the divine struggle to achieve a historical and genuine liberation in our abnormal society.... For only a God who is able to satisfy human spiritual and sociopolitical needs can qualify to be that God whom the oppressed Blacks can accept as their source of life here and now and their hope for the future life."[43] This recognition of the particular situation of oppressed blacks portrays the urgency of connecting theological principles to the liberation struggle. The SACC focuses on the particular need for blacks to know that God is working with and through them to achieve liberation.

For the SACC, the fundamental failure in these systemic injustices is their refusal to treat black people as people. For instance, Tutu defends the idea of "black consciousness" in 1982:

> Black consciousness is of God. Our Lord said the two majors laws are 'Love God and thy neighbor as thyself.' A proper self-love is an indispensable ingredient to love of others. Black consciousness seeks to awake in the black person an awareness of their worth as a child of God. Apartheid, oppression, injustice are blasphemous and evil because they have made God's children doubt that they are God's children. Black consciousness is deeply religious. It is not anti-white. It is pro-black and only if it succeeds will it be possible to have any reconciliation. Reconciliation happens only between persons not between persons and dehumanized half-persons.[44]

For Tutu, the point is that black consciousness, and an awareness of dignity based on being God's children, has been denied to blacks and must be reclaimed. This is a contrast to AE, which emphasizes an equality of need across racial lines despite different experiences, and to PACSA, which takes these insights about black consciousness and adapts them for white people's consciousness of their complicity in such a system.

Even as the SACC focuses specifically on the black experience of oppression, leaders like Tutu also affirm that the theological principle of God's solidarity with the marginalized also matters for whites who have been dehumanized by being oppressors. But, in contrast to AE's primary focus on whites' emotional and spiritually powerful experience of black forgiveness through cross-racial encounters, Tutu connects the message of liberation and solidarity to the need that whites have to reclaim their human dignity apart from their position as the powerful. He writes,

> I thought I was coming back mainly to tell blacks that God loved them, that they were of infinite value in His sight and that they should enter into their inheritance as the children of God, taking a proper pride in their blackness and assert their personhood as blacks because only so would they be able to participate in real reconciliation, [which] is a deeply personal and costly enterprise.... I was amazed to discover that in many ways, it was whites who needed to hear this message about self-assurance and self-acceptance, that oppression dehumanized the oppressor as much as, if not more than, the oppressed; that white people needed to hear and know that their value as persons was intrinsic to who they were, by virtue of having been created in God's image.[45]

In fact, if whites in South Africa can be liberated into their full humanity, then they will be able to realize the dignity of others. Tutu goes on to say, "Maybe some day it will dawn on the white Afrikaner Christians that nobody hates them, that the world is waiting eagerly to accept them once they give up this one obsession. Once the whites accept for themselves that their value as humans depends not on the colour of their skin, or on the value of their possessions, but is intrinsic, they will also accept that about others."[46] There is a similar logic here concerning what is deemed necessary for both blacks and whites. The focus on whites' personhood, self-value, and the fundamental dignity that comes from recognizing one's belonging to God is a mirror image to the call for blacks to recognize their own personhood and dignity. At the same time, while there is attentiveness to different racialized experience, in the context of the SACC's discourse overall, white experience is not centered in the same way that it is in AE, as I show below.

In fact, sometimes the SACC's discourse not only focuses attention on the black experience; authors also speak directly from the position of the black oppressed. The SACC's published newsletters sometimes articulate a collective voice that explicitly identifies with the blacks who want to be heard and liberated. In one of the many depictions of the horror of forced removals, black people's capacity for love and forgiveness is expressed: "Standing in the rain there was the prayer of the one old man who said: 'Thank you God for still loving us.' How can one, on the eve of being finally removed pray, and then pray for God's thanksgiving presence? Our people are peaceloving to a fault. It is one of the greatest miracles that blacks still talk to white people."[47] To note that "our people" still have the capacity to express thanks for God's provision is a representation of a collective black voice and experience, expressing both awe at this man's response and a particular identification with the plight of blacks being forcibly removed.

A concern with trying to get white people to understand and respond to the plight of blacks also characterizes this identification with the black oppressed. For instance, Tutu laments, "What more must we do so that our white brothers and sisters will hear us? What more must we say that they will listen to our cries? All we want is to be seen to be human. We do not want to drive the white people into the sea.... What must we do? Must we all go into exile? Please help us before all of us are saying that the only good white person is a dead white person."[48] Again this plea to recognize the fundamental humanity of blacks, this call to be treated as people, emerges from the SACC's identification with the liberation struggle. Here, an appeal to whites to listen ends with the stark observation that the situation is going to escalate in hatred and violence if whites cannot listen to the "we" that is articulated here.

The SACC's theological convictions about a liberating God who takes the side of the oppressed intersect with their particular posture toward different racial groups to shape their actions. As they focus on the need for the church to enter into suffering solidarity with the oppressed, they also sometimes speak from and center a collective black experience. Their theological convictions about liberation are institutionally embedded in ways that shape the SACC's actions of close identification with the suffering black population that seeks freedom from oppression.

AFRICAN ENTERPRISE

Identity and Actions

As I described in the introduction, AE was founded in order to evangelize the cities of Africa. While their primary emphasis has been on evangelism, they have also devoted significant attention to describing the connections between preaching the Gospel and attending to social issues. Founder Michael Cassidy resonated with concerns articulated by evangelicals from the Global South in the global Lausanne Congress of 1974, in which he participated, about the prioritization of evangelism apart from addressing the social conditions of people's lives.[49] As such, Cassidy was adamant that conversion could not only be seen as a matter of saving souls, but must also involve reconciling people's relationships, working for justice, and pursuing love and forgiveness. In contrast to the SACC's focus on liberation from oppression, for AE the call for Christian engagement against apartheid coalesces around the idea that evangelism and social change are compatible, and that spiritual reconciliation with God also necessitates social reconciliation with one another. AE's theological culture centers on reconciliation.

This emphasis on reconciliation is linked to the organization's characteristics and leadership. Cassidy, as well as others within the organization, had a political consciousness from a young age. Before founding or participating in the organization, Cassidy and several of the other longtime AE leaders were either drawn to or were active participants in political activism against the apartheid regime.[50] But they also experienced the limits of pursuing purely political mechanisms of social change. Born out of their own experiences encountering people across racial divides, they perceived that God's intention for society necessitated both spiritual and social reconciliation.[51]

AE's theological culture of reconciliation shaped their actions. In the early years of their existence, especially, apartheid's racial segregation policies posed a direct challenge to the team's efforts to preach the Gospel. For instance, in one of the earliest evangelistic events ("missions") that AE conducted, in the city of Ladysmith, they capitulated to the government policy prohibiting interracial gatherings and set up a separate space for blacks to gather. But, convinced that this was a practice that was antithetical to their preaching of the full Gospel, which promised not only spiritual reconciliation with God, but also social reconciliation with one another, AE vowed never again to do so.[52]

Indeed, AE attempted to foster connections across both denominational and racial factions in South Africa. In 1976, they organized a gathering of Christian leaders from across the continent of Africa, which they called the Pan-African Christian Leadership Assembly. Inspired by the way this group came together across denominational boundaries and experiences, AE decided to attempt something similar in South Africa, in what they called the South African Christian Leadership Assembly (SACLA).[53] AE's internal history documents the resistance they faced in this effort, as they were "castigated as political by right-wing whites and as irrelevant by militant blacks."[54] Nevertheless, despite this opposition, approximately six thousand church leaders gathered in 1979, with both multiracial and multidenominational representation.[55] For AE, SACLA both symbolized and enacted the possibility that people really could come together across divides and seek reconciliation.

As the 1980s saw increased violence and repression, AE leaders expressed some discomfort with *The Kairos Document* for its direct confrontation with the state, and for not centering the possibility of racial reconciliation.[56] Instead, they designed a Day of Prayer for reconciliation and sent teams into places of unrest to preach the Gospel and call for reconciliation, as part of what they termed the National Initiative for Reconciliation. Cassidy recounts a meeting with President P. W. Botha in which he refused to publicly condemn *The Kairos Document*, despite Botha implying a threat to Cassidy's life if he refused to denounce it. For Cassidy, while he did not "agree with all the theology of the document," he nevertheless contended that "it represents a deep cry from the black world which the government and all whites must hear."[57] And yet, he and other AE leaders also expressed their own conviction that the way forward was to promote a theology of reconciliation, not direct confrontation.[58] There was a cost to this as well—AE teams reported being stopped by security police and interrogated as they went to preach the Gospel in townships.[59] But they remained committed to promoting reconciliation as the best path forward.

In addition to these efforts to promote nationwide reconciliation, AE's work also involved the development of two local programs. First, they incorporated and expanded a program called Bonginkosi, which is Zulu for "Praise the Lord."[60] This program had been begun by two women—one black, one white—to establish a feeding program in a local black township where children were experiencing significant food insecurity. Discussions of the Bonginkosi program emphasize the significance of this effort as uniting black and white women in their efforts to provide for the children's needs.[61] Second, beginning in 1981, they started hosting Bridge Building Encounters, an initiative that brought youth of different racial backgrounds to AE's Conference Center and facilitated cross-racial dialogue.[62]

I show in the analysis below that AE's distinct theological emphasis on reconciliation intersected with their racial positioning to shape these actions. AE's theological convictions center on God's reconciling power and the church's responsibility to enact cross-racial reconciliation. They articulate this belief system from the posture of those who are listening to the cries of those who suffer. This intersection of theological conviction and social positioning meant that AE sought to foster cross-racial connections in order to challenge the injustice of apartheid and seek social change.

Theological Convictions: Reconciliation with God and with People

For AE, as for the SACC, apartheid was in opposition to God's character and plan for human flourishing. But where the SACC emphasizes the need for liberation from oppression, AE's theological culture centers on reconciliation. Their theological convictions center on the belief that God has ordained a particular way for society to be ordered. God's design is for peace, mutual understanding, and healthy relationships among people of various racial and ethnic groups. For AE, apartheid violates God's intended plan for right relationships, and so people of different races have different experiences. In order for God's way for society to be enacted, people are called first to be reconciled to God, and then to reconcile with one another. Indeed, the reconciliation described in AE's documents is both a spiritual and a social one. For the SACC, Jesus's life, death, and resurrection primarily evidence the significance of identifying with people on the margins. For AE, by contrast, Jesus's death on the cross has an equalizing and a politically neutralizing power.

For instance, a devotion by John Smyth for an AE Team Conference described in the April 1985 newsletter affirms that the cross is "the centre of the Christian message."[63] Further, the cross is "the sinners [sic] place," which means "it is my place and your place—we leave it at our peril. We are constantly in the presence of sin, even though we have been saved from the guilt of sin."[64] Everyone needs to stay near the cross—but not because being in solidarity with Jesus's suffering means occupying a place of marginalization, as was true with the SACC. Rather, for AE, the cross is significant because all of humanity is tainted by sin. This saving presence from sin is not simply a spiritual reconciliation with God; in fact, from this place of recognizing the ubiquity of sinfulness, the cross is also characterized as "the place of two-way forgiveness—where God forgives us and we forgive each other. Only when we glimpse Christ's love ... can we forgive others."[65] A supernatural experience of forgiveness from God empowers believers to be able to forgive others.

Indeed, newsletters often indicate that there are two priorities for AE: converting people to faith in Jesus by preaching the Gospel and recognizing the relational implications of that conversion. This is seen, for instance, in a January 1986 newsletter that celebrates donors' financial support for the new National Initiative for Reconciliation by affirming, "We are on the right track in terms of bringing together the twin concerns of evangelism (which is our priority commitment) and reconciliation, which is the horizontal outflow of healing in the relationships of those who have come to Christ."[66] The financial commitment from donors is seen as affirmation that AE's work to build reconciled, healed relationships also warrants programmatic attention, in addition to missions and evangelistic campaigns.

The theological imperative expressed in AE's discourse is understood to have practical implications for the church. But where the SACC focused more on the capacity of the church to identify with the marginalized and enter into the quest for liberation, for AE, the church has a unique capacity to preach and embody reconciliation. For instance, in August 1985, Cassidy's letter in the newsletter contains this call to action: "My own view is that the Church of Jesus Christ in South Africa is far and away the most powerful instrument for change, healing, reform, and progress. Indeed only God through His Church in this land can pull our nation out of the abyss."[67] As is true with the other organizations, Cassidy recognizes the particular and unique role that the church might play in calling for and enacting a different model for society.

But the theological beliefs that undergird AE's identity also mean that Cassidy perceives the specifics of that role differently than the other two organizations. He goes on to write, "But the Church is largely unaware of its enormous power and capability to help dialogue, build relationships, and forge understanding in our shattered and burning land."[68] This is not a call for the church to enter into solidarity with the liberation movement to overturn oppression, as both the SACC and PACSA contend. Rather, for AE the priority is on restoring right relationships with God and with one another. Dialogue, relationships, and understanding are the path forward. The way of God is the way of reconciliation, and the church is to enact and advocate for such a path to a more just society.

In fact, AE's emphasis on spiritual and social reconciliation also means affirming a particularly Christian solution to the problem of racial division, one that transcends racial difference and struggle. For instance, the newsletter from April 1988 states, "In some ways what we are facing in South Africa is not just a black/white power struggle, but a struggle between different philosophies and types of power.... God's way to power, however, is quite different from ours. It does not involve a development or capacity for confrontation or collision, it rather happens by the cross and an emptying of oneself, so that in weakness we may be filled with the power of Christ."[69] Here, there is a difference between God's way and humanity's way, but it expands beyond race to consider power more generally. This is also a contrast to the SACC: This analysis of power does not align Christ's suffering on the cross with black experience and portray his own marginalization as significant for the oppressed, as was the dominant message in the SACC. Rather, for AE, everyone is to be humble and embrace weakness, rather than engage in a power struggle, so as to follow the way of Jesus.

As the possibility of a political transition to democracy became more certain, this emphasis on God's way for society continues in AE's publications, with the warning that Christians are not to get too caught up in the political promises being made. Cassidy writes in October 1989: "I believe the Church needs to be in solidarity with those in this country who are calling out for an end to the apartheid system. We need to be clearly identified with that call and part of the processes of change. But as a Christian I believe the social revolution in which we are caught up now should be channeled into a Christian direction and controlled by Christian principles and presuppositions."[70] This provides an interesting contrast to the SACC: While calling for the church to be in solidarity with the liberation struggle, Cassidy also calls for "Christian principles and presuppositions" to rule the day.[71] This kind of distinction is not as salient for the SACC, where the whole point is that there is a theological mandate to enter into solidarity with the marginalized. AE's concern, in contrast, is to assert that there are also Christian principles that transcend political powers. Unless those principles are enacted, there will be social disaster.

The concern for AE is twofold. One concern is that, in the quest for political freedom and equality, Christian values will not be honored and God's intention for society will be sidelined. The second concern is that unless people of different racial groups can be reconciled to one another through healed relationships, any political promises and actions will be futile. AE's theological convictions center on the idea that Christians are called to follow God's way, which involves not only spiritual conversion, but also has social implications. Those who follow Jesus are to pursue reconciled relationships in the midst of alienation, injustice, and violence. I show next how these theological convictions intersect with a posture that focuses attention on white experience even as it also highlights the emotional release that comes from cross-racial encounter, as a sign of the power of the Gospel.

Social Positioning: Different Racial Experiences, Equality of Need

AE's theological conviction of the importance of reconciliation intersects with their posture toward different racial groups. In contrast to the SACC, where authors both focused more attention on and identified with the black experience, AE's discourse identifies more with a white collective experience that is relatively distant from black suffering. And unlike in PACSA's discourse, there is very little attention to the complicity of whites in an unjust system. Healing comes not from white people taking concrete action to enter into black people's suffering and directly confronting the state's injustice, but through the pursuit of right relationships, both with God and with one another. AE's theological convictions about reconciliation intersect with this social positioning to stress that blacks are in need of healing from the wounds of apartheid, while whites are in need of black love and forgiveness.

Rather than emphasizing God being on the side of the oppressed and focusing on inequities in black and white experience, as the SACC had articulated, for AE, both whites and blacks can have a problematic response that is fundamentally at odds with the Christian way. A piece in one of their publications, *AE Witness*, contends, for instance:

> It's much easier, if you're white in this country, to shrug your shoulders and say 'well we can't do anything about it so let's go with the *status quo*.' And in our private

ethics we can treat our brethren of other races with respect but [if we] make no attempt to change the system, that is copping out of the problem.

If we're black a number of options are open to us—we can passively put up with the situation and say 'Well, it will be better in heaven;' or we can nurse bitter resentment in our hearts; or we can join the political activists and put that in the driving seat and our Christian values in the back seat.

Neither attitude, white or black, is thinking Biblically, both have abandoned the Christian mind.[72]

There is an equality of poor thinking between the white and black people imagined in this description, though for different reasons. Neither has adopted "the Christian mind" that they should, which is to recognize both that "there is a strong Biblical basis for social concern and action" and that "God has made of one stock all races that dwell on the face of the earth, and we belong together."[73] In this account, whites are not adopting this Christian principle because their private ethics do not result in working to change the system, and blacks because acquiescence, resentment, and political activism devoid of Christian values are insufficient.

Interestingly, there is also an identification with both racial groups here. The use of "our" and "we" brings readers into the experience of both. At the same time, "Christian values" and "the Christian mind" are to transcend such racial differences. This use of a collective voice for both racial groups reinforces AE's fundamental conviction that Christian principles transcend racial differences.

This awareness of difference in racialized experiences also emerges in accounts of what happens when people from different racial groups are brought together. For instance, in a report on a planning session for a National Initiative for Reconciliation event, Cassidy's newsletter article depicts a vivid contrast across different groups: "We had black ministers who left their burning and suffering townships, we had a large contingent of Dutch Reformed Church members. . . . We had those who came saying 'I have no hope' and those who came longing to learn and understand, so that they could go away better equipped to help their people contribute to healing and change in South Africa."[74] Within this diversity of perspective and position, Cassidy observes, "But notably, there was a humility, and a listening ear, and a willingness to repent of all the wrongs of the past."[75] The assumption underlying this observation is that in order for racial reconciliation to occur, spiritual reconciliation has to happen, too. Indeed, the spiritual practices of humility and repentance are a necessary step for any hope of social reconciliation. At the same time, though, the initial explicit acknowledgment of racial difference is then masked by general descriptors of hopelessness or learning and wanting to promote "healing and change."[76] This discourse both stems from and reinforces AE's assertion that there is a Christian way to follow that transcends racial difference.

Sometimes a clear identification with a white experience is also evidenced in AE's published newsletters. For instance, when black theologian Bonganjalo Goba gave "the Black perspective of the situation," Cassidy writes, "we were forced to hear the cry of pain from the Blacks, who come from townships where the suffering and social upheaval are massive and largely hidden from white eyes and experience. We agonized with those who...spoke of their own situations."[77] The contrast between life in the townships and the white experience is highlighted here, and whites are called upon to encounter the realities of black experience.

There are also important differences from the SACC's discourse. Where the SACC's "we" spoke from the margins, here the "we" is listening to the cry of blacks, speaking from a white collective position. And the fact that the township life is "largely hidden" from that white collective perspective is also an important difference.[78] AE's calls for reconciliation come not only from a distinct theological conviction about spiritual and social reconciliation, but are also shaped by a white posture that has been distant from the realities of apartheid's violence and is listening to the cries of black people in townships, seeking to be enlightened.

Unlike in PACSA's discourse, where white ignorance is problematized as complicity in a violent and unjust system, AE's discourse tends to emphasize the need for whites to experience black love and forgiveness, and for blacks to find healing primarily through their faith in Jesus. For instance, a description of a mission to Port Elizabeth in the October 1985 newsletter establishes that the "*most poignant experience*...was to preach in the black township of New Brighton to a *packed group* of traumatized and hurting people.... 'Why do the whites fear us so much?' asked one old patriarch. I found myself crying inside that so few whites could have a *first-hand experience of black love, forgiveness and hospitality*."[79] The voice taken here represents a white collective experience that is listening to the trauma and hurt of black people.

Indeed, while there are resonances here with the SACC's attention to the plight of the oppressed, the narrative for AE shifts attention from the trauma and hurt of black people to a sense of grief that white people are unlikely to experience all that black people have to offer. While the SACC also expresses concern with the impact of apartheid on whites, their focus is on the need for whites to be liberated from the dehumanization that comes from being the oppressor. Here, instead, a white leader is "crying inside" that so few of the members of his own race can "experience black love." The narrative focuses on how whites could benefit from receiving black love.

In addition, for AE, the solution to the trauma and turmoil that blacks experience is fundamentally a spiritual and relational one, not a political and structural one. For instance, a discussion of youth coming from "troubled townships" in Port Elizabeth to the AE Conference Center in Pietermaritzburg recounts the many activities they did, and how important it was for them to talk about the realities of their lives.[80] The newsletter reports, "Most important they spent hours with AE team members talking out the issues facing them as young blacks in the township turmoil.... Many of them were very hurt and broken by the violence of life...and we rejoiced when about 21 of them responded to David Peter's call to submit their lives in a new way to Jesus Christ."[81] This statement implies that devotion to Jesus is key for responding to the brokenness and violence of apartheid. An acknowledgment of the racial discrimination and violence experienced in the townships is met with gratitude for the spiritual reconciliation these young black people might receive by committing to Jesus.

In addition, spiritual change for blacks is not the only kind of change that happens through this experience. The newsletter goes on to note that local white young people were also impacted by the presence of the young black people: "They also spent quite a bit of time with white teenagers from some of Pietermaritzburg's local youth groups. The impact they had on the white kids was evident on the night they left to return to [Port Elizabeth]. A group of white kids stood crying around the bus while the [Port Elizabeth] teenagers leaned out the windows calling goodbye and promising to write."[82] This model of cross-racial encounter resulted in plans to do more of these events in the future and, in fact, these events turned into the Bridge Building Encounters that became a signature part of AE's practical actions.

AE's theological conviction about the power of spiritual and social reconciliation is evidenced here, as it also intersects with a particular posture toward racial groups. Commitment to Christ changes lives, but it does so in different racialized ways. Indeed, white experience is centered as the account stresses how impactful the black youth's visit was for the white, local teenagers. Black youth find healing as they encounter the Gospel, and white youth express powerful emotion as those black youth return home.

In AE's discourse, the encounter among these individual people is the main point. Unlike in the SACC's discourse where there was a clear path of confrontation with the unjust regime, for AE there is more of an emphasis on the individual-level and relational impact that cross-racial encounters can have. For instance, another newsletter narrates a different example of bringing young blacks to the AE Conference Center, quoting a letter from one of the black youth who wrote after the event, "'At AE we were living, we were freed from hatred, freed from suspecting other human beings, freed from keeping our distance away from a fellow brother, and freed from mistrust.... Now we know that in us we have the gifts that can make peace in our country. Now we know that we must have the love that is more than skin deep to cure the problems.'"[83] AE's solution is evidenced in this letter: rather than emphasize policies and economic reforms, the promise is held out that if blacks and whites can reconcile with one another; cease to fear, hate, and mistrust one another; and find a deeper love than race, then apartheid can be cured.

The language of healing, emotional response, and relational connection are prominent here. As racial divisions have caused a kind of social sickness, social reconciliation that is made possible by spiritual reconciliation is the medicine required to cure the disease. Interestingly, again in contrast to the SACC, the kind of freedom articulated here is seen primarily in relational and emotional terms. The solution for AE is not to confront the state and pursue freedom from the structures and policies that dehumanize, but to facilitate freedom from the emotional toll that living separately and in violent spaces has wrought.

The fundamental hope underlying AE's discourse is that there is a deeply spiritual solution to the problem of apartheid. In a newsletter leading up to a Day of Prayer sponsored by the National Initiative for Reconciliation, Cassidy articulates his hope that this day set apart for prayer will be "a great day in the history of our nation—when we turned away from cataclysm and sought the solution of Christ."[84] And the primary solutions are both spiritual and social: "Keep praying for our leaders of all races, as you have never prayed before. And let all Christians at this time identify with one another in pain and seeking to understand the plight of those suffering in our country."[85] This call to reconciliation acknowledges different racial experiences, and proposes both prayer and identification with one another as the solution. In fact, the solution is to recognize that "all" are in need of prayer and "all" are in pain, even as there is also particular attention to "those suffering."[86] AE's theological convictions about reconciliation intersect with their posture toward different racial groups. All people experience an equality of need across racial difference, and this call to prayer is articulated from a position of relative difference that needs to "understand the plight of those [who are] suffering."[87] Trusting in a connection between the spiritual and social, AE's discourse reflects a fundamental tension between recognizing different racialized experiences and identifying with a relatively distant, white position.

AE's theological convictions about God's design for society intersect with their posture toward different racial groups. As they focus on cross-racial encounters as a key mechanism for implementing God's vision for reconciled relationships and advocate for a Christian response to the injustice of apartheid that transcends racial differences, they also sometimes speak from and center white experience. AE's theological beliefs are institutionally embedded in ways that shape their actions to bring people together in a seemingly neutral space to experience reconciliation with God and with one another.

PIETERMARITZBURG AGENCY FOR CHRISTIAN SOCIAL AWARENESS

Identity and Actions

PACSA was founded by white Christians in 1979—the latest of the three organizations—in order to "conscientize" other white Christians about the evil of apartheid. This founding mission has had a significant impact on their call for social engagement over time. Influenced by the Black Consciousness Movement's emphasis on the need for white people to have their own consciousness awakened and transformed, PACSA has stressed the importance of connecting awareness with action.[88] Initially motivated by an intention to focus specifically on other white Christians, their mission expanded to work more closely with black people in the city of Pietermaritzburg and in rural areas outside the city, seeking to alleviate the suffering of those who were most impacted by the cruelty of apartheid policies and to address political violence in KwaZulu Natal.[89] Where the SACC emphasizes liberation from oppression, and AE stresses racial reconciliation, PACSA's theological culture centers on transformation. Writers envision a society whose racist and economically oppressive structures are transformed from dealing violence to promoting life.

As with the other two organizations, this theological culture is shaped by the organization's characteristics. PACSA was a multiracial, but also predominantly white, organization, especially in its early years. PACSA was led by Peter Kerchhoff, a white South African who quit his job as chief chemist at an aluminum factory to become the organizing secretary of PACSA.[90] They began as a relatively small group of mostly white people that gathered for monthly liturgies, where they would pray, sing, and share a meal.[91] Authors in PACSA's newsletters articulate ideas that resonate both with the SACC's focus on God's solidarity with the poor and oppressed and with AE's focus on the power of encounter across racial difference. But their distinctive emphasis is on the contrast and contradiction between structures that promote death (both literal and metaphorical) and the possibility of a transformed society that brings life out of suffering.

PACSA's actions emerge from the intersection of their theological convictions and their posture toward both privileged whites and marginalized blacks. Their actions centered first on raising awareness, particularly among white Christians. PACSA sought to raise awareness of how apartheid policies were being implemented in their own locale and hurting the poor and marginalized, starting with forced removals in nearby rural areas. To do this, they created and disseminated "factsheets."[92] Staff created documents that explained the features of a particular issue (e.g., hunger, children in crisis, detentions) and aimed to present basic facts about realities that others, especially fellow white Christians, might not be aware of or understand. This attention to raising awareness of the reality on the ground also manifested in their work and partnership with international organizations. For instance, newsletters and internal histories describe how they hosted visitors from international agencies like Amnesty International.[93]

Over time, PACSA integrated more practical solidarity with the resistance movement into their work, shifting from promoting awareness to action after the 1983 Tricameral Constitution was instantiated. This constitutional reform established separate parliamentary assemblies for white, coloured, and Indian members of Parliament, while still excluding black Africans from political representation.[94] Cycles of repression and violence escalated during this time, including the apartheid state instigating and supporting conflict between African National Congress and Inkatha factions in KwaZulu Natal.[95] PACSA founded a Detainees Support Committee in 1985, and worked with other NGOs to provide practical support (ranging from legal to medical) to people who were detained (often without trial) and were victims of violence.[96] As PACSA became a key node in this network of organizations trying practically to help and intervene in the violence and injustice, their own staff were targeted. For instance, under the state of emergency in 1986, founder Peter Kerchhoff was detained without trial, spending thirty-two days in solitary confinement and a total of ninety-six days in prison, without ever being formally charged or brought to trial.[97]

In the analysis below, I demonstrate how PACSA's distinct theological emphasis on transformation intersected with their posture toward different racial groups to shape these actions. Their theological convictions center on God's transforming power for systems of oppression and death. Leaders of PACSA did not speak or act from a detached or neutral position as they articulated these beliefs, but from the perspective and position of those who were privileged in the society and wanted to become more proximate to suffering. This intersection of theological conviction and social positioning meant that they sought both to raise awareness among fellow white Christians and to relieve the suffering of the marginalized black population.

Theological Convictions: Transformation of Suffering
and Death into Justice and Life

PACSA's theological culture centers on transformation. Authors perceive that the forces of death, oppression, and evil that characterize the apartheid system set out to destroy people; but there is yet a possibility that such a system can be transformed into one that is characterized by life, equality, and goodness. Christians are called to recognize their involvement in the system and to align themselves with God's mission in society, modeled through Jesus's crucifixion and resurrection. This narrative and theological metaphor of death being transformed into life is echoed in all three organizations, but it plays a particularly central role in PACSA's discourse.

PACSA authors describe apartheid as problematic because it involves a combination of systems, structures, and relationships that are oppressive and that promote death and hate rather than life and love. For instance, John Aitchison writes in the March 1980 newsletter: "The sinful powers that bind and oppress people, laws and systems that do not protect and conserve but destroy, barriers that prevent or frighten people from loving and sharing—these are all too real. . . . But beyond our powerlessness is a greater power [that] can break all bonds and barriers—even that of death. There is a source of renewal and re-creation that is working through all things. Christians know, through the resurrection of Jesus, that they can share in this transformation."[98] For PACSA, the resurrection of Jesus ushers in the ongoing transformation of destructive powers and systems into life-giving ones. Aitchison ties this conviction directly both to PACSA's own mission and to that of Christians more generally: "Hence we can, in hope, see that beyond the suffering and dying there is the power of life. PACSA exists as an agency to assist Christians to become more aware of how the power of God is at work in society and how we can align ourselves with what God wants in our world and South African society."[99] PACSA calls Christians to partner with God in the work of transforming evil and death into goodness and life, which is what God intends for society.

A key feature of this work of Christians aligning themselves with God's intention for society is for Christians to see that individual people are caught up in broader systemic issues—indeed, that everyone is involved in the system. As Joan Kerchhoff, Peter's wife, observes, "If I adjust to an unloving, unjust society, I oppose God and reject his values. But if I oppose and reject the social order, I can accept God's image and adapt to the perspectives of His kingdom—a kingdom of humility, joy, solidarity, peace, love and compassion—where the hungry are filled with good things, and death and sin have been overcome."[100] Similarly to AE, PACSA suggests that Christians are called to adopt God's values and perspective. But for Joan Kerchhoff, the focus is not on reconciliation across spiritual equals. Instead, in a way that is more resonant with the SACC's theological culture, aligning with God's values also means attending to the hungry and witnessing death and sin being transformed into a kingdom based on solidarity, love, and compassion.

Authors for PACSA frequently express a concern both with the disconnect between God's kingdom and the present reality, and with trying to make the Christian message relevant in the South African situation. For instance, in the Easter 1982 newsletter, this theme is taken up in reference to the biblical passage of the Beatitudes (Matthew 5; Luke 6), in which Jesus pronounces that those who are poor, meek, and mourning are blessed. Graham Lindegger reflects on the paradox between this theological affirmation and the reality of suffering in the world as he writes, "What evidence, at all, is there that it is the poor, peacemakers, merciful, hungry and thirsty for justice, who will inherit this kingdom? In fact the present order suggests exactly the opposite: it is apparently the wealthy, the elite, the complacent, the comfortable and the oppressors rather than the oppressed who have inherited the kingdom. The poor, mourning, hungry, the oppressed and strivers for justice seem to be the last who are 'blessed' or 'happy' in the present order."[101] Writing with a pastoral concern for Christians who may be tempted to dismiss the relevance of their faith, given the bleakness of the situation, Lindegger contrasts the kingdom of heaven with that of earth, reflecting on how these different "orders" highlight the inequities in the current order of society.[102] Similarly to the SACC, PACSA's discourse calls attention to social inequality, using language about justice and oppression to highlight the stark disconnect between how things ought to be, and how they are.

Lindegger suggests that the key to pressing into that tension and still holding on to faith is to be grounded in a liturgical and theological affirmation: "It seems to me that the Easter Celebration is an invitation to a recommitment to the values of the kingdom of God.... The Easter message is an affirmation that resurrection will triumph over death, good over evil, the oppressed over the oppressor."[103] In this understanding of God's intended order for society, there is hope in the promise that death can be transformed into life, and the oppressed can triumph over their oppressors. For PACSA, Jesus's crucifixion functions primarily not as an indicator of his own marginalization, as the SACC articulates, nor as a bridge that reconciles all sinners, as AE contends. Rather, Lindegger writes, "The Cross stands as a sign of contradiction and hope."[104]

For PACSA, this understanding of the paradox of Jesus's death and resurrection directly implicates the church and its mission. In the April 1984 newsletter, John Aitchison contrasts the church's joyful celebrations of Easter with the reality of death and suffering that permeates the context. He then describes the ways that Easter does, in fact, resonate with the painful reality on the ground in this way: "God had so identified with the man Jesus that when Jesus died death was taken into God. The experience of death is at the heart of God. Death is no more the ultimate in distance from God, the source of life, but, in Jesus, a route of direct access. Jesus took death into God. According to the reports of the few, God transformed death into resurrection. The church, we its members, have to take death into ourselves."[105] This call to enter the depths of death in order to have transformed life highlights the idea that God can empathize with those who are suffering and experiencing death in order to transform it into resurrection. The Christian community is called to enter into this journey of transformation, taking death into itself and finding life.

Similarly, in the March 1983 newsletter, Neville Richardson suggests that those who respond to the South African situation with a concern for their own wellbeing are missing Jesus's invitation: "If there is to be a resurrection there must first be a crucifixion.... We must see that Jesus continues to suffer and die in and for our society. His invitation is that we take up our cross and join in the fellowship of his sufferings. Only THEN can the glory and victory of Easter BEGIN to be seen—a love encompassing the very worst of the world and yet bringing joy, peace and abundance at an entirely new level."[106] Christians are called not to be concerned with their own wellbeing and not to preach peace where there is none, but to enter into the ways in which Jesus "continues to suffer and die in and for our society" in order to see the transformation of death into life throughout the society. This is a different portrayal of the significance of Jesus's death than appears in AE's publications, in particular, where Calvary is the place for reconciliation. Here the theological message is more similar to the SACC, with a reflection on the model that a suffering Jesus holds for Christians in the current situation. But, as I show next, PACSA's posture toward different racial groups also provides a contrast to the SACC, as they stress white complicity in the system and sometimes speak from a white collective experience.

Social Positioning: White Complicity and Solidarity with Black Marginality

PACSA's theological emphasis on death being transformed into life, and of the role of individual people in broader systems, manifests in a focus on black suffering and white complicity. PACSA newsletters also contain multiple voices in their discourse, in contrast to AE, especially. Some identify specifically with a white collective experience and position, calling for the relinquishment of comfort and distance and, instead, becoming proximate to black pain and suffering. In contrast to the SACC, PACSA authors tend to speak from a posture of relative distance to those who are suffering. While this posture is similar to AE's, it also manifests differently from AE because of their different theological convictions. AE called on people to pursue the Christian way as they seek to be reconciled with one another, but this sometimes also centered white experience in a way that prioritizes individual-level healing rather than systemic change. By contrast, PACSA authors call on white people, specifically, to go to places of suffering and to relinquish their privilege in order to forego their complicity in an unjust and violent system.

Focusing attention on the ways in which black suffering aligns with Jesus's suffering is an important component of PACSA's discourse. For instance, in the Christmas 1985 newsletter, Alex Bhiman, a leader of the Institute for Contextual Theology, writes, "Black people in this country can only understand a Christmas which is a time of celebrating God's solidarity with them and so God's vindication of their liberation struggle.... May [Christmas] be a time when we affirm solidarity with the way of the poor towards justice, peace and a new nation."[107] For Bhiman, Christmas marks the contrast between God's intended order and the present reality, and it provides an opportunity to show God's solidarity with "the poor and oppressed" because "Jesus Christ was born into their class."[108] This statement aligns more closely with the theological concerns of the SACC than AE, focusing on the realities of black suffering and the need for a Christian message that resonates with that experience.

But PACSA's posture toward the different racial groups is also different from the SACC's, as they sometimes speak from the position of the privileged. PACSA's emphasis on the need to get proximate to suffering, following the model of Jesus whose suffering and death were transformed into life, also shapes their depictions of the racial violence of apartheid. This is also a difference from AE. In AE's discourse, change happens as black people leave the townships and encounter white people in neutral spaces, where they can all be changed by the Gospel. PACSA calls specifically for white Christians to seek out places of pain and suffering.

For instance, in the Easter 1986 newsletter, Theo Kneifel, a German priest in South Africa who was exiled in the 1980s for his anti-apartheid activism, describes encountering a young black child who dies from malnutrition. He writes, "I then promised this little black girl that I wouldn't get used to her death, and to death like hers. I want to fight this kind of useless, unnecessary death with all my strength."[109] Acknowledging his own lack of understanding and possible questioning of faith, Kneifel asserts that Easter expresses God's "protest against the power of death."[110] Jesus's life and death are then aligned with the experience of a corrupt political system: "When everything seemed lost, when Jesus of Nazareth was executed as a criminal and a political agitator, when the cause of the Kingdom seemed defeated, then God intervened, and did the impossible, and the only necessary thing: He raised Jesus from the dead.... That is why there is sense in all the nonsense around us.... God does not forget: God does not get used to death."[111] Here, the quest to find meaning in senseless violence takes place through the power of the Gospel message of transformed death into life. And Jesus is depicted here as "a criminal and a political agitator," aligning with the experience of those who are protesting, resisting, and experiencing the violence of apartheid.[112] This alignment of Jesus with the marginalized is similar to the SACC and different from AE. But Kneifel also speaks from a place of relative distance from the black girl who has died, and makes a specific theological affirmation of God's commitment to transform death.

In addition to focusing attention on black suffering, PACSA's discourse also highlights the need for white Christians to recognize that they are implicated in the system. Sometimes they do this by speaking explicitly from a white perspective and experience. For instance, James Massey states, "I am White. I share the benefits of being White in South Africa. I share the responsibility for the deep divisions and inequalities in our society. I share the feelings of foreboding and guilt—and anger—in our community."[113] Massey explicitly names his whiteness and all the privileges that this involves. In so doing, he models PACSA's commitment to fostering awareness of one's own position in an unjust system. This is a clear contrast to AE's social positioning with respect to race, in which the emphasis is not so much on white responsibility but on the emotional needs whites have to experience black love and forgiveness.

Similarly, Colin Gardner asserts that "religion cannot be regarded as simply a question of the salvation of isolated, pious individuals: as believers we are involved with all our brothers and sisters, with the society that we are a part of, and therefore with every aspect of this society."[114] This affirmation of the interwoven fates of all Christians is followed by a reflection on the role of the white church in gaining awareness and working for social change. Gardner writes, "I think that in the last three years many white Christians have become distinctly more aware of the socio-political meaning, in South Africa, of Jesus's teaching. As against that, however, it is still sad and frightening to consider how many devoted white Maritzburg churchgoers are still largely or even wholly unaware that being a Christian means really responding, deeply and seriously, to the lot of one's suffering fellow citizens."[115] This discussion of the white church in Pietermaritzburg highlights PACSA's conviction that the church must connect Jesus's teachings to sociopolitical realities. White ignorance is problematized here. This is a contrast to AE's discourse, where there was more of an emphasis on white ignorance as a benign, even innocent, factor that could be changed through their own encounters with black people into spiritual connection and healed relationships. For PACSA, this ignorance involves complicity, and a concern that awareness will not lead to action to address black suffering.

This same newsletter presents the results of a survey that PACSA conducted to give direction to their work. Peter Kerchhoff writes that "a black participant saw

PACSA as part of the Church and said it 'made the Church credible.'"[116] This is followed by a list of reasons why the organization's work is necessary, and the first one is "Awareness is necessary to enable white Christians to fulfill the practical application of Christianity."[117] This inclusion of the voice of a black participant gives more power to the assertion that white Christians need greater awareness. The credibility of the church's witness is at stake. And, implied in both comments is the notion that the possibility for a transformed society is hindered by inadequate engagement from the white church.

PACSA's concern with the distance between white Christian and black Christian responses resonates throughout their discourse. Sometimes white authors explicitly name the problematic features of their position of privilege. In a reflection on how the image of childbirth can be applied to the political situation, Gunther Wittenberg notes, "It is the Black Christians who groan and agonize, while we whites in the main opt out and enjoy the good life. Can there ever be unity in the Church if there is no sharing of suffering?"[118] There is a parallel here to AE, with this concern with the unity of the church and the depiction of the agony and suffering of blacks. But there are also important differences: The path to unity is not reconciliation, but, rather, for whites who are enjoying privileges to share in the suffering of blacks. The black and white church are divided in their experiences, and transformation can only happen if "we whites" are willing to enter into the suffering of blacks.[119] Unlike with AE, where there was a similarity of need despite different experiences, with PACSA there is more emphasis on the requirement for whites to relinquish privileges and enter into black suffering.

This sense of the disparity between white and black reactions to the sociopolitical realities of apartheid, and the need for the church to respond if transformation is to occur, appears throughout PACSA's discourse. For instance, a June 1986 reflection on the ten-year commemoration of June 16, 1976, when schoolchildren in Soweto were killed as they protested having to learn in Afrikaans, posits this question: "How will white South African Christians react to the day? Will they feel that this is not their concern? Will they carry on with business as usual and view the ongoing violence in the townships as something that could just as well be happening on the other side of the globe? It is our task in PACSA to communicate something of the urgency of our present crisis to the churches in Pietermaritzburg. June 16 may very well be a day for renewing and rededicating our commitment to this task."[120] This "urgency" for white Christians to respond to and engage with the issues is juxtaposed with white ignorance and distance.[121] PACSA calls for the white church to become more proximate to black pain.

Similarly, reporting on an open meeting held at PACSA that addressed the ongoing state of emergency, Mark Butler discusses a keynote address given by Father Smangaliso Mkhatswa, the chair of the Southern African Catholic Bishops' Conference. One key problem Mkhatswa names is that "the white community in general is happy to remain ignorant of the real situation."[122] White ignorance here is portrayed as the auto-response, because it is easier (they are "happy") to remain unaware; awareness will require sacrifice and affiliation with suffering. Yet Christians need to "take, very seriously, the 'preferential option for the poor' and identify with the poor and oppressed in their struggles."[123] The problem of white ignorance that is named in all three organizations, but especially in AE and PACSA, has different solutions. In fact, there is a similarity here to the SACC's emphasis on the need to identify with the poor and oppressed. But because PACSA's racial positioning is different from the SACC's, this commitment is expressed differently.

Further reflecting on the event that Butler describes, James Hlongwa notes that "it was clear also how ignorant people are especially about what is happening in the current violence in the townships."[124] Hlongwa posits a practical solution: "It was clear at the evening that there is no excuse for not going out to hot places and discovering for ourselves what is really happening."[125] Unlike in AE, the solution is not to invite black people to leave the townships and enter into a different, neutral space. And unlike in the SACC, the solution is not to invite white people to claim their own dignity and humanity. Rather, PACSA writers perceive that raising awareness involves white people not being content to rest in their ignorance, but actively seeking out places of suffering, identifying with those who are suffering, and seeking to transform that suffering.

As with the other two organizations, PACSA's theological convictions intersect with their social positioning with respect to different racial groups to shape their actions. Their primary theological emphasis on the possible transformation of death into life is institutionally embedded. While they share a theological concern with the SACC about God's solidarity with the oppressed, this conviction intersects with their racial positioning as whites who are relative outsiders to the situation. PACSA calls upon white people to leave their comfortable conditions and enter into solidarity with blacks' suffering. While PACSA shares a similar white racial positioning to AE, this posture is expressed differently because of their theological convictions. They problematize white ignorance as complicity in a violent and unjust system and call for white people to become more proximate to black pain and suffering in order to work for the transformation of such marginalization.

CONCLUSION

This chapter shows how the organizations' theological cultures shape their actions against apartheid. All three organizations contend that the Christian Gospel necessitates combating the injustice and violence of apartheid. They draw on this conviction to argue that apartheid contradicts God's intention for society, that Jesus provides a model for understanding how and why an alternative vision of justice is possible, and that the church has a particular role to play in the cause of justice. While the organizations share these basic convictions, there are also important differences in both their discourse and actions.

The organizations' different patterns of social action are shaped by the intersection of their distinct theological convictions and their social positioning with respect to racial groups. The SACC's support for political detainees and role as an international funnel of financial support to victims of apartheid emerge from their theological commitment to liberation and their focus on the experience of the oppressed. AE's efforts to promote cross-racial encounters at their Conference Center and bring Christian leaders together across racial divides stem from their theological commitment to reconciliation and their focus on an equality of need in the midst of different racialized experiences. PACSA's factsheets and practical support for victims of violence stem from their theological commitment to transformation and their focus on black suffering and white complicity.

Identification with particular racialized groups matters, also. The SACC's calls for and efforts to support liberation emerge from their close identification with the black oppressed population. While both AE and PACSA tend to identify with a white collective experience, this white racialization manifests in different ways in their discourse and actions because of their different theological convictions. As AE includes narratives that demonstrate the power of cross-racial encounter, they also portray the emotional cost of white ignorance, emphasizing the need for white people to receive black love and forgiveness. For PACSA, by contrast, a theological emphasis on transforming death-dealing systems into life-giving ones means that white ignorance is problematized as complicity in a violent system.

These patterns of distinct religious convictions that intersect with racial positioning illuminate the importance of seeing race and religion as mutually constitutive, and not reducible to each other. The courageous actions taken by each organization in a context suffused with increased political repression, violence, and instability show both the possibility and the fragility of channeling religious convictions into social change. As they challenge the existing racial hierarchy and point to a different way, the organizations draw on distinct religious convictions that are also institutionally embedded in ways that reflect and even sometimes perpetuate distinct racialized positions. The links between race and religion are both flexible and durable, contingent and powerful.

The key questions moving forward are these: What dimensions of these theological cultures that were forged in the context of significant tumult in both the churches and the broader sociopolitical context survive across time? How are they carried through to the organizations' responses to GBV? And to what extent do these same theological convictions intersect with the organizations' social positioning when it comes to other social groups, including gender?

I will show in the chapters that follow that the answer to these questions is partly historical and partly contextual, to varying degrees for each organization. On the one hand, the specific intersections of religion and race in the apartheid era establish a particular trajectory that each organization follows, which influences their discourse and actions around GBV and gender itself as a category of justice. On the other hand, there are also important shifts that occur in these intersections of social positioning and theological convictions, and the changing context also influences the subsequent development of ideas that have consequences for the organizations' discourse and actions around GBV.

Chapter 2 considers what happens once apartheid is no longer the primary target of theological claims about justice. Does the pursuit of justice mean something different in the transition to and early years of the democracy, or does it stay consistent? Once the oppressed black majority holds political power, what does this mean for the organizations' focus on and identification with various social groups? Examining patterns of continuity in the organizations' theological cultures amidst a changing environment will allow us, then, to understand how and why these groups vary in their responses to GBV.

2 · CONTINUITY OF THEOLOGICAL CULTURES IN AN EMERGING DEMOCRACY

> As representatives of the Christian Church in South Africa, we confess our sin and acknowledge our part in the heretical policy of apartheid which has led to such extreme suffering for so many in our land. We denounce apartheid, in its intention, its implementation and its consequences, as an evil policy, an act of disobedience to God, a denial of the Gospel of Jesus Christ and a sin against our unity in the Holy Spirit. —The Rustenburg Declaration

In November 1990, South African church leaders convened in the city of Rustenburg to reflect on the role the church could play as the demise of apartheid became more certain.[1] At the conference, a key representative of the white Dutch Reformed Church, Willie Jonker, presented a dramatic confession of guilt not just for his own part in the system, but also on behalf of his entire denomination.[2] Some, including Desmond Tutu, greeted this confession with appreciation. Others criticized it. Some fellow white church leaders asserted it went too far, while some black church leaders were unconvinced that such a statement would lead to practical or lasting change.[3]

Responses to the Rustenburg Declaration, which was published as a result of the convention, were also complicated. The Declaration contained confessions of guilt and repentance for various sins. This included acknowledging how some had used scripture to justify apartheid, while others had condemned it in word but not in action.[4] The Declaration also affirmed the importance of pursuing God's intended justice, and committed to supporting efforts to enact a new democracy.[5] But among those who had cultivated a strong stance against the apartheid regime, there were concerns that the Declaration muted the prophetic voice of the church and settled for "cheap reconciliation" that would not lead to lasting and sacrificial change on the part of those who had been complicit in the oppressive regime.[6]

These events and their variable interpretation illuminate the fragility of religion's influence in a changing sociopolitical context.[7] This chapter examines how the SACC, PACSA, and AE's theological cultures shape their actions in the political transition to, and early years of, the new democracy. I argued in chapter 1 that the organizations' varying actions emerge from the intersection of their theological convictions with their posture toward different racial groups. In this chapter, I analyze whether, how, and to what degree these theological cultures change as the organizations navigate an environment of expanding possibilities and sociopolitical turmoil. I show that the theological cultures follow a distinct path across time and across different issues.

To examine the process that establishes the continuity of the theological cultures, I draw on insights from political and historical sociology concerning the social significance of political transitions. We know that political transitions can not only implement new political and economic structures, but also usher in new imagined possibilities for social life.[8] At the same time, we know that political transitions do not always result in broader social and cultural transformation, and that democratization can coexist with significant, ongoing social and economic inequalities.[9]

These dynamics of both progress and constraint have certainly been the case in South Africa. Prior to the Rustenburg Conference in 1990, under President F. W. de Klerk the apartheid regime had unbanned political parties and released a number of political prisoners, including Nelson Mandela. Political negotiations signaled the impending end of apartheid and transition to democracy. There was considerable political violence and unrest during this time. Indeed, as historian Saul Dubow writes, South Africa's transition period from these events in 1990 to the first democratic elections of 1994 was "the most turbulent in the country's already deeply fractious history."[10]

Though high rates of political violence in the transition era jeopardized the possibility of successful implementation of a representative democracy, peaceful elections were held in 1994.[11] Political leaders subsequently crafted what many have considered to be one of the most progressive constitutions in the world.[12] South Africa also implemented a Truth and Reconciliation Commission (TRC) to try to name and reckon with various human rights abuses under the apartheid regime, a process that inspired other countries to similarly try to address society-wide traumas.[13] These events were shaped by cultural imaginaries of hope, interconnectedness, and the triumph of love over hate and justice over injustice.[14]

At the same time, even as the political transition opened up new possibilities for articulating and enacting the possibility of a nonracial democracy, South Africa has experienced ongoing challenges. Chief among these has been the persistent level of very high economic inequality.[15] In addition, the efficacy of the TRC in enacting true reconciliation and justice has been a subject of considerable discussion and debate.[16] And new social issues have also emerged, including the HIV/AIDS epidemic that was linked to apartheid's migrant labor system and intersected with cultural beliefs and practices about gender and health that contributed to its high prevalence.[17] High levels of crime and corruption among government leaders are among other concerns that have threatened the fragile democracy.[18]

The key question for this chapter is, What do the SACC, PACSA, and AE say and do in the midst of this hopeful and tumultuous environment? Do their theological convictions and social positioning change in light of both the new possibilities for equal and just social relations, and the devastating political violence, persistent social inequality, and various social problems? I argue in the analysis that follows that the theological cultures that each organization cultivated to respond to apartheid forge a path for their responses to the violence in the political transition and the new challenges that emerge in the early years of the democracy.[19] By that I mean that the institutional process that produces the intersection of their theological convictions with their postures toward various social groups is reproduced over time and across social issues. This process of path dependency results in a remarkable continuity in the organizations' theological cultures and their actions.

I show in the analysis below that the organizations' theological convictions remain both consistent and powerful. The SACC's primary theological conviction around a liberating God who enters into suffering solidarity with the oppressed affirms that this same God now provides guidance through a time of wilderness wandering. They perceive an ongoing theological mandate to be in solidarity with the marginalized. AE continues to be grounded in their primary conviction that God ordains a particular way for society to be ordered and invites both spiritual and social reconciliation. PACSA continues to draw on their conviction around a transforming God who is at work to change death-dealing systems into life-promoting ones, and who requires the church to alleviate suffering. These theological convictions are all applied to both the possibilities and tumult of the transition and early democracy.

Once again, these theological convictions are not produced in an institutional vacuum. They also intersect with the organizations' social positioning. The organizations' posture toward various social groups reflects some of the dynamics of the changing context. The SACC shifts from a focus on racial groups and identifying with the oppressed black population that is fighting for freedom, attending more to economic marginalization and adopting a posture of critical solidarity with the new regime. AE's social positioning is more consistent. Of the three organizations their posture toward the new government is the most critical. They express concern that the new dispensation is also not aligning itself with God's way but is ushering in decline in the realm of personal morality and values. AE continues to focus primarily on racial divisions, though there is also some more attention to economic empowerment as well. PACSA continues to focus on and sometimes identify with the complicity of the privileged. Similarly to the SACC, they also attend more to economic marginalization, insisting on the ongoing requirement of the church to align itself with the poor.

In what follows, I take each organization in turn, identifying key features of their work in the transition and early democracy. I then explain how their actions are shaped by the continuity of their theological cultures in the changing environment. Recognizing the path that is forged for the organizations' responses across time and across social issues helps us to understand how religion plays a fragile yet powerful role in the pursuit of justice amidst sociopolitical change.

SOUTH AFRICAN COUNCIL OF CHURCHES

At their 1991 National Conference, the SACC drew on the biblical narrative of the Israelites following Moses out of enslavement in Egypt into an extended period of wilderness wandering before reaching the Promised Land. The conference theme, "From Egypt to the Wilderness, the Ecstasy and the Agony," applies this biblical narrative to the South African context that was suffused with significant hopes, as well as tumult and violence. The newsletter that reflected on the conference theme notes that it "reminded us of the long wilderness journey of the Israelites once they had left Egypt. Not only do we have to leave the slavery of Egypt but also endure the wilderness journey before we reach our promised land goal. In South Africa we have left the bondage of the old style apartheid but have entered into a wilderness of violence and mistrust, confusion and conflict."[20] This description of the conference theme aligns the South African situation with the biblical narrative of turmoil that follows liberation. In so doing, it draws on the central message of the liberation theological culture to remind those gathered at the conference that their experience remains resonant with the biblical witness.

The newsletter adds that "the theme also reminded us that the Lord provided for the people of Israel as they journeyed through the wilderness. The Lord was before them and behind them, guiding and caring. In our wilderness journey we are reminded of the care and love of God made known in Jesus Christ so that we can still rejoice and say Emmanuel, God with us."[21] The SACC's theological conviction of a liberating God who joins in suffering companionship with the marginalized is transposed onto this time of wilderness wandering, as the audience and readers are reminded of God's presence even in the tumult of the new era. The SACC's liberation theological culture forges a path that shapes their discourse and actions in the transition and early democracy.

Identity and Actions

This continuity in the SACC's theological culture is interesting and important given the significant changes the organization had to navigate in this time period. They experienced a substantial decline in funding. Much of the SACC's income in the apartheid era was from international donors, and, in fact, they had been a primary conduit for channeling international funding into the country to assist the resistance movement.[22] With the change of regime, the activities supported by these international bodies declined as funding decreased. The SACC also restructured organizationally, incorporating the work of their regional offices into the national office as a way to consolidate resources.[23] Finally, key leaders took on positions in the new government, including Frank Chikane, who served as general secretary of the SACC from 1987–1994.[24]

To help navigate these challenges, the SACC sought to reestablish connections with their member churches around spiritual formation, rather than making social engagement their primary work as had been true during apartheid.[25] But they also still sought to be a vibrant presence in the civil sphere. The organization set up a Parliamentary Liaison Office in Cape Town to advocate for key legislation in the democracy and supported the TRC, including hosting a conference on the churches and the TRC.[26] They also developed public critiques of some government policies. For instance, they criticized arms trade deals that they saw as contributing to further violence, as well as the government's proposed economic policy, Growth, Employment and Redistribution (GEAR), for not actually being concerned with improving the lives of the poor.[27]

One of the SACC's chief programmatic efforts that emerged during this time was a Development Ministries program.[28] Their Inter-Church Aid program, which had been the primary program through which they supported victims of apartheid, was one of the precursors to this work on development.[29] This new focus on economic inequality and development is thus a continuation of the SACC's concern with supporting the marginalized. The new Development Ministries program involved funding small-scale projects (e.g., sewing and handcraft projects), as well as supporting training in bookkeeping and other practical skills.[30] Newsletters sometimes highlight these various projects, including interviews with the people their programs support, continuing the organization's focus on the experiences of the marginalized.[31] In addition to the SACC's development work, their Justice Ministries branch developed five specific programs, focusing on Education for Democracy, Human Rights, Covenant and Land, Peace and Justice, and Reconciliation and Healing.[32] They also tried to develop programs to address the HIV/AIDS crisis, though this was difficult given their funding constraints.[33]

In what follows, I explain how these programmatic efforts emerge from the continuity of the SACC's theological culture. In particular, their commitment to solidarity with the marginalized remains a consistent theme. As they respond to the changing environment, they interpret this commitment to require a shift in attention from solidarity with the liberation movement to promoting economic development. But the SACC's underlying theological commitment remains intact. This consistency demonstrates the path dependency of the theological culture. In the midst of significant change, we see the enduring power of religious ideas that are institutionally mobilized to respond to pressing social issues.

Continuity of Theological Convictions: Ongoing Solidarity with the Marginalized

As I showed in chapter 1, during the struggle against apartheid, the SACC's theological culture centered on the conviction that the biblical story conveys the power of a liberating God who takes the side of the marginalized in their struggle for freedom from oppression. During apartheid, they contended that God was in solidarity with the suffering black population in their quest for liberation from apartheid. In the transition and early democracy, the SACC's theological convictions follow a path from their call for liberation from apartheid to the metaphor of wilderness wandering I described above, in which a broad and bewildering range of issues now need attention. This path is governed by a consistent theological commitment: the church must be in solidarity with the marginalized. In the changing context, the SACC's sensibility around the marginalized shifts from an explicit focus on race-based oppression to a focus on economic deprivation and inequality. As they had emphasized the contributions of contextual theology during apartheid, they continue to draw attention to the role of a distinctly African theology for responding to the issues that emerge in the transition and early democracy. Far from being detached from their prior convictions, the SACC's discourse during this time is dependent upon and continuous with their original theological culture.

One key articulation of these theological commitments is a statement by the World Council of Churches (WCC) and SACC a little less than a year after the first democratic elections. Following a conference on the church's role in the changing context, the groups issued a statement entitled "Reconstructing and Renewing the Church in South Africa." They write that "African theology is intentionally inclusive; it does not accept a permanent underclass of squalor and fear."[34] They describe the ways the church has "failed to be the Church of the poor" and recommit to that mission.[35] And they suggest that a distinctly African theology is the key both to addressing the legacies of the past and moving into the future. The statement notes that "African theology is rich with vitality, charisma and diversity. We commit ourselves to draw on these resources as we seek to turn away from the legacy of the past."[36] Addressing the contemporary tumult requires recognizing the enduring impact of the apartheid system and drawing on African theology to respond to the situation.

For SACC leaders, a key aspect of African theology is the concept of *ubuntu*, a Nguni Bantu term that signifies shared humanity and interconnectedness.[37] Reflecting on the significance of this theological principle for the TRC process, General Secretary Brigalia Bam notes that "the healing process can never be an individual course of action. It is a community exercise. This is where our African sense of belonging to one another—ubuntu—is so important."[38] She goes on to describe the importance of embracing this notion of interconnectedness as a way to reckon fully with the realities of the past: "We have been blessed in this nation with the possibility of moving out of a dark and putrid past which was destroying us all into a light and blossoming future in which all have the opportunity of life to the full."[39] Calling for the recognition and embracing of *ubuntu*, Bam perceives that the TRC process will require more than simple truth-telling. The belief that people belong to each other is also grounded in the conviction that people belong to God.

Bam writes, "We now have the miracle of healing within our hands as they are within the hands of God. God will not let us go or let us down. That is our starting point, the foundation upon which truth and reconciliation are possible."[40] The possibility of healing from the injustices and violence of the past is rooted in the affirmation that shared humanity and solidarity are the way forward. The SACC's theological convictions follow a path from a God whose liberating power frees from oppression to a God who entrusts humanity with the gift of healing, and who will not abandon these people who have been freed and need to heal.

In addition to drawing on *ubuntu* to promote healing from the wounds of the past, leaders also refer to the concept to articulate the ongoing need for an ecumenical movement to respond to the demands of the time. For instance, the SACC's head of the Communications Unit, Bernard Spong, writes, "Ecumenism is about caring for one another as brothers and sisters under God.... It is not a question of the haves giving to the have nots to salve conscience or as an act of security. It is about being tied together one with another in the family of God's people. The nearest ideal to this in African tradition is, of course, *ubuntu*. It relies on an acceptance of community as the basis of dealing with one another and not individualistic give and take."[41] Here, Spong perceives a difference between those with privilege and advantage bestowing things on the needy, and the principle of interconnectedness among members of a community. The church's response to poverty and economic injustice requires the Christian affirmation of human dignity to intertwine with the African sensibility of community and interconnectedness.

Indeed, the SACC expresses an ongoing theological commitment to solidarity with the marginalized. For instance, a newsletter discussion of a Church Leaders Forum notes, "For its part, the Church had to continue to speak out for and identify with the poor, the destitute and the oppressed. It had to remind the affluent (including those in the Churches) that they had a civic and moral responsibility to equip the disadvantaged so that the quality of life could be improved for all people living in the country."[42] This statement of the church's continued obligation to advocate for and empower the marginalized perceives the need also to call on the privileged to recognize that their economic status is caught up with the status of those on the margins. Even as they broaden their focus on race-based oppression during apartheid to a more explicit concern with economic injustices, the SACC's central underlying theological commitment continues: the Church's responsibility is to be on the side of the marginalized and disadvantaged.

This continuity of theological conviction in the midst of upheaval is sometimes also grounded in affirmations of the need to honor the legacy of the struggle against apartheid. For instance, in a talk on "South Africa in Its Regional and

Global Perspective: Being the Church Today" in March 1995, General Secretary Bam describes the vastness of the emergent issues. She then intertwines the SACC's theology with the importance of shared memory, asserting that, "The need is to ensure that these huge issues do not paralyze us. We dare not let this happen. Our ancestors who gave so much, sometimes life itself, for the creation of a new South Africa will not let us rest, and even if they did the faces and voices of the marginalized and hungry people of our land would not allow it."[43] In the midst of its wilderness wandering and the daunting issues that need to be addressed, the church is reminded both of what it owes those who fought for liberation, and of its consistent theological imperative to be in solidarity with the poor and oppressed.

The SACC's particular focus on the economic marginalization that many South Africans experience is grounded in their recognition that liberation itself has been attained, but the church needs to continue to follow its mandate of attending to the needs of the poor. The WCC and SACC joint statement notes, "We look at our history and the need for its redemption. It tells the story of a long and painful struggle against one common enemy: the apartheid system. Today we are free of those chains, but find there are other enemies . . . such as exploitative economic systems."[44] The statement draws on the liberation theological culture to celebrate freedom from oppression, and shifts to focus on a multitude of enemies, especially economic marginalization.

Thus, in the midst of significant sociopolitical change, the SACC's discourse forges a distinct path in which their response to the oppression of apartheid shapes their response to the dizzying issues now emerging in the new era. That path is marked by the guiding principle of the church's solidarity with the marginalized, as they navigate this time of wilderness wandering and affirm the ongoing relevance of a distinctly African theology. As I show next, these theological convictions intersect with the SACC's social positioning to shape their actions, especially their work on economic development.

Social Positioning: Focus on the Marginalized, Critical Solidarity with the Government

The SACC continues to focus attention on the experience of the marginalized in the transition and early democracy. The way they articulate and embody this commitment is shaped by their changing posture toward the government, as they move from opposition to critical solidarity. And, as I alluded to above, their focus on and identification with the oppressed shifts from racial groups to economic ones. The SACC's social positioning both reflects the uncertain dynamics of the time and is also dependent upon a consistent posture of attention to marginalization.

Sometimes the SACC affirms the importance of solidarity with the marginalized as an ongoing commitment as they respond to criticisms that the churches are politically biased. For instance, the December 1991 newsletter reported on a meeting between the state president, F. W. de Klerk, and church leaders, in which they "were told that they were seen as biased and not impartial."[45] Desmond Tutu, the former SACC general secretary who was then serving as the archbishop of Cape Town, responded, "The churches were not partial when it came to party politics, but... they were when it came to standing for peace with justice, for truth and standing on the side of the poor, the oppressed and the marginalized. For that partiality is of God in Christ."[46] In response to the accusation that they were not politically neutral, the leaders' theological affirmation remains the same: even as the political situation changes, the church is mandated to retain its commitment to standing with those on the margins of society.

Just as this commitment to the marginalized persists in a nonpartisan way, so it should also be enacted in a nonracial way. Frank Chikane clarifies that, as the church continues to foster this posture of solidarity with the oppressed, "it is not taking sides because some people are black and others are white. It is not taking sides with the particular group of human beings—It is taking sides with the victims of society."[47] While many in the SACC would have affirmed this theological principle even under the unjust, race-based political structure of apartheid, Chikane's clarification in this time of political transition is also shaped by the SACC's changing positioning with respect to race. As they shift from focusing on and identifying with the suffering black population in the quest for liberation and toward a solidarity with any victim in the pursuit of nonracial democracy, they broaden the scope of their institutional imagination for marginalization.

The SACC's leadership acknowledges that this is complicated terrain to navigate. In early 1992, their newsletter notes that General Secretary Frank Chikane spoke at a Theology Colloquium, where he reflected on the church's changing posture and role. Chikane notes that, while there are some who might argue that after its time of being "at the forefront of the struggle against apartheid... the church had now to 'retire into prayer,'" this was not a satisfactory answer.[48] It "raised the question, however, of the church's ministry to the poor and the powerless. Are their needs looked after well enough in the changing scene of South African politics? Or is it the church's ministry to ensure they are not sidelined again and again?"[49] Here, once more, the SACC points to the need to engage in solidarity with the poor as a timeless theological commitment. And, indeed, in contrast to what they perceive others to be calling for, this is not the time for the church to retreat, but to continue to enact solidarity with "the poor and the powerless."

As the SACC's discourse draws particular attention to those suffering from economic deprivation, they also call for support of the new government's efforts to address economic injustice. In his address to the SACC's 1994 National Conference, General Secretary Chikane argues that there needs to be continuity with the church's moral obligations of the past. He states, "The church has to take a stand and remain a conscience of the nation. It has to actively participate in the program of reconstruction and development with a particular bias to achieve justice for all the people, especially those who are at the bottom of the ladder."[50] Arguing that the church's ongoing role as the "conscience of the nation" is now to be manifested in their support of new governmental policies around economic reconstruction and development, Chikane articulates a particular concern around economic marginalization.

Indeed, the SACC's social positioning shifts not only from focusing primarily on race-based oppression to economic injustice, but also in relation to the state. Rather than adopt an oppositional stance against an oppressive regime, the SACC now seeks to be in a posture of "critical solidarity" with the new government. Their leaders perceive that there are tensions here, as they discern a consistent theological mandate to be in solidarity with the marginalized even as their own posture to the government is different. Put simply, while they seek to support the new democratic government, they also call on the church to hold the new government accountable to its responsibility to care for the socially and economically disadvantaged.

For instance, when he was head of the Justice Ministries program, Eddie Makue affirmed that "justice issues do not disappear because we have a Government that is committed to justice. We have to insist that Government fulfill its promises, hear the voices of those who still remain silent, and change justice ideals into reality."[51] Resisting the temptation to leave the work of justice to the new government, Makue calls on the church to continue to hold the government accountable. Naming both economic disparities and violence as two specific issues that the church needs to exhort the government to rectify, he states that "economic injustices are so severe and rife that we would want to address them immediately. Not to do so would be a denial of our ministry to the whole person. In the same way the issue of violence is one that has to be dealt with."[52] Situating the concern with economic injustice within a broader commitment to recognize and respond to the needs of the "whole person," Makue contends that the church needs to continue holding the government accountable to its mandate to enact justice.

This posture of critical solidarity with the state while continuing to advocate for the marginalized remains consistent across time for the SACC. In his opening remarks to the 2001 Annual Report, for instance, General Secretary Molefe Tsele expresses concern that the church has retreated too much from political engagement and needs to revitalize its efforts to promote social and political action. He states, "Our involvement in the public sphere does not seek to replace the role of other players in society," including government officials and business leaders. Yet the church does have a specific role to play: "Our business is derived from the *task of ensuring that the poor and marginalized do not become victims of power systems, or rendered non-persons or simple objects of abuse and exploitation by these systems.*"[53] Tsele recognizes that the responsibility of the church is different than it has been in the past, and that it needs to not replace the work of other entities in society. But, even as the SACC's social positioning shifts from confrontation to partnership with the state, he continues to affirm the SACC's core theological commitment to act in solidarity with those who are victimized and marginalized.

Indeed, leaders like Tsele continue not only to call the church to act in solidarity with the marginalized, but also to represent the perspective of the marginalized. At the end of this exhortation to remain focused on the marginalized, he notes, "The vantage point of the Council is the pulse of pain, vulnerability, and poverty."[54] Tsele's message and exhortation reflects the SACC's ongoing commitment to speaking on behalf of, and representing the voices of, the marginalized.

The SACC's theological convictions center on a liberating God who continues to guide the church in a time of wilderness wandering as they reaffirm the importance of solidarity with the marginalized. These theological convictions intersect with a posture that shifts from focusing attention to racial injustice to those experiencing economic marginalization. And their posture to the government shifts from opposition to the unjust apartheid regime to critical solidarity with the new government. In the midst of these adaptations, the core commitments of the theological culture remain intact. The liberation theological culture follows a clearly established path across time and social issues.

AFRICAN ENTERPRISE

AE's June 1991 newsletter celebrates the publication of Michael Cassidy's new book, *The Politics of Love*. In it, Cassidy expresses his conviction that the tumult of the transition will only be successfully navigated if Christian principles are embraced. He writes, "If you begin your reasoning that whites have got to survive at all costs, or if you begin from the view that blacks are going to get revenge, then you are going to have a whole bunch of consequences following from where you started. But if you start your reasoning from Calvary you ... can have only a mandate of love, forgiveness and active compassion and care for our society."[55] Cassidy affirms AE's central theological conviction that the reconciling power of God is enacted through a nonracial and nonpartisan Gospel.

Cassidy contends that this ethic of treating one another according to the logic of Calvary has far-reaching ramifications: "So, then, from the cross, you take Christian principles and the biblical love ethic of thinking of the other person and the other group first and you build that into economic and political structures in terms of justice, compassion, dignity and freedom."[56] People must follow God's way, one that commits to self-sacrifice and putting others first. This is true not only interpersonally, but also for the way that economic and political structures can and should function. As with the other two organizations, AE's theological culture is remarkably consistent across time and issues. God has established a particular way for societies to be ordered, and cross-racial reconciliation provides strong evidence of God's reconciling power.

Identity and Actions
AE's conviction about a distinctly Christian way to organize society in line with God's intention for humanity continues to resonate in the midst of sociopolitical

change, as does their assertion that spiritual reconciliation has the power to enact social reconciliation. As with the other organizations, their theological culture forges a particular path for their response to the changing context. AE experienced some leadership changes during this time. Cassidy stepped away from AE South Africa for a while and did more with the AE International Team. Subsequent leaders were brought in, but none of them lasted very long in the position of AE South Africa's Team Leader, despite the optimism expressed at the time of their appointment.[57] The organization also developed a socially conservative stance vis-à-vis the state. For instance, Cassidy joined with other conservative Christian leaders who were concerned with the new government's expansion of marriage rights to include same-sex couples. They formed the Marriage Alliance of South Africa, an initiative aimed at preserving heterosexual marriage. While this was a separate group from AE, Cassidy led and chaired it.[58]

During apartheid, AE had put their theological principles into action through events and programs that fostered cross-racial encounters and large gatherings of church leaders, in addition to their evangelistic missions. Similar patterns can be seen in the transition and early democracy. AE's geographic location outside Pietermaritzburg, in the province of KwaZulu Natal, significantly impacted their actions. This province had the highest levels of political violence during the transition and has had the highest rates of HIV/AIDS in the country.[59] AE's theological culture impacted their response to this reality. Drawing on their conviction about the importance of facilitating connection across lines of social difference, AE leaders brought representatives of various political factions together, away from media scrutiny, to build interpersonal connections across their differences.[60] AE also hosted a regional gathering of church leaders, at a KwaZulu-Natal Church Leaders Assembly, in early 1996 to try to bring religious leaders together to address the pressing social issues of the time.

AE's commitment to running evangelistic "missions" continued, even as they also developed new programs. They started a Social Empowerment and Development certificate program, developed by Marilee James and Marit Garratt, and formed an African Leadership Development Initiative run by Phineas Dube.[61] In this way, AE's initiatives reflected some of the broader social context and programmatic efforts of the time, as they worked to promote economic development and skills training for leadership in the new democracy. They also started a program called "Foxfires" for youth evangelists. Multiracial teams of about ten youths worked together for a yearlong program, visiting such locations as schools and youth groups to share the Gospel with their peers.[62] These various programmatic efforts reflect consistency in AE's commitment to bring people together across their differences and to minister in both "word and deed" by linking evangelism with social action.

These actions are rooted in the intersection of AE's theological convictions and social positioning. AE's theological commitments remain centered on the belief that God's plan for humanity involves a particular way for relationships, societies, and political systems to be ordered. The way to resolve the alienation that violates God's way is to first seek spiritual reconciliation with God, from which social reconciliation across racial divisions, especially, can be found. These theological convictions intersect with AE's posture toward different racial groups. They continue to emphasize the power of blacks' forgiveness of whites, as evidence of the power of the Gospel. Their posture toward the state is more consistent across time than the other two organizations, as their theological convictions around God's way translate into a concern that the new regime is ushering in a decline in the realm of personal morality and values. This continuity in the midst of significant change shows how the reconciliation theological culture follows a distinct path for both their discourse and actions in the transition and early democracy.

Continuity in Theological Convictions: God's Way for Democracy

As I showed in chapter 1, AE's reconciliation theological culture is built on the conviction that interpersonal relationships and nation-states should be arranged in accordance with God's way. For AE, apartheid was a fundamental denial of God's intention for humanity, and it needed to be changed by addressing alienation and pursuing reconciled relationships. This central conviction continues in the political transition and early years of the democracy. Cassidy writes in the early years of the transition, for instance, "The point in life is that there is a Jesus Way, and if nations follow it they are exalted—for righteousness exalts a nation. Take the non-Jesus way, and a nation is on the way down and out! South Africa should take note."[63] Cassidy continues to contend that following the "Jesus Way" has significant consequences for whether a nation will thrive or not.

This primary theological commitment about following the Jesus Way also shapes a central concern for AE. Their leaders believe that implementing a nonracial political regime is a good thing because it corrects the alienation wrought by apartheid's racial separation, aligning the new regime with God's intention for human relationships. But they also perceive that this change is ushering in an unacceptable departure from God's way in the realm of personal morality and values. A couple of months before the first democratic elections, Cassidy contends, "While the war in South Africa against racism has been fought by forces of nonracialism, there is an ongoing civil war in which the whole Western world is caught up. This is a war of values."[64] Cassidy registers concern with the lack of recognition of this bigger war that is about "defining the nature of Ultimate Reality and Final Authority."[65] This concern is rooted in a perceived contrast between the forces that have been marshaled to enact nonracialism and the dearth of forces that have been marshaled to address values. But God's way is to be followed in all of life. There is continuity here with AE's primary theological conviction of the past: people need to follow God's intended way for societies to function, and not only with respect to racism but also moral values.

For AE, these theological convictions are articulated as a contrast to what is being promoted by the new political regime. During apartheid, God's way was being violated by a regime that alienated people on the basis of race. In the new democracy, God's way is being violated by a regime that is slipping up in the realm of values and personal morality. Cassidy states in April 1995, for instance, "I have a fear that while we are finding our way politically we are busy losing it morally and becoming a society adrift from its moral moorings in Judeo-Christian faith and principles."[66] He goes on to note that his concern was sparked by seeing a news headline that was "trumpeting forth to us, as if it were some triumphant and noble breakthrough for the spirit of freedom, democracy and liberalism, that almost all forms of censorship and pornography laws are probably set to be abolished."[67] AE's central contention that there is a Jesus Way to order societies has ramifications not only for political life, but also for personal morality. So, while appreciating movement toward implementing God's way for democracy in the political realm, Cassidy articulates a concern that this political success is also giving way to a decline in traditional values.

Cassidy is not the only leader in AE to express this conviction. In the November 1995 newsletter, for instance, interim team leader Soh Chye Ann observes that "the changes taking place in our society are happening so fast it is as if, as a relative latecomer to the world of free nations, we have allowed the pressures exerted upon us to propel us to dizzying heights of social, political, religious and economic transformation."[68] As new opportunities open up, dramatic changes are occurring. But these new freedoms are ushering in problematic patterns of individual and social action. He continues, "In the area of morals and ethics, the notions of 'freedom' and 'rights' have put in place new frontiers of behavior. Rules of life are changing as core values affecting individual integrity and choices, business and professional ethics, family structure and morals, religious freedom and expressions are challenged as never before."[69] Again, there is a concern here that the opening up of political opportunities is also coinciding with a decline in personal morality and values. God's way must be followed in all aspects of life, and by all political regimes.

These theological commitments remain consistent over time. For instance, Mike Odell, a long-standing member of the leadership of AE, steps in as interim team leader of AE South Africa after Cassidy transitions to head up the International Team. In a 2000 newsletter, Odell recognizes the broader tumult of the sociopolitical context but then reminds readers that "the important thing is to focus on what God says—not what the politicians, economists and secular leaders of the day might have to say."[70] He then references the biblical text of Colossians 3:1–4, which refers to Christians being raised with Christ and setting their hearts on heaven. But, Odell notes, "this does not mean we opt out; instead, it gives us the right perspective on our world and the assurance that, ultimately He is in control."[71] There is a strong continuity of message here: Christians remain called to follow God's intention for society. Following God's way, not what is promoted by any politician or leader, is the most important thing they can do.

Similarly, Mark Manley, who became AE South Africa's team leader in January 2002, reports on efforts to gather Christian leaders together again in a second

South African Christian Leadership Assembly (SACLA), as they had done in 1976. He writes that this second SACLA provides the opportunity for the church to reflect on "what God has in mind for us. Could it be a nation ... without Aids, without crime, a nation that is godly, humble and an example to others from a servant perspective, a nation that is fully reconciled to each other and to God. We have to find out what the truth is, so we can hold onto it. How do we do that? We have to find God."[72] While not using the specific language of "God's way" that Cassidy deployed earlier, this message nevertheless continues the central theme in AE's discourse: God has ordained a way for relationships and societies to be ordered, and pursuing reconciliation with each other and with God is the way to enact that way—here, described as God's truth.

As with the SACC and PACSA, AE's theological convictions follow a clear path from apartheid to the transition and early democracy. The insistence on God's way for ordering relationships and social systems that undergirded AE's focus on the power of the Gospel for reconciliation during apartheid shapes their ongoing sense of mission in the midst of sociopolitical change. At the same time, the theological culture also adapts, incorporating more explicit concerns with personal morality. AE's posture of criticism of the apartheid regime for its violations of God's intention for society by creating racial alienation is transposed into a criticism of the democratic regime for its violations of God's intention for society by promoting a decline in personal morality and values. As I show next, these theological convictions intersect with AE's social positioning to shape their actions, especially their ongoing work on cross-racial reconciliation.

Continuity in Social Positioning: Enacting God's Way through Reconciliation

AE's theological culture is built on the conviction that following God's way means seeking reconciliation, both with God and with one's neighbors. During apartheid, this theological conviction intersected with a particular focus on the power of black people's forgiveness of white people, often centering white ignorance and emotion. This pattern continues in the transition and early democracy. In contrast to the other two organizations, whose posture focuses attention on the marginalized, especially in terms of economic deprivation, AE remains primarily focused on the possibility of cross-racial reconciliation.

For AE, cross-racial reconciliation is only possible because the Gospel is a politically and racially neutral force. They call people to embrace a different set of values than their race-shaped perspectives would otherwise lead them to enact. For instance, in July 1992, at a time when the political violence in KwaZulu Natal was intensifying, the emphasis is on the need for understanding and forgiveness. Cassidy writes, "We must resist all alienation—and forgive. . . . All over the place, people are letting alienation and disillusionment with one another take over their ever-hardening hearts. We all need again to hear our Lord's word that the unequivocal Christian mandate is reconciliation and forgiveness."[73] AE's consistent emphasis on all people being in need of the Christian Gospel continues here. Their theological conviction that people have a shared spiritual need is seen here in the exhortation that "all" forms of alienation, everywhere, and among everyone need to be resisted. All people's hardened hearts can be healed through Christian reconciliation and forgiveness.

This insistence that all people are in need of the Gospel results in a tendency to downplay social inequalities in favor of an emphasis on unity.[74] As I described above, AE facilitated an effort to gather political leaders together away from media, where they could simply tell one another their life story. Reflecting on the success of such events, the March 1993 newsletter notes that these experiences "have brought home to us afresh the need for South Africans of every colour and all creeds or none and at every level to take on board self-consciously the spirit of togetherness."[75] Cassidy goes on to observe that this invitation is a contrast to the apartheid years: "This spirit of pulling together is the very opposite and antithesis of the apartheid notion of apartness at every level of life and action. If South Africa is to be saved we had better grasp that we either swim together or sink apart."[76] In contrast to apartheid's policies of separation, the mandate is for all people to come together and realize their connectedness.

This language of a "spirit of togetherness" sounds similar to the SACC's advocacy of embracing *ubuntu*. But the meaning is different here. Cassidy advocates for a togetherness that is predicated on everyone reaching beyond their differences to be in relationship with one another. Common humanity transcends difference. By contrast, the SACC argued that the African theological emphasis on interconnectedness resulted in particular responsibilities of the privileged to not take advantage of the marginalized. Social inequality and difference of experience matter.

For AE, the primary mechanism for facilitating this sense of togetherness is by cultivating interpersonal relationships across difference. Cassidy writes in August 1993, "Everywhere alienated people must take initiatives [sic] to find each other in real relationship. Only in this way will we come through. . . . Just get a bunch of opposites together—let the Lord in—get away with each other and let Christ's chemistry do the rest."[77] Without calling attention to specific ethnic and political factions involved in the conflict, Cassidy's call to simply gather "opposites together" envisions both a spiritual and social reconciliation that can defuse the violence. Fostering relationships will enact wider social change. This consistent message within AE—that is, that even while people have different experiences, they have a shared spiritual need—signifies a key difference from both the SACC and PACSA. The other two organizations often call for those who are more powerful and privileged to instead enter into solidarity with the marginalized, and increasingly they shift to a focus on economic marginalization and other social issues. By contrast, AE's discourse continues to stress the equality of need that people share despite their different experiences, especially in terms of race.

AE also continues to document the redemptive power of black people's forgiveness of white people who have wronged them. The other two organizations' social positioning shifts from focusing on race to economic groups. AE's social positioning remains centered on racialized categories. Not only this, but for the other two organizations, particular responsibility is placed on white, privileged people. AE focuses primarily on the forgiving initiative of blacks.

Sometimes AE's narratives stress black people finding spiritual solace as they forego the personal bitterness they feel toward whites. For instance, in 1992 AE sponsored a Pan-African event where church leaders from other parts of Africa visited South Africa and met with leaders of various political factions. These black African church leaders' own experiences of trying to forgive white supremacists and Afrikaner supporters of apartheid become a testament to the Gospel's power for changing individual hearts. The newsletter describing this event notes how a prominent East African church leader, John Gatu, "was able to detect hatred and bitterness in his heart."[78] This sin was directed both "towards Afrikaners generally and the Conservative Party" and to "Dr Truernicht particularly"— that is, Andries Truernicht, a Dutch Reformed clergyman who had helped craft apartheid policies.[79]

Gatu "confessed" this "personal bitterness" to Truernicht, "without, of course, compromising any of his convictions relating to the mechanisms of classical apartheid."[80] This confession is rooted in Gatu's conviction about the consequences of holding on to this resentment because he "knew that his Lord and the Scriptures could not condone personal bitterness."[81] As Gatu confesses that his bitterness was preventing him from seeing Afrikaners the way that God would, the newsletter observes that "a mighty onus of reflection and self-examination is thus also placed upon the person hearing such a confession."[82] From AE's perspective, forgiveness is not only for the one who has been harmed, but also for the one who has done harm. And yet, the newsletter does not actually recount the response of Truernicht or the others present. Instead, the narrative centers a black person's spiritual reconciliation as he lets go of personal bitterness.

These stories sometimes also depict black forgiveness of white perpetrators of violence as a catalyst for white people's salvation, centering white experience. This motif that was common during apartheid remains a remarkably consistent narrative pattern over time. A later newsletter documents the conversion of a member of the Afrikaner Weerstandsbeweging (Afrikaner Resistance Movement), a neo-Nazi, far-right political party. While in prison, the white supremacist heard Malawian evangelist Steve Lungu preach. He approached Lungu afterward and "said he had hated blacks with all his heart but on hearing Steve say that he forgave whites, he had decided to commit his life to Christ."[83] This brief vignette about a black person's forgiveness prompting a white person's salvation captures AE's consistent message. Embracing the Gospel's mandate to enact forgiveness can change personal bitterness and individual hatred. This process starts with a black person. The main burden of change and reconciliation is on blacks who offer forgiveness to whites, even—or perhaps especially—those whites who were not innocently ignorant, but who had actively constructed the system and facilitated its violence.

As with the other two organizations, AE's theological culture follows a clear path from their response to apartheid and their navigation of the transition and early democracy. Their theological convictions center on the assertion that God ordains a particular way that relationships and societies must follow. This affirmation of the Jesus Way intersects with their social positioning as they remain focused on the possibility of cross-racial reconciliation, narrating the power of black people's forgiveness of whites as a sign of the efficacy of the Gospel. And it shapes their portrayal of a concerning decline in personal morality and values that the new government is supporting. AE's theological convictions intersect with their social positioning to shape their ongoing work in preaching the Gospel and enacting cross-racial reconciliation.

PIETERMARITZBURG AGENCY FOR CHRISTIAN SOCIAL AWARENESS

In February 1992, PACSA's fieldworker Sikhumbuzo Mbatha was assassinated. Mbatha was working to "rebuild communities destabilized by violence," intertwining work on development and peace-building in a community rife with inequality and violence.[84] PACSA's response to this tragedy was to draw on their transformation theological culture. Acknowledging the grief of the death of their colleague and friend, Neville Richardson writes, "A central truth of Easter is that the love and creative power of God can reach and transform the human condition, no matter how bad it may be."[85] In fact, in the face of the violence around them, Richardson reminds readers that "the Easter message is that [Jesus's] nonviolent way triumphed over the violence that was done to him."[86]

This message of the possibility of peace triumphing over violence has ramifications for Christians to embrace and enact: "The Easter faith, in a God whose love and creative power reach us anywhere, grips us and does not let us give up. Instead it spurs us on against the odds in our sick and very violent society, to loving service, following a living God who still says: 'Go, in my name. I am with you always.'"[87] Richardson draws on PACSA's distinct theological convictions as he calls on "the Easter faith"—a faith that is rooted in the power of the Gospel for seeing violence and death transformed into peace and life—to encourage Christians to engage in ongoing "loving service." PACSA's transformation theological culture forges a path that shapes their discourse and actions in the transition and early democracy.

Identity and Actions

In the transition and early democracy, PACSA authors continue to draw on the theological conviction that systems that deal violence and death can be transformed into ones that promote peace and life. As with AE, PACSA's navigation of the tumultuous sociopolitical climate was significantly shaped by their geographic location in the province of KwaZulu Natal. In March 1990, the "Seven Day War," which started as a confrontation between the United Democratic Front and the Inkatha Freedom Party, broke out in areas around Pietermaritzburg. During the conflict, over one hundred people were killed and between twenty and thirty thousand had to flee their homes.[88] PACSA set up a crisis center for victims and partnered with local churches to provide practical support.[89]

As part of PACSA's partnership with others working to ensure peaceful elections in the midst of the political violence, Peter Kerchhoff was called upon to head up the Monitoring Division of the Independent Electoral Commission, and various PACSA volunteers were trained as election monitors.[90] As with the SACC, PACSA also was involved in the TRC, both expressing support of the process and providing tangible assistance by taking statements from victims.[91] In the years of transition and early democracy, PACSA continued to be situated in close proximity to the suffering of the marginalized and to try to support efforts to address the tumultuous context.

As with the other organizations, PACSA also experienced leadership and staffing changes during this time. In 1999, the organization's founder, Peter Kerchhoff, died unexpectedly, after sustaining injuries in a car accident. Karen Buckenham, who had been in charge of PACSA's gender work, stepped into the role of director for several years. She was succeeded in 2003 by Daniela Gennrich, who had also led PACSA's gender work.[92] Where the SACC experienced significant decline in their staff and resources for programming, PACSA's staff actually grew during this period. With funding from international sources, including Diakonia Sweden and Norwegian Church Aid, the organization transitioned from a small staff that was supported by volunteers to hiring multiple coordinators of various programs along with fieldworkers and interns to help carry out their work.[93]

PACSA's ongoing commitment to raising awareness and accompanying the marginalized was expressed as their organizational structure and programming expanded. They developed new programs and initiatives to address voting and peaceful elections, human rights, and economic inequality and poverty.[94] In response to HIV/AIDS, they conducted a research study, developed educational programs, and provided practical support to those who were experiencing it.[95] And they continued to center their mission on the importance of raising awareness, publishing factsheets and hosting workshops and presentations on various social issues.[96]

PACSA's experience was not always smooth. Annual Reports and newsletters acknowledge that their staff undertook times of organizational discussion and debate to find the best path to take in the changing environment. This included organizational discussions of PACSA's mission and future throughout 1992.[97] Peter Kerchhoff's death in 1999 also raised significant questions about the future of the organization.[98] And, in part due to donor demands, they eventually shifted they work toward community development.[99]

In the midst of these changes, PACSA's theological culture forges a path that guides their mission and actions. They continue to emphasize both the importance of the possibility of transformation of injustice and the Christian mandate to be on the side of the marginalized. Their conceptualization of the structures in need of transformation expands to incorporate the range of social issues that emerge in the transition and early democracy. And they continue to focus both on the complicity of the privileged and the need to enter into suffering solidarity with the marginalized. This pattern of continuity amidst significant upheaval demonstrates the path dependency of the transformation theological culture for shaping PACSA's actions.

Continuity of Theological Convictions: Transformation of Death and Injustice into Life and Justice

As I showed in chapter 1, PACSA's theological culture centers on the conviction that death can be transformed into life, and that Christians are called to partner with God's transforming work as they seek to alleviate suffering and usher in a more just world. Especially in the midst of the political violence during the transition, this theological narrative continues to predominate in their discourse. It is also carried into the early years of the democracy and applied to the wide range of social issues that they believe the church needs to confront. PACSA's transformation theological culture expands to incorporate the new constellation of social issues. As they do so, they express an ongoing commitment to solidarity with the marginalized.

The contrast between life and death, and peace and violence, is a consistent dimension of PACSA's theological convictions. For example, in the December 1992 newsletter, Robin Hutt highlights "the Christmas good news that God is in our world sharing the reality of its joys and its pains and bringing the light of the Resurrection beyond the darkness."[100] Hutt draws on PACSA's central beliefs about the contrasting forces of light and darkness, peace and violence, goodness and evil. He writes, "We believe in the resurrection and the victory of goodness over evil and life over death. Keep on going along the way of faith and courage, honesty and justice, of love and peace. This is the way of God, the way of the light that no darkness can put out."[101] God's transforming power brings light out of darkness, and Christians are to continue to follow that way of light and life.

This continuity in PACSA's theological convictions is consistent across time and issues. For instance, Karen Buckenham explicitly connects the message of life triumphing over death to the TRC in the Easter 1996 newsletter. She begins by affirming PACSA's central interpretation of the Easter narrative: "At Easter we celebrate the fact that life is more strong, more real, more lasting than cruelty, pain, evil and death."[102] Buckenham then notes that this message resonates in particular ways with the launching of the TRC: "This year, Easter has coincided with the beginning of the hearings of the Truth Commission. People are telling their stories, cleaning wounds, sharing pain, and looking for justice. They are affirming life.

So too are those who are listening, allowing themselves to absorb the pain and feel the suffering of the speakers."[103] Buckenham's interpretation of the TRC draws on PACSA's theological culture that includes attention both to those who are suffering and to those who bear witness to such suffering.

Buckenham concludes by explicitly invoking PACSA's emphasis on the transformative power of the Gospel: "May God transform the anguish of lives taken, and blood spilled, into resurrection life."[104] During apartheid, PACSA contended that the violence and oppression of the system could be transformed into peace, justice, and life. As she affirms that God transforms death and suffering into life, Buckenham directly applies these theological convictions to the new issues and processes emerging in the new democracy.

While this direct application of the transformation theological culture predominates in PACSA's discourse, authors in the newsletters sometimes also reflect on the ways that the changing South African context complicates such an application. Tim Nuttall reflects in the Easter 1997 newsletter, for instance, on the continued relevance of the resurrection narrative, but he also acknowledges that without the specific enemy of the apartheid regime, applying this theological commitment is not as straightforward. He writes that in the late 1980s "it was a relatively simple matter to equate the Easter idea of resurrection (restoring from death to life) with the political liberation of South Africa from the grip of apartheid. Now, just over a decade later, it is less easy to conceive of this symmetry."[105] In particular, he notes, "we are living through the shift from the politics and morality of anti-apartheid resistance to the more messy and compromised arenas of social and economic reform."[106]

What does this shift mean for the ongoing resonance of the transformation theological culture's emphasis on the power of resurrection? Nuttall writes, "In my own thinking, the resurrection simile for dramatic societal revival and restoring of life has given way to less spectacular guiding notions of caring and serving, and of deepening the cultures of democracy and development."[107] Still affirming the significance of the resurrection narrative in the transformation theological culture, Nuttall notes that the changing sociopolitical environment also invites Christians to embrace the more mundane, "less spectacular" ways of recognizing and working for that transformation. The central themes of the transformation theological culture are adapted to the changing environment.

Even as authors sometimes call for ongoing consideration of how PACSA's theological commitments should adapt to the changing context, there is also remarkable continuity in their discourse across time and across social issues. For instance, the Easter 2003 newsletter opens with a reflection on children living with or impacted by HIV/AIDS. Reverend Livingstone Ngewu draws on PACSA's transformation theological culture as he affirms that "in becoming human God assumed our humanity to the extent of being subjected to the worst form of humiliation.... When Jesus assumed our humanity, this was not some kind of stage show. The intention was to transform it and thus he penetrated human despair by offering hope. As Christians we need to carry the cross as Jesus carried it."[108] And for this particular issue, Ngewu notes, "God who reaches out towards us requires us to clothe the naked children on the cross."[109] Here, Ngewu echoes PACSA's long-standing message of God entering into the human condition and transforming it. And Christians are called to do likewise. The social issues may be changing, but the underlying theological commitment remains the same.

PACSA's primary theological commitments remain consistent in the midst of the sociopolitical tumult. Authors acknowledge the complexities of applying their theological culture to the changing sociopolitical environment. Their focus on the transformative power of the Gospel still grounds their interpretation of and response to a range of issues, including political violence, poverty, the TRC, and HIV/AIDS. As with the other two organizations, the theological convictions that were cultivated during apartheid forge a path for PACSA's response to the tumult and hope of the transition and new democracy.

Continuity of Social Positioning: Focus on the Marginalized from a Position of Privilege

PACSA's theological culture stresses not only the relevance of the Christian account of the transformation of death into life for the South African context, but also the importance of the church engaging in actions of solidarity with the poor and the oppressed. In this respect, their discourse is quite similar to the SACC's. At the same time, there are subtle but important differences between the two organizations. As described above, the SACC's posture shifts from being closely aligned with the liberation movement itself toward a posture of critical solidarity with the government. In that context, they reinterpret and expand their conviction that the church is mandated to engage in solidarity with the marginalized. For PACSA, while their organizational posture also shifts in some ways, they do not experience the same degree of change as the SACC. In fact, in the midst of broader change, PACSA authors often continue to recognize that they occupy a posture of relative privilege, as they had perceived and grappled with during apartheid. They call on their constituency, often presumed to hold the same kind of privileged position, to take concrete, meaningful Christian action in the world.

One of PACSA's early contentions in the political transition is that the church will have an ongoing, consistent imperative to advocate for the marginalized. As Sid Luckett writes in the August 1991 newsletter, "The church . . . has the responsibility of ensuring that the voices of the poorest and most marginalized people and society are always heard: we may not relax our vigilance for justice simply because basic human rights become enshrined in a Constitution."[110] Instead, the church will need to help ensure that the new Constitution is practiced in ways that honor the dignity of the marginalized: "A just Constitution will always need to be vigorously implemented in favor of those who are powerless and suffer at the margins of society and against the vested interests of those who hold power and wealth."[111] Arguing that the church will need to play a key role in holding political structures accountable to the poor, Luckett recognizes that a new Constitution will not cause power differences to evaporate. Rather, the new political systems will need to advocate for the interests of the powerless and poor, rather than the powerful and wealthy.

Similarly, a few months after the first democratic elections, John Aitchison argues for the church's continued presence in the civil sphere, in contrast to the politicians who are now taking center stage: "Off the stage, what will Christians and their organizations do? Surely what they were always supposed to do—be with the people who are always off the stage, the poor, the marginalized, the forgotten, the alienated and the rejected. And those people will still be around."[112] While celebrating the new democracy, Aitchison aligns the mission of the church with those on the margins. Indeed, the church needs to recognize that, again, a new democratic regime does not mean that injustices and inequalities will disappear. Christians are called not to step into the limelight, but rather to enter into solidarity with the marginalized who will still be there.

This emphasis on ongoing solidarity with the marginalized is rooted in PACSA's theological emphasis on transformation. In the October 1994 newsletter, Moshe Rajuili reflects on a course he taught on some of the biblical prophets, and highlights the prophet Amos, in particular. He writes, "Amos would remind us that God is a great transformer.... He changes people, systems and nations. We have witnessed that in the last two to three years in this land. The challenge to us is that if we have credible dealing with that God we are to be transformed and show real signs of new life."[113] And what is the evidence of such "new life" that has been transformed? Rajuili goes on to observe that "Amos challenged the people of Israel not to trample the poor while they build themselves stone mansions and plant lush vineyards. He did not spare them for oppressing the righteous and depriving the poor of justice in the courts."[114] This biblical witness of the prophets not only reaffirms the importance of seeing the possibility of broad social transformation, but also points out that the fruit of such transformation must be ensuring justice for the poor. Rajuili also exhorts those who have material resources not to "trample the poor," continuing the transformation theological culture's emphasis on the complicity of the privileged.

In the midst of social and political change, this expression of the Gospel's good news remains constant. In the Easter 1995 newsletter, Mzwandili Rodrigo Nunes contends that "times change and fashions change but the call of Jesus remains the same. Support the poor, the weak, the marginalized and the exploited for whom the Gospel is always good news."[115] And Christians are once again called to take concrete action in order to see life-giving social change happen: "Denounce corruption, greed, fraud and selfishness as you try to persuade yourself and those around you to work and to sacrifice in order to build a new world—A world where God's will is done so that there is real equality and freedom for everyone without regard to gender, age, physical ability, color and language."[116] PACSA thus argues that Christians are to maintain their commitment to following Jesus's call to attend to and advocate for those who are marginalized and, in so doing, usher in a new world.

PACSA authors also sometimes explicitly speak from a position of privilege. This pattern originated during apartheid and continues through the transition into the new democracy. For instance, in July 1996, Beverley Haddad, a local Anglican minister and theology professor at the University of KwaZulu Natal who later joined PACSA's staff, draws a contrast between the clarity of the prophetic voice of the church during apartheid and the muted presence of the church in the new democracy. She notes, "During the apartheid era, the prophetic voice of the church constantly called us back to the suffering, pain and dehumanization experienced by the poor. This voice constantly challenged our apathy and our indifference. It reminded us that the church needed to work towards eradicating systems of injustice, not to collude with them."[117] This narrative clearly speaks from the posture of the privileged, highlighting "*our* apathy and *our* indifference." Employing an expansive notion of who "the poor" are, Haddad speaks from the posture of those who have been apathetic and indifferent to injustice, even colluding with it.

Haddad goes on to note that this strong prophetic voice of the church has become much quieter: "In these post-liberation days, it seems that the prophetic voice has become a mere whisper, and the Church has gone back 'to being the Church'—a place where people are not challenged, but comforted as they are lulled back into apathy and indifference. Yet the poor are still with us."[118] Again, the people imagined in this discourse are those who had previously been disengaged and have also now been "lulled back" into that same posture. PACSA authors continue to speak from and to the position of the privileged. This is an important point of continuity in their theological culture's emphasis on challenging white complicity and calling those with privilege to relinquish it.

Sometimes this clear identification with the privileged is named more explicitly by PACSA authors. For instance, in a reflection on the significance of Christmas for the poor, Renate Cochrane notes that, in contrast to the way she experienced the nativity story as a child, "the nativity story told in the context of real-life poverty contains such a different meaning. Among my poor parishioners, I can sense real empathetic suffering with the holy couple."[119] Describing Jesus's own experience of poverty, Cochrane goes on to note, "The dehumanizing poverty in the nativity story is brutally real to those who labor and are heavy laden. And the same story is so magically unreal to our children who grow up in the wealthy suburbs. Isn't it amazing how we, as rich Christians, do not even feel the pinch of pain when we hear the nativity story?"[120] As Cochrane identifies with those who are rich, she speaks from the posture of the privileged in ways that resonate with PACSA's apartheid-era discourse as well. The emphasis here on economic privilege is consistent with the messages of the past, as they continue to call for white and wealthy people to wake up to the deeper realities of the world's suffering, and then to follow the Christian call to action.

Cochrane also draws on PACSA's central theological conviction about the power of the Gospel for transformation: "The nativity story... expresses our deepest longing for a transformed world in which hierarchically oppressive structures have been overcome."[121] Narrating her own interactions with "poor parishioners" in her congregation, Cochrane then articulates a keen awareness of the structures and systems that oppress people and need to be transformed. For PACSA, a commitment to ongoing solidarity with the marginalized remains an integral part of their theological culture.

This recognition of the contrast between the experiences of people on the margins and those who have more economic resources only sharpens as South Africa moves further into the democracy. For instance, the front page of the Easter 2000 newsletter contends, "Our Christian faith gives us hope that any system that significantly deprives the majority of people of resources while rewarding a small elite with super abundance does not find favor with God and will not last."[122] The newsletter then invites readers to "pray for the coming of the Kingdom of Justice and Peace, for the redistribution of the resources of the earth to all human beings and especially to those who are now deprived!"[123] This call for redistribution of resources emerges from PACSA's theological culture that stresses the need to be in solidarity with the suffering and marginalized in the society, and to pursue a comprehensive transformation of the society's systems and resources.

PACSA's theological culture centers on the conviction that God can transform systems that deal death into ones that promote life. They continue to call the privileged to accompany those who are suffering, bearing witness to and working to transform their pain. This transformation theological culture expands to incorporate various issues that emerge. As with the other two organizations, PACSA's transformation theological culture forges a path that shapes their discourse and actions in the transition and early years of the democracy.

CONCLUSION

This chapter demonstrates the path dependency of theological cultures amidst significant sociopolitical change. Each of these organizations has to navigate a complex environment that is marked by new hopes, new challenges, funding constraints, and political instability, as well as their own structural and leadership changes. In the midst of these changes and challenges, their theological cultures prove to be remarkably consistent across time and across social issues. The organizations' varying actions emerge from the ways their distinct theological convictions are institutionally produced and reproduced.

The SACC's theological culture follows a particular path from their call for liberation from apartheid, with its focus on racial groups and opposition to the apartheid regime, to the affirmation that the God who liberated them was still accompanying them in a time of wilderness wandering. And this same God continued to invite the church to be in solidarity with the marginalized. Their social positioning shifts from an explicit focus on racial groups to economic marginalization, and their posture of opposition to the apartheid regime shifts to one of critical solidarity with the new regime. The SACC's intersecting theological convictions and social positioning result in efforts to address economic inequality through development work.

AE's theological convictions remain grounded in the affirmation that people and nation-states are supposed to follow God's way. While the other two organizations adopt a posture of critical solidarity with the new government, AE's theological convictions lead them to perceive that God's way may also not be followed by this new regime, which instead is ushering in a problematic decline in personal morality and values. In addition, where the other two organizations shift toward more focus on economic inequality, AE remains primarily focused on racial groups. A key feature of their discourse is consistent over time: black people's forgiveness of white people is the impetus for cross-racial reconciliation. AE's theological convictions around the Jesus Way intersect with their social positioning to shape their continued actions of fostering cross-racial reconciliation.

PACSA's theological convictions remain grounded in the affirmation of a God whose transforming power can change death-dealing systems into life-promoting ones. Their theological culture expands to incorporate economic inequality and other issues, as they maintain their theological and practical commitment to the socially disadvantaged. While they share the SACC's conviction that the Gospel mandates solidarity with the marginalized, this commitment is expressed differently because of both their theological convictions and their social positioning. Their emphasis on the transforming power of the Gospel is different from the SACC's account of wilderness wandering, and they also continue to both focus on and sometimes identify as white, economically privileged people who need to relinquish their complicity in an unjust, violent system. PACSA's actions to raise awareness and assist victims of violence stem from this intersection of theology and posture toward various social groups.

Thus, my argument is not only that theological convictions are institutionally embedded in ways that shape actions, as I have demonstrated both in chapter 1 and in this chapter. Theological cultures also follow a clear path that shapes their actions over time and across social issues. They are not immune from changes in the broader context, and they prove to be adept at adapting to that context. But they do not fundamentally change over time or across social issues.

What is the significance of these patterns of continuity in the organizations' theological cultures for their responses to GBV? Part II examines the implications of these theological cultures for GBV and gender justice. In chapter 3, I demonstrate that the organizations vary in their institutional imagination of women who experience violence. These different responses are due to the ways that the organizations' primary theological convictions intersect with their posture toward women as a social group. The theological cultures shape both their discourse and actions around GBV as an issue of gender justice.

PART 2 THE POWER OF THEOLOGICAL CULTURES FOR GENDER-BASED VIOLENCE AND GENDER JUSTICE

3 · THEOLOGICAL CULTURES AND GENDER-BASED VIOLENCE

> Issues of violence against women violate the image of God in humanity. The church in Africa should be concerned deeply with the way the image of God is being destroyed through violence against women. —Isabel Phiri

In November 1995, the international NGO Human Rights Watch released a damning report about violence against women in South Africa. Documenting a pervasive pattern of egregious violence, the report was picked up by local, national, and international news sources, with various entities referring to the country as the "rape capital of the world."[1] Since that time, public debates have ensued within the country about both the extent and the causes of the problem.

Some of these debates have circulated around high-profile cases. For instance, in 1999 there was a public confrontation between President Thabo Mbeki and journalist Charlene Smith after Smith went public with her experience of rape and stabbing.[2] Mbeki defended accounts that the country's crime rates were, in fact, decreasing and that they were effectively combating all manner of crime. He also accused Smith (a white woman) of deploying racist rhetoric to overplay the significance of GBV.[3] In 2005, then–deputy president Jacob Zuma was accused of raping a woman. A judge allowed the defense to include extensive questioning into the plaintiff's sexual history, and the court sided with Zuma's contention that the sex was consensual.[4] And in 2013, the Paralympian Oscar Pistorius shot and killed his girlfriend at home, defending himself by saying he thought she was a dangerous intruder.[5] Each of these cases was laden with debates about the extent to which race and "culture" played a role, both in the violent encounters themselves and in public perceptions of and responses to them.[6]

Since South Africa's crisis of GBV initially brought international and national scrutiny, and as these high-profile cases have magnified debates over its severity, causes, and consequences, researchers and policy experts have established that the country has a persistent and very high rate of both rape and intimate partner homicide.[7] The problem has been widely acknowledged, albeit still debated in some circles, and numerous governmental programs and NGOs have sought avenues of addressing it.[8]

In the midst of public discussions, debates, and controversies about GBV, and as the high prevalence of various forms of GBV in South Africa has been substantiated numerous times, an important voice in the civil sphere has largely been missing. As SACC general secretary Brigalia Bam acknowledged in an address in March 1995, "The silence of the Church on violence against women and children is deafening."[9] This silence seemed to linger more than fifteen years later when I went to South Africa to begin this project. As I described in the introduction, shortly before my trip, a gang rape of a mentally disabled girl in Soweto made international news headlines. The incident was still reverberating when I was there. In a Cape Town restaurant one afternoon, I had a lengthy conversation about the church's role in democratic South Africa with a journalist who had been involved in the anti-apartheid movement and has also been deeply invested in gender issues. I observed to her that the public awareness of GBV seemed very high to me, based on my observation of multiple newspaper and other public responses to the incident. She rejoined, "Was the church—did you hear the prophetic voice? In the public domain?" I reflected for a moment, and answered, "Well, no. Not really in the public domain." She responded, "That's my problem." She went on to decry the lack of a clear prophetic Christian voice against this form of violence, seeing it as a sign that the church has faltered in its attempt to continue to be a source of conviction and power in addressing injustice.

This chapter takes up her question and observation, and investigates why. That is, what factors explain how and why religious organizations that had condemned and sought to take action against racial injustice and violence may falter when it comes to addressing GBV? And what factors facilitate their recognition of and response to the problem?

These are important but vexing questions, and not only in South Africa. Research on the role of religion in GBV in various empirical contexts has documented the ways that religious leaders and organizations can exacerbate the problem by their unhelpful responses, especially those that rely on religious teachings that support women's subservience to men.[10] But we also know that religion can sometimes be protective against GBV and can provide survivors with a sense of meaning, support, and healing.[11] These patterns have been evident in South Africa, specifically. Religious leaders, churches, and faith-based organizations have sometimes emerged as key actors who offer both spiritual and practical support to try to address the problem, but these efforts are complicated by the ways that these religious entities can also perpetuate the subordination of women through their teaching and practices.[12]

Existing scholarship has thus helpfully illuminated the ways in which religious leaders and organizations can be complicit in GBV yet can also mitigate it. But we know less about the institutional pathways that shape the connections and disconnections between religious organizations' responses to racial and gendered violence. As I discussed in the introduction, one of the crucial insights of intersectional theory has been that violence plays a significant role in legitimating and upholding intersecting systems of power, including racism and sexism, and that these processes happen not only among individual people but also within social institutions and organizations.[13] Prominent intersectional theorists such as Patricia Hill Collins have alluded to the fact that religion is an important institutional space in which conceptions of violence are created and maintained, and that defining and responding to violence is a key source of the power of intersecting systems of oppression.[14] Yet little in-depth attention has yet been paid to the distinct features of religion that contribute to these processes.

I argue that in order to reckon with the capacity of religious institutions both to be complicit in and to challenge the systems that rely on racial and gendered violence to maintain power, we need to attend to the ways that particular theological convictions intersect with religious organizations' postures toward women who experience violence. I show in this chapter that there is a fragile but powerful connection between the theological cultures that the SACC, AE, and PACSA produce to respond to the racial injustice and violence of apartheid and their responses to GBV. As the woman I talked with in Cape Town highlighted, the religious belief systems that are mobilized to respond to some pressing social issues may not translate to others.

A central dimension of the issue at hand is the extent to which GBV is understood as a distinctly gendered phenomenon, rather than a problem that can be reduced to other aspects of social life, including racism. As Helen Moffett contends in her analysis of narratives about rape in South Africa that perceive it primarily through the lens of race and the legacies of apartheid, "Rape is about many things, including the toxic after-effects of apartheid; but it is probably one of the few burning social issues in South Africa that is fueled not by narratives about race, but rather by vitriolic patriarchal imperatives."[15] Reckoning with the distinctly gendered dimensions of the problem is essential if we wish to address it.

This chapter demonstrates that the theological cultures of the SACC, AE, and PACSA shape the extent to which they perceive GBV to be an issue of gender and power. I analyze patterns of connection and disconnection in the path that the theological cultures follow from the racial violence of apartheid to the tumult of the transition to GBV. In chapter 4, I explain why the process differs across the organizations. There, I argue that the theological cultures facilitate and constrain the organizations' capacity to cultivate a conception of gender justice more generally. Then, in chapter 5, I analyze the implications of these patterns for the organizations' actions with respect to GBV and gender justice.

PACSA's transformation theological culture facilitates a strong response to GBV. Their theological convictions around a transforming God who can change death-dealing systems into life-promoting ones intersect with a posture of solidarity with suffering women and critique of complicit men. PACSA perceives GBV to be rooted in inequities of gendered power, and they contend that the Gospel has the potential to transform this form of violence into full freedom and life.

AE's reconciliation theological culture constrains them from recognizing the gendered roots of the problem. Their theological convictions concerning the power of spiritual reconciliation shape their response, as they perceive that women and girls who are raped need the healing power of the Gospel. But AE's posture toward these victims does not also include attention to those who perpetrate the violence against them. Where the reconciliation theological culture included narratives of the power of cross-racial reconciliation, there is no parallel gender reconciliation.

The SACC's discourse reveals the loosest connection between the theological culture and their response to GBV. GBV is perceived to be a crime, a violation of human rights, and a problem rooted in economic and racist structures. Sometimes the theological principles of equal dignity emerge, as does a concern with the church's lack of response to GBV. But, in a clear departure from the path the SACC's theological culture follows from apartheid into the democracy, they do not focus on women as a marginalized group with whom the church should enter into suffering solidarity. These patterns demonstrate the importance of reckoning with the ways that theological convictions intersect with the organizations' posture toward women victims of violence to shape responses to GBV.

PIETERMARITZBURG AGENCY FOR CHRISTIAN SOCIAL AWARENESS

Gender-Based Violence in Need of Transformation

The front page of PACSA's Easter 2001 newsletter immediately arrests the reader's attention. An image of a body on a cross occupies most of the space: a body with a nail piercing the hand, a crown of thorns puncturing the head, and a face in utter agony. But rather than portraying the person of Jesus, the crucified body is that of a woman.[16] Sister Susan Rakoczy begins her reflection on this front page of the newsletter, "To Carry the Death of Jesus," by noting that there were witnesses— "a few women and one man"—who watched Jesus's brutal death.[17] She then writes, "Women were at the cross with Jesus and women are crucified today by rape, physical, psychological and spiritual violence. Stretched between their hopes for a better life and the pain inflicted on them, often by someone they know and profess to love, their bodies and spirits are torn in a violent crucifixion."[18] With the dramatic image of a woman on the cross as the backdrop to her words, Rakoczy aligns the familiar Christian narrative of Good Friday with the violence that women experience.

She then draws explicitly on PACSA's theological convictions concerning the transformation of violence and death into resurrection life, observing that "the women at the cross went home and a few days later their lives were transformed by the news that Jesus is risen. What transformation awaits women who are battered and bruised, violated and rejected?"[19] Rakoczy answers this question by drawing on two key features of PACSA's theological culture: an affirmation of the possibility of death being transformed into life and a call to Christians to take action to address suffering. She writes, "We who already know that death leads to life in Christ are called not to walk away, but through compassionate presence and action to bring life."[20] PACSA's theological convictions about God's transforming power intersect with a posture that centers the experience of women victims of violence to call for those who witness such violence to take actions of empathetic solidarity. The transformation theological culture follows a clear path here from the violence of apartheid, through the political violence during the transition to democracy, to GBV. Rakoczy contends that Christians must be proximate to suffering women and work to transform their death into life.

Rakoczy also draws on the Easter narrative of women sharing the good news with others to anchor her reflection: "Mary Magdalene brought the incredible news that Jesus is risen to the other disciples" rather than "keep silent or go home and quietly reflect on her experience of Jesus in the garden."[21] Rakoczy then echoes PACSA's long-standing commitment to expose the realities of hidden social issues in her exhortation to her readers: "We are called to 'break the silence' that supports sexual violence against women, to speak the word of truth that 'this is wrong, evil, sinful,' to announce the good news that such death which is so prevalent in our society must end."[22] She writes, "We who are the Body of Christ carry the death of Jesus in every effort to … work to bring life where the words and actions of death carry so much power."[23]

Death can be transformed into life. Christians must break the silence that masks attention to issues that require action. They must then enter into compassionate solidarity with the suffering and take actions that facilitate this transformation. This is a clear, direct, and powerful application of PACSA's transformation theological culture to GBV. Rakoczy draws on the central theological narrative that had grounded PACSA's anti-apartheid work and continues to resonate in the new democracy. Christians, once again, are to face the ugly reality of devastating violence and take actions to resist the power of death. These convictions intersect with the organization's posture of attention to the experiences of the marginalized. Women experiencing violence are such a group. PACSA's theological convictions intersect with their social positioning to create a strong response to GBV.

An Early Call to Action

This clear and direct application of PACSA's theological culture to GBV was not inevitable. As I will show below with both AE and the SACC, organizational awareness of a pressing social issue does not necessarily translate into a clear and powerful theological response to it. How and why was PACSA able to develop such a robust theological response to GBV, one that clearly draws upon the central features of their transformation theological culture?

To answer this question, we need to trace the path that PACSA's transformation theological culture follows over time to facilitate their response to GBV. The earliest mention of GBV that I found in PACSA's public discourse is in their June 1985 newsletter, which reprints an address that Peter Kerchhoff gave on "Christian Responsibility Today."[24] While Kerchhoff does not engage in an in-depth analysis of the problem, he does name "child and wife abuse" as one of many social issues facing South Africans. The problem is named in a speech that exhorts Christians to be engaged in the world around them.[25] From the very beginning of PACSA's public acknowledgment of GBV, the issue is incorporated into the organization's theological culture.

Kerchhoff begins by acknowledging that "the social problems in South Africa today are so great that you may think you cannot do anything about them."[26] "That," he reminds his audience, "may certainly be a human response, but as Christians wanting to grow in unity and maturity that certainly, I believe, is not an option."[27] He then names the various issues that people may be aware of and concerned about, including "divorce, deteriorating relationships, child and wife abuse."[28] How do people respond to these and other issues? Christians may "become directly involved in dealing with people, encouraging, healing and caring."[29] And yet, he states, this is not a sufficient response. In addition to recognizing problems and trying to step in to help, "a further step is needed in order to understand more fully the problem, and to see the picture as a whole. This further step is that of social analysis, and should in fact be the initial step, for we respond to a problem according to how we see it."[30] Kerchhoff goes on to explain that such a social analysis requires four main steps: "insertion" into the real lives of people; "social analysis" that attends to power relations; "theological reflection" on scripture and God's action; and "pastoral planning" for particular, practical responses.[31] This first mention of GBV in PACSA's public discourse situates the problem within a call for Christians to cultivate a posture of empathy, understanding, and solidarity.

Kerchhoff goes on to critique the church's failure to engage in robust social analysis in its attempts to enact positive social change, and to insist on the church's mandate to engage in justice work. He writes, "At present the Church's social concern seems limited to welfare work, and to trying to be a reconciling force and bridge builder—without any social analysis [and] without regard first and foremost for justice."[32] But, Kerchhoff observes, "there will never be true peace or true reconciliation while injustice and oppression are prevalent. The Church will never truly live out its God-given mandate in the world as long as it sides with the rich and powerful." What is the church to do instead? "If we are to know, love and serve Jesus, we need to get our hands dirty, we need to get involved in working and praying for justice."[33]

On the surface, it may be hard to imagine that this very brief mention of abuse in a reprinted talk on Christian social responsibility in 1985 would have a strong causal influence on PACSA's subsequent robust theological response to GBV. But there are two important things to note here. First, this is a relatively early public acknowledgment of the reality of abuse. As I noted in the introduction to the book, while organizations such as Rape Crisis had been founded in the late 1970s to address rape and domestic violence, the issue did not garner widespread public attention until the late 1980s and early 1990s.[34] The fact that, however brief, there is acknowledgment of the problem at this time is significant, especially as this marks a contrast to both AE's and the SACC's public discourse.

Second, and more important for my argument about the power of theological cultures for shaping institutional action, it is also significant that GBV is mentioned here in the context of PACSA's overall mission to enter into proximity with the suffering, raise awareness of social issues, and exhort the church to move from a posture of passivity or inadequate theological and social response and toward a commitment to, as Kerchhoff put it, "get our hands dirty," and engage in sacrificial action.[35] This brief mention of GBV occurs in the context of a call for Christians to engage in actions that do not side with the powerful but work for justice for the marginalized instead. GBV is incorporated into PACSA's theological culture from its first mention.

Patriarchy as the Cause

In fact, as broader public awareness of GBV grew in the early 1990s, PACSA's staff members were already poised to recognize it as the significant social issue that it was, and to apply key aspects of the transformation theological culture in their response. And they perceived gender inequities to be central parts of the system that needed to be transformed in order to respond to GBV. PACSA contends that there are clear logics of oppression that govern different systems, and that patriarchy is a system that contributes to GBV. This is a contrast to the SACC: as I show below, they tend to treat GBV as rooted in other systemic realities rather than in sexism and patriarchy.

In particular, Karen Buckenham, who was initially hired as PACSA's human rights worker, devoted significant attention to the problem. In the October 1994 newsletter, she begins an article entitled "Domestic Violence and the Church" by affirming that "the Spirit of God has been blowing throughout the world to free women and men from traditional unequal relationships."[36] Attributing the global movement for gender equality to the initiative of the Spirit of God, Buckenham then writes, "We know that oppression dehumanizes both the oppressor and the oppressed. Realizing that this applies to relationships between women and men, realizing the extent and manifestation of sexual oppression in our society, getting to the core of patriarchy and uprooting it in our society and church, is something that some in South Africa are beginning to take seriously."[37] One of the central features of PACSA's theological culture is their contention that transforming unjust systems involves both the oppressed and oppressor. Buckenham applies this insight explicitly to gender.

Describing GBV as a form of this patriarchal injustice, Buckenham writes that "one manifestation of oppression is sexual violence," which "is a pervasive and still hidden dimension of violence in South Africa."[38] How should the church engage the issue? Buckenham draws on central features of PACSA's theological culture to answer this question. The church must "take it out of the realm of 'private affair,' see why it happens, and deal with it."[39] That is, as with other issues that PACSA has addressed, the church must become aware, do a thorough social analysis, and then take steps to address it. Buckenham applies PACSA's posture of empathy with the marginalized to suffering women. She writes, "The church must recognize and feel the pain, agony, confusion and loneliness of assaulted women."[40] Buckenham perceives that women who experience GBV are a marginalized group who require the church's proximity, empathy, and solidarity. The transformation theological culture follows a path that connects PACSA's responses to various forms of violence and injustice.

But Buckenham also recognizes that the church itself has been complicit in GBV. She writes, "Some Christian teaching has been used to keep women in abusive relationships, saying she must 'obey' or that it is God's will for her."[41] Highlighting the role of theological beliefs that keep women in a subordinated position to men, Buckenham states that the church, in fact, has "a pastoral responsibility" to accompany women who have been assaulted and that it should provide "education for men and women about respect and love."[42] Here, Buckenham draws on another key feature of PACSA's theological culture: the importance of working with the privileged and perpetrators as well as those who are victimized and oppressed.

Indeed, the work to address GBV will require not only solidarity with suffering women, but also teaching men how to relinquish power and embrace different dimensions of themselves. Buckenham writes that in addition to knowledge that can empower women and girls, "education is also needed to help men discover and value characteristics inside them that are tender and vulnerable."[43] There is a clear consistency in PACSA's social positioning here, as Buckenham focuses attention on both the experience of the marginalized and those who are complicit in such systems. Indeed, she grounds the response to GBV firmly in PACSA's transformation theological culture as she emphasizes the need to break silence, raise awareness, engage in empathetic solidarity, and to focus not only on victims but also perpetrators, especially through education.

PACSA's staff recognize that there are tensions and difficulties in reckoning with gender oppression and its connections to GBV. For instance, Buckenham later reports on a workshop on the church's response to violence against women that she led with PACSA's gender fieldworker, Lihle Dlamini, at a January 1999 conference on issues facing South Africa, sponsored by the South African Missiological Society. She again calls attention to the role of theological beliefs that are complicit in GBV, acknowledging the difficulty in "challenging traditionally-held religious beliefs about ordering of relationships between women and men."[44] She then points out that while such beliefs in a natural ordering of human relationships have been challenged with respect to race and power, similar beliefs about sex and gender remain deeply entrenched. She writes that "Biblical scholarship examining historical context and present day beliefs about slavery and ethnic oppression, with liberating ways to read the Bible in the context of Christ's message of freedom and life for all, is accepted by most when discussing issues of race and systems of racial domination."[45] However, "questioning domination based on sex and tradition is usually resisted—by both men and women—so deep are the assumptions of what is normal and the justification for these."[46]

Identifying this parallel between systems of racial and gender oppression, yet also the tendency to resist an acknowledgment of such parallels, Buckenham's social analysis then moves into a discussion of the possible pathways of challenging these norms. She draws on PACSA's consistent social positioning of both focusing attention on the experiences of the marginalized and calling the privileged to recognize their position. She writes, "Those on the receiving end of sexual oppression must continue to speak their reality. Those benefiting by sexual oppression need to learn to see and even feel the consequences of such theology."[47] Attending both to the experiences of those who are victimized and those who are complicit in and contributing to the problem, Buckenham grounds her suggestion of how to address the problem in PACSA's theological culture as she emphasizes the power of cultivating empathy that can result in social change.

Buckenham concludes by pointing to the possibilities that can emerge from drawing comparisons between experiences of racism and sexism. She writes, "Comparisons between being on the receiving end of racism and sexism (not putting them in opposition) reveal more similarities than differences. I believe such comparisons are valuable. Drawing on our own experiences of what we have felt ourselves, it is easier to walk in the shoes of another, imagine what it feels like, see the subtle and not so subtle manifestations of our learnings and assumptions, and then learn to challenge ideology or theology that would defend either system 'in the name of God.'"[48] This call to engage in empathy and to see points of connection across different systems of oppression relies on PACSA's long-standing commitment to focus on the experiences of the marginalized, and for those who are privileged to be informed and recognize their complicity in oppression.

These discursive patterns continue in other pieces that call for the church to address GBV. When Buckenham reports later on another conference at which she and Dlamini presented on domestic violence, she draws on the transformation theological culture's central theme of solidarity with the suffering to answer the question "What can the uniqueness of the Christian faith community offer in response to violence against women?"[49] She writes, "In thinking about this, I came up with the word solidarity. The Christian faith community is by no means of one mind about the acceptability or 'non-acceptability' of violence against women. But solidarity is a step that is possible—to listen to women. Everyone working on the problem together, women, men and children—with the starting place being listening really and entirely present to bleeding, crying women. And with women leading with the vision of what they want to happen."[50] Even as she acknowledges the challenge of the church's own ambivalence toward abuse, Buckenham suggests that the main contribution the church can make is to listen to and accompany those who are suffering. This call to engage in empathetic solidarity is consistent with PACSA's approach and mission since the beginning of their work. Central to their theological culture is the conviction that privileged people need to be made aware of the violence that those who are marginalized experience, and to then accompany them in ways that can lead to sustained change. PACSA's posture toward women experiencing violence is consistent with their responses to other issues. The transformation theological culture facilitates a clear and strong response to GBV.

Buckenham acknowledges that the church's own witness here is complicated since "the Christian tradition is not innocent of a certain amount of culpability in perpetuating abuse and oppression of women."[51] However, "the gospel is freedom and life, and so the Christian tradition is also a strength and resource."[52] Buckenham draws on PACSA's theological conviction that the Gospel itself is about "freedom and life," not death or violence, and she articulates a posture that focuses attention on women's experiences of violence. Even as she acknowledges the church's complicity in the problem, Buckenham also affirms that the Gospel itself is a source of freedom and life for suffering women. In this account, GBV is firmly situated within the context of PACSA's transformation theological culture.

These themes continue under the work of Beverley Haddad, an Anglican priest and theology professor who led PACSA's gender program after Buckenham became the organization's director. In a 2001 call for churches to participate in the international 16 Days of Activism campaign to end violence against women and children, Haddad writes, "In South Africa the high rate of violence against women and children morally compels the church to break the silence and act against this scourge in our society."[53] She goes on to point out that religious leaders have a unique role to play in addressing the problem, observing that "as spiritual leaders we are often in situations where we know more intimately than most the crises of families under our pastoral care and we therefore have a particular responsibility to be involved in this campaign. As church, we are in a strategic position to both educate and act in breaking the cycle of violence against women and children that has gripped our communities."[54] Recognizing the distinct opportunity that churches have to intervene in this crisis, Haddad evokes the legacy of the church's past activism against the apartheid regime, stating that "the church needs to be at the forefront of eradicating this social evil, as it was in the fight against apartheid."[55] In this call for churches to work to address GBV, Haddad draws on PACSA's theological culture's emphasis on the importance of both education and action.

One of the consistent messages within PACSA's discourse is that attending to experiences of marginalization and violence must go hand in hand with raising awareness and education among groups who benefit from and are complicit in the systems that create such marginalization. Unsurprisingly, over time we see significant attention to the importance of working with men. Kesavan Kisten, who was hired to help PACSA do research that would specifically focus on men, follows Haddad's statement with a reflection on the need to invite men into the process of challenging the norms that support violence. He perceives a parallel between the logics that supported apartheid's racism, particularly its policy of separate development, and the realities of patriarchy and sexism. He writes that "part of the strategy of patriarchy was to separate people [by] gender and to keep the male gender on a pedestal of domination, power and control over the female gender which was conditioned to be weak and subservient to men."[56] Kisten then acknowledges that men may "feel suspicious and resistant towards men's initiatives that support women."[57] But, as with the past, the church continues to have a role to play: "The Church has the potential to bring about effective change as it has been doing in the past regarding other issues of social injustice."[58]

As part of the 16 Days of Activism program, men are invited to join a White Ribbon Campaign, wearing a white ribbon as their "personal pledge to never commit violence against women and children, never condone acts of violence, not to make excuses for perpetrators of violence, never think that any woman 'asks for it,' not to remain silent, [and] challenge other men to act to end violence."[59] In making these statements, Kisten draws on PACSA's consistent social positioning that attends not only to the marginalized, but also to perpetrators and those who are complicit in the system that is causing harm. He recognizes that working to change systems of violence and injustice necessitates working with those who benefit from the system and perpetrate harm, challenging them to relinquish their privilege and change their behavior.

From Peter Kerchhoff's brief early mention of the problem to Susan Rakoczy's dramatic alignment of women victims of violence with the crucified Jesus, PACSA's theological convictions and social positioning intersect to facilitate a robust response to GBV. It is a social problem that is dealing death to women and yet it could be transformed into life. It requires education, awareness, and empathy. PACSA's authors focus attention both on those who are victims of the violence and those who are perpetrating it, stressing the importance of believing and accompanying the marginalized. Indeed, Christians are called to engage in solidarity with suffering women rather than continue to be complicit in the problem. The transformation theological culture results in a strong response to GBV.

AFRICAN ENTERPRISE

Gender-Based Violence and the Power of the Gospel

In July 1995, a team of AE's evangelists from various parts of Africa went to Kigali, the capital of Rwanda, to minister to people who had recently experienced the horrific genocide there.[60] In the newsletter that reports on this mission, Ralph Jarvis highlights the deep emotional response that the evangelists had to the intensity of the violence and its aftermath. One leader "chokes back tears," while another "weeps" as they share stories of witnessing mutilated bodies and hearing accounts of church leaders' complicity in the violence.[61] The string of brief narratives concludes with one of them describing "a young pregnant woman, who, raped during the fighting and hating the child she bears, hears the Gospel and forgives the rapist."[62] And then, "a wave of weeping sweeps the meeting as others break down."[63]

Jarvis goes on to note that AE founder Michael Cassidy's interpretation of this emotional response to the trauma the evangelists encountered was that it "symbolized a breakthrough in the mission. From then on, there was a greater understanding, and a greater love for the suffering people to whom they had been sent to take the message of Jesus Christ."[64] Emphasizing the ways that the strong emotions of the moment were a sign of the power of the Gospel at work, this narrative draws on key features of AE's reconciliation theological culture. The story highlights their theological convictions concerning the deep need that people have to experience the Gospel, and the capacity of the Gospel to prompt forgiveness. The deep emotions people experience as they encounter the Gospel and one another demonstrate the power of the Gospel for changed lives.

At the same time, an interesting puzzle emerges regarding AE's social positioning. It is striking that this inclusion of a narrative about GBV focuses attention on the woman and then on the impact of the stories on the evangelists, not on the perpetrator or on men who were coming to terms with their ignorance of the situation for women. As I showed in chapters 1 and 2, AE's discourse about the power of the Gospel for cross-racial reconciliation often centers on the impact of a black person's forgiveness on a white person who had perpetrated violence or white people who were ignorant of the situation. Here, the narrative states that the victim does forgive her perpetrator, but he is not actually present in the encounter that is described.

I show throughout the examples below that this is an important pattern of AE's discourse. AE's theological convictions have a profound impact on their response to GBV. They see the issue as a symptom of broader social ills that show the need for the Gospel. They include narratives like this one of the pregnant woman in Kigali who forgives her rapist to show the power of the Gospel for spiritual conversion and healing for the one who has experienced such violence. The narrative also shows the impact of encountering such emotionally fraught experiences on the listeners.

But, while their theological convictions are consistent here, AE's social positioning is different for GBV. In contrast to the ways that AE perceived a link between spiritual reconciliation and social reconciliation with respect to race, GBV is not treated as an issue that necessitates social reconciliation of men and women. Unlike PACSA, for AE the problem is not seen to stem from divisions and inequities related to gender and power. Rather, in keeping with the ways that their emphasis on following God's way is manifested in the democracy, they portray GBV as part of a broader problem with a decline in personal morality, especially concerning sexuality. AE's theological convictions concerning the healing power of the Gospel intersect with their posture toward women victims of violence in ways that constrain their ability to recognize GBV as a gendered issue that requires a robust response. They do include some narratives that focus on the victim and those who encounter her story—but not on the men who perpetrate such violence.

Gender-Based Violence as a Sign of the Need for the Gospel

We can see this pattern in examples from AE's public discourse in which GBV is mentioned as a sign of the need for the Gospel. For instance, in April 1999 AE's deputy team leader Abiel Thipanyane, one of the first black evangelists, begins his letter by describing how everything seems to be falling apart if one follows the news: "fatal road accidents, corruption, disturbances in education, rampant crime, lawlessness, declining economy, abuse of women and children, labor strikes, violence, unusual weather conditions, increasing joblessness, and so on!"[65] He connects this deterioration to the situation of the country in that historical moment, when the question is what the future might hold: "The present looks dark! The future looks even darker! Some people even say there is no future!"[66] But, Thipanyane states, the Christian response must be hope. The hope that Thipanyane describes is the "tough hope" of the biblical Abraham, one that "generates action. We are not immobilized by the hopelessness around us. We have this hope as an anchor for the soul, firm and secure."[67] This is the response to those who look at the present condition of the country, including violence against women, and are afraid for its future: Christian hope, an "anchor for the soul," is the antidote to the chaos and bleakness.

Thipanyane draws on the central theological convictions that ground AE's theological culture. The various social problems that are evident in the broader context are enough to make people feel deep despair. And the solution is a spiritual one of cultivating a posture of hope. GBV appears here as a sign of the need for the Gospel, as evidence that the society is a disintegrating mess. Christians are called not to be overwhelmed by the vastness of these problems but to cultivate a spiritual response that will equip them to navigate the perilousness of the times.

In their depictions of GBV as one of many issues that evidence the need for the Gospel, AE also sometimes describes the problem as an issue that young people, especially, are experiencing. For AE, this is a moral crisis, in keeping with the ways their theological culture forges a path for their responses to issues in the democracy, as I described in chapter 2. It is not a systemic issue that is rooted in sexism and power. A later newsletter, for instance, includes rape in a list of multiple issues in South African society that bear evidence of biblical accounts of the "last days" that Christians need to figure out how to navigate. Team Leader Greg Smerdon writes, "To the murders, the theft, the alcohol and drug abuse, add the rapes, the teenage pregnancies, the abortions, the AIDS crisis, the child-headed households . . . and the list goes on and on as the country (and in fact much of the world) faces a moral catastrophe amongst its teens. The Apostle Paul's description of the last days is a wake-up call, as this reality has dawned on South

Africa."[68] Rape is one component of the "moral catastrophe" that young people are experiencing. It is evidence of the dramatic need for the Gospel and a sign of the times.

In addition to the inclusion of rape as part of a list of social ills that demonstrate the need for the Gospel, sometimes narratives add more detail to the reality of GBV in the communities to which AE ministers. They do so in a way that focuses on the spiritual needs of the community, not on the possibility of encounters across difference that could also be changed. This is a contrast to their posture toward racial groups and the possibility of cross-racial encounters that could spark social reconciliation. AE's theological convictions are consistent, but their posture toward women victims of violence does not include the possibility of social reconciliation with respect to gender.

For instance, a newsletter depiction of the surrounding context ahead of a mission notes that the team observes people drinking and shouting, while "others are kept awake by the wife next door who gets beaten quite often by her intoxicated husband. She screams long enough to alert the neighborhood that another session of bashing has begun. Otherwise it has become commonplace; no one ever intervenes."[69] Abuse is framed here as part of the typical experience of people in the community, such that nobody intervenes to address the violence, illustrating the need to preach the Gospel. In contrast to AE's discourse about the racial violence of apartheid, in which the setting pointed to the need for cross-racial reconciliation, here GBV shows the need for the Gospel, but it is not a prelude to changed lives with respect to gender relations.[70]

Gender-Based Violence as a Sign of the Healing Power of the Gospel

GBV is not only presented as a sign of the need for the Gospel. AE's public discourse also focuses on how the problem shows the power of the Gospel for spiritual healing. This is an important continuity: AE consistently describes the power of the Gospel being evidenced as people encounter one another, share their stories, and experience healing. But, unlike with their discourse about cross-racial encounter, the perpetrators of the violence do not appear in their discussions of GBV. AE's social positioning is different for race and gender. With respect to racial groups, there was a focus on both whites and blacks who need the healing Gospel. With GBV, AE's discourse focuses on girls and sometimes women who find healing in Jesus and emotional release in telling their stories. But the possibility of such spiritual reconciliation leading to social reconciliation is muted. Where it is present, the social reconciliation that is depicted has more to do with the people who listen to and witness the victim's possible healing, while the perpetrators are absent.

For instance, a newsletter report about a mission in Port Elizabeth that worked with youth describes how a young woman evangelist, who is visiting from Norway, "almost broke down as she told of her own feeling of inadequacy when trying to deal with some of the pain she saw in many of the young, mainly black, people to whom she spoke."[71] She says, "'Some of the girls raised the issue of rape and I prayed for them for protection [and] for the healing of their pain.'"[72] She goes on to say that the young people challenged her assertion that God would provide for them because she comes from a wealthier country and has never been in want. After she acknowledged the validity of their challenge to her, she notes, "'I didn't have an altar call because they were all sitting around crying. I don't know what God did that day, but it was very powerful. I was emptied.'"[73] Rape is a sign of the need for the Gospel, and it is understood to require spiritual intervention through prayer.

There is also an interesting rhetorical positioning here, as the newsletter highlights the impact these narratives of rape have on the person listening to them. This is similar to the positioning taken during apartheid, as I discussed in chapter 1, with the narrative sometimes centering on the one listening to those who are in pain rather than the one who is experiencing the pain. But here, regarding GBV, the listener is not part of the group who has been inflicting harm (whether intentionally or not), as was the case with AE's discourse about race. Social reconciliation may occur across the lines of difference between the young woman from Norway and the youths who challenge her on her economic privilege. But there is no attention to the possible social reconciliation between young men and women that might address the young women's experiences of rape.

This pattern of highlighting the power of emotional storytelling as a possible avenue for experiencing spiritual healing from the hurt that rape causes occurs even in stories that do not mention the Christian Gospel explicitly. Interestingly, one of the places where this happens is also the one instance I found where AE explicitly portrays GBV as a gendered issue. The April 2001 newsletter discusses how AE staff member Clive Lawler led a two-day leadership course at a school for deaf pupils. The newsletter notes that, in addition to other activities, the students "had a session where they discussed gender relations," in which "some of the most worrisome issues emerged."[74] The newsletter reports that one of the teachers who was present recounted that "'rape, abuse, and pregnancy came out as some of the most disturbing problems for them. This was a very sensitive issue, they had not discussed this with anyone before. But they were courageous enough to speak openly in the group.'"[75] As a result, the teacher says that they "'came out of the discussion confident enough to stand up against harassment, abuse and rape'" and that "'this has been a step forward that will encourage the pupils to break the silence and get help to stop abuse.'"[76]

On first glance, this sounds like something we might see with PACSA, with the emphasis on sharing stories in order to break silence. But, rather than developing this story into an account of the need to address unequal gender relations that contribute to the problem, AE frames the response in terms of individual empowerment. And it is significant that the one example I found where AE perceives GBV to be an issue of "gender relations" does not include explicit attention to the power of the Gospel for changing the situation. AE's theological culture shapes their attention to GBV in ways that constrain the possibility of seeing the problem as a gendered issue that requires a robust theological response. There is no sense of the possibility of social reconciliation among boy and girl pupils to address the problem.

The emphasis in AE's theological culture on the power of encounter across social differences does occur in their attention to GBV. But this happens without explicitly naming gender itself as a feature of difference that needs to be bridged, the way that they had perceived racial division to be a barrier to connection. An April 2003 newsletter story, for instance, describes how the AE leadership incorporates exercises from their Bridge Building Encounters program to help train youth evangelists in their Foxfires program, who are sent out to evangelize and work with fellow youth. Describing the process, the story notes a natural progression as the events take shape: "The end of the second day arrives and the group [of Foxfires] recognizes that one of the barriers to their togetherness is lack of sharing and vulnerability. Many painful memories are haunting the group. The third morning we shift direction. We sit for about 2 hours hearing story after story of such hurt and pain. The effects of divorce, rape, rejection by mother and/or father etc. It is almost too much to bear."[77] The newsletter identifies rape as one of the various experiences of rupture in family or relational life that negatively impact these young people, with consequences for their sense of "togetherness." The newsletter then reports that "after all who wanted to share had done so, we took the papers they had written on and torn up and burnt them as the group began to let go and give them over to God. The power of the cross became apparent to all of us there."[78]

This narrative includes rape as one of the painful experiences that serves as a barrier to strong relational connections, stressing once again the power of vulnerability and encounter as people hand their challenges over to Jesus. This story is grounded in AE's affirmation of the power of spiritual reconciliation for social reconciliation. Spiritual surrender to God is a way of experiencing "the power of the cross" that will, in turn, change the group's connection with each other as they share the Gospel with others. But such an account of the possibility of spiritual conversion for relational connection and healing does not translate to the social context in which the abuse is happening. In contrast to AE's application of their theological culture to race relations, here there is no reconciliation between the victims of GBV and their perpetrators.

Similarly, after an event in Pietermaritzburg, the leader of the Foxfires team describes her impression of what she considers the "highlight" of the event, an open-air ministry at St. Peter's Square. She comments, "You seldom realize the desperation of the people in the street. When you look at their faces, you can see they are wearing a mask saying they're fine—till the invitation [to come forward and receive Christ] is given. Two young girls gave their lives to Jesus, and one woman came forward. She was so sick. She had financial problems and was being abused at home. She received the Lord and asked for prayer. She left there knowing that she had met Christ."[79] The newsletter story ends with this statement of the power of spiritual conversion for the woman experiencing abuse. This woman simply leaves "knowing that she had met Christ." We do not hear what comes next. Does the person perpetrating violence against her also hear the Gospel, repent, and cease abuse? Does her own conversion prompt a reconciled relationship that is free from violence? We do not know. This is a consistent theme across AE's discursive attention to GBV. We do not hear about the power of the Gospel for the perpetrators of this form of violence.

Gender-Based Violence apart from Gender

These various examples demonstrate that AE's theological culture shapes their discourse about GBV. They are aware that GBV is an issue, and they draw on key elements of their theological culture to make sense of and respond to it. At the same time, especially in contrast to PACSA, GBV is not treated in a deep or substantive way in AE's discourse. Where it is named, the problem is mentioned briefly in narratives that make a broader point about the need for the Gospel and the potential power of the Gospel for changing lives. There is not a conception of the need for reconciliation with respect to gender the way that there was for racial reconciliation. Why do we not see a more robust response to GBV?

The simplest answer to this question is that AE does not perceive GBV to be about sexism the way they had perceived apartheid's violence to be about racism. This lack of attention to gender as a relevant dimension of relationships that are in need of healing is evidenced in AE's discourse about steps that churches should take to address various social issues. The earliest mention of any form of abuse I could find in AE's discourse was about child abuse. In 1990, they hosted an event at the Conference Center called "Facing Crisis Issues." The newsletter names four major issues that need to be addressed: "Human Sexuality," "Violence," "Care in Grief," and "Family Disintegration."[80] The newsletter then mentions particular challenges within each category, and situates "child abuse" as a problem under the "Human Sexuality" umbrella issue, along with HIV/AIDS and "teenage promiscuity."[81] This is striking given the other categories that are named. Abuse is not included under the category of violence, which stresses "the support of victims" and "witnessing in the face of violence."[82] Nor is it situated within the category of family life, which stresses "issues affecting the young and the old, communication and family support, and divorce."[83] This framing of abuse as related to human sexuality rather than violence or the family stunts the possibility of developing a more robust response that would attend more fully to the reality of abuse in various kinds of relationships. There is no recognition of gender and power here.

Similarly, in 1995, AE was asked to "lead a special 'task force' of Church leaders in violence-ridden KwaZulu-Natal" to pave the way for a provincial conference that would take place in 1996. This ecumenical gathering to begin the conversation about what issues needed to be addressed in South Africa, and especially in the province of KwaZulu Natal, prompted discussions of what the church's role should be in addressing various social issues. These areas "in which the Church was seriously concerned" included abuse and rape close to the top of the list: "political intolerance, violence, abuse, rape, youth indiscipline, the role of adults in the cause of the problems of youth, spiritual warfare, the need for courage on the part of the Church, prayer, the need to face a power that is greater than politics, the great need for Church unity, forgiveness, confession, repentance, restitution, AIDS."[84] A panel then decided on the nine themes that this long list of concerns represented. "Family life" was one, as was "AIDS and education in sexuality."[85] However, gender as a category was not included, and violence was not explicitly listed as a theme either. Subsequent newsletters reporting on the planning and implementation of this particular event include the themes of "family life" and "sexuality," but they do not name rape and abuse again. And, unlike with what we see in PACSA's discourse about various forms of GBV, gender is also never named.

The reconciliation theological culture constrains AE's response to GBV. The issue is presented as one that exemplifies both the need for the Gospel and the power of the Gospel to change people's lives. In keeping with the path their theological culture follows in the transition and democracy, AE authors recognize and condemn GBV as an issue of sexuality and morality. Left untouched here, however, is an awareness and analysis of the ways in which gender and power contribute to the problem. I argue that this lack of robust response to GBV is because of the ways AE's theological convictions intersect with their social positioning. That is, the theological convictions are remarkably consistent, but their posture toward the social groups involved is different here, compared to what we see with race in chapters 1 and 2. While they include some attention to girls' and women's experiences of victimization, they do not focus on boys' and men's perpetration (nor even their innocent ignorance) of GBV. As such, the connections between spiritual and social reconciliation that were so clear for AE's account of racial injustice are not seen with GBV.

SOUTH AFRICAN COUNCIL OF CHURCHES

Gender-Based Violence as a Sign of a Fragile Democracy

With both PACSA and AE, we see how the theological culture has a strong impact on their response to GBV. The SACC, by contrast, presents an interesting and surprising puzzle. They clearly recognize the problem. But women who experience violence are not depicted as a marginalized group requiring the church's solidarity. The SACC does not draw on this central feature of their theological culture that persists across time and across other issues in their response to GBV.

For instance, in March 1997 the president of the SACC, Bishop Sigqipo Dwane, gave a presentation to the SACC's Central Committee that included his reflections on the significance of a program sponsored by the World Council of Churches (WCC), an "Ecumenical Decade of Solidarity with Women." This initiative of the WCC, which took place from 1988 to 1998, aimed to encourage churches around the world to prioritize women's issues and to enact gender equality.[86] Some elements of the SACC's liberation theological culture are present in Dwane's speech. In particular, the president affirms women's equality and dignity in their quest for freedom. For instance, he states that "we will want to thank women in the church for their patient but persistent calling of men to walk with them, on the road towards the [realization] of freedom and human dignity for all."[87] Grounding this quest in theological language, Dwane celebrates the ways that "women have helped the church to come to grips with the reality that in Christ, there is equality and partnership between women and men."[88] He goes on to describe how these principles of equality are now enshrined in the new Constitution, which the church should also celebrate.[89]

Dwane then describes GBV as an issue that shows the fragility of such efforts. He states, "We have no reason to be complacent because, though there is much for which we should be grateful, we know too well that there is much more to make us ashamed and sorrowful. The horror of rape and the magnitude of this form of abuse in our society is enough to silence us."[90] But, Dwane asserts, "it is not enough to express shock and indignation, but we must pull our energies together, and aim to uproot this evil."[91] The president's remarks on the WCC's gender program conclude with this statement.

Dwane's comments do not include one of the central features of the SACC's liberation theological culture: the requirement of the church to enter into suffering solidarity with the marginalized. The invitation to join together to uproot the evil of GBV is simply that. It is not a theological exhortation to recognize that God is on the side of suffering women who need the church's solidarity. In fact, the emphasis is on the partnership of men and women rather than on power differences between men and women that require actions of solidarity with the oppressed. While the speech contains some affirmations of women's equal dignity, Dwane also draws on language that stresses the "complementarity" of men and women. He states that, this "campaign [has] been successful in driving home the point that there is indeed a mutuality and complementarity between women and men. In their togetherness and partnership, women and men manifest the image of God."[92] This theological framing that celebrates the accomplishments of women—the very accomplishments that also reveal GBV to be such an egregious problem—is not an affirmation of equality and the empowerment of women. Nor is it a recognition of the ways that women, too, might need to be liberated from oppressive social systems that dehumanize them. Rather, it is an affirmation of the image of God that is expressed through men and women's "mutuality and complementarity."

This speech illuminates important themes and tensions in the SACC's discourse about GBV. The SACC recognizes GBV as an issue that emerges in the time of wilderness wandering that I described in chapter 2. They sometimes draw on their theological convictions about dignity, equality, and freedom. But their posture toward women victims of violence is different from their posture toward those experiencing the racial violence of apartheid and economic deprivation in the new democracy. The SACC does not focus on women victims of violence as a distinct marginalized group that requires the church's solidarity.

Gender-Based Violence and Other Systemic Realities

What explains both this clear recognition of GBV and this lack of application of this central feature of the SACC's theological culture? To understand this disconnect, we need to examine how the SACC portrays GBV as related to broader social systemic realities. The SACC clearly condemns GBV as a crime and as a violation of human rights, one that is connected to deep social systemic injustices. But these accounts do not portray GBV as an issue of gender and power.

For instance, the earliest discussion of GBV that I found in the SACC's newsletters portrays rape as part of a more general increase in criminal violence. In the November 1989 newsletter, Mbulelo Linda describes an anti-crime campaign in Soweto that had been organized by the SACC. GBV is the first type of crime specifically named in the piece. In framing the need for this gathering of community organizations that seeks to address the problem of criminal violence, Linda notes, "In recent months the rape of young girls by gangs of armed gangs [sic] has caused particular concern and outrage in Soweto."[93] But rather than frame this problem as a moment for the church to engage in solidarity with a marginalized group, this form of GBV is instead connected to "criminal violence" more generally: "SACC general secretary Dr Frank Chikane said he had received disturbing reports of criminal violence. 'This has manifested itself in clashes between students and teachers, drug abuse by students, the kidnapping of girls at school and their homes and raping them, sexual abuse of school girls by teachers and the sharp increase in car theft and robberies in shebeens and shops. . . . No one feels safe in Soweto.'"[94] GBV is described as a problem of criminal violence and, similar to AE's diagnosis of the problem, as particularly common among youth.

But unlike AE, the problem is also seen to be rooted in social structural conditions. For instance, Linda describes how those at the conference named "the poor physical state of the township," "the inferior education system," "the absence of adequate parental control and care," and "unemployment" as "interrelated factors" that were all "contributing to the criminal pattern."[95] Interestingly, though, unlike PACSA, the SACC's response here does not name gender itself as part of the problem. Women are seen to be a possible part of the solution, as one idea from the conference was the creation of a "'Women Unite Against Crime' campaign."[96] But the gendered inequities that can contribute to GBV are not named here.

This lack of attention to gender as a social structural reality that contributes to the problem is shaped by the SACC's depiction of GBV as symptomatic of a broader social crisis. That is, unlike in PACSA's discourse where GBV tends to be conceptualized as a problem that is rooted in the system of sexism that is also in need of transformation, the SACC's discourse is more similar to AE's in naming

GBV as one challenge among many. This perception of GBV is shaped by the path the liberation theological culture follows from apartheid to the democracy. That is, calls to the church to join in the quest for liberation from oppression are transposed into concerns with the many issues that are now presenting themselves in the transition and early democracy, as part of a wilderness wandering experience that shows the need for healing from wounds inflicted by past systemic injustices.

This perception of GBV as one issue among many does not necessarily draw on the SACC's core theological convictions. For instance, the 1999 Annual Report by General Secretary Charity Majiza names GBV as one of "a number of challenges locally, regionally and internationally" facing the country.[97] After describing how poverty and unemployment threaten the country, Majiza notes that "while incidences of political violence have declined remarkably, we saw the rise of other forms of violence in society. Of major concern was the rise in violent abuse of women, to the degree that South Africa became known as the rape capital of the world."[98] Majiza goes on to decry the HIV/AIDS crisis, and the challenge of people from neighboring countries seeking refuge within South Africa as they flee war and poverty in their own lands.

These challenges are seen to be rooted in social structural patterns. But gender itself is not named as one of them. Instead, these various challenges are primarily understood to be rooted in the historic intersection of racism and economic injustice that continues to impact so much of the social fabric. Majiza posits, for instance, that one of the explanations for these various challenges is the way that "the apartheid policy and colonialism before it left our society differently endowed," and points to the fact that "Black communities remain without adequate infrastructure in all spheres of social need, be it housing, education or health."[99] As she names the historical legacies that have deprived black communities, especially, of access to the resources that they need to address these challenges, it is striking that gender itself is not named. And, this recognition of social structural conditions that shape such social issues as the refugee crises, HIV/AIDS, and rape is not framed with explicitly theological language. GBV is seen to be rooted in economic injustice. This is due to the way the SACC's social positioning shifts over time, as I demonstrated in chapter 2, as their theological culture follows a path from focusing on the racial injustice of apartheid to the economic injustice that persists. Gender is not given the same attention.

Reflecting some of the broader public discourse about GBV, the SACC does grapple with the paradox that rates of GBV skyrocketed under a new Constitution and Bill of Rights that make explicit provision for women's human rights. But even when this kind of deeper attention is paid to the issue, the intersections of gender and power are not fully addressed. In the Annual Report from 2001, for instance, "domestic violence and child abuse" are discussed as part of the SACC's Human Rights program. After noting that "having a progressive Constitution and Bill of Rights is not an end in itself," the report both acknowledges a gender disparity in the likelihood of who will be the perpetrator of the problem, but posits that economic structures are at its root: "In most instances men are the perpetrators of these heinous crimes and victims who seek recourse in the legal system are unhappy with the outcomes. Squalor, poverty, centuries of dehumanization are all contributory factors to this evil that plagues our society."[100] Acknowledging the gendered dimension of the problem—at least in terms of who is more likely to be a perpetrator—the report sees broader social conditions at the root of the problem. But it does so without explicitly naming and problematizing gendered inequities. And, once again, the issue is not perceived to require a theological response. Women are not seen as a marginalized group with whom the church must enter into suffering solidarity.

Instead, the SACC invokes the promise of equality that should be assured through human rights. The report states, "Through our ongoing human rights work we hope to inculcate a culture of human rights where the rights of women and children would be respected equal to the rights of any other person. In our search for this equality we have integrated human rights in all other programmes."[101] The SACC's discourse contrasts with both AE's and PACSA's. Unlike AE, there is a clear recognition of social structural realities that contribute to the problem. Unlike PACSA, gendered power, itself, is only vaguely acknowledged. Rather, GBV is framed as an issue rooted in past and ongoing economic inequities. The promise of equality as a human right is expressed—but not as a theological tenet around which the church should mobilize.

This is not to say that the SACC's discourse contains no attention to gender as a contributing factor in GBV. Where gendered power is recognized, GBV is understood as a sign of the fragility of the rights that are supposed to be granted to women in the democracy. In the 2003 Annual Report, for instance, GBV is described as evidence of the problematic exclusion of women who are being denied their "rightful place": "Like many other countries we have not allowed women to take their rightful place in the Church and in society. We are experiencing disgraceful levels of women abuse even in the safety of homes. For democracy to be real the majority in any society should benefit from the fruits of such democracy. Although women are the majority in our society and in the church they are excluded from effectively benefiting from democracy and excluded from decision-making processes and structures."[102] Rape and abuse are seen as the failure of both the church and broader society to fully honor women's rights. Women are not portrayed as a marginalized group, per se, but as a "majority" whose rights need to be fully exercised. The problem is framed not primarily in theological terms, but in democratic ones.

The Church's Response

What, then, does the SACC suggest the church should do in response to GBV, if they are not drawing on their central theological conviction about the importance of the church entering into suffering solidarity with the marginalized? Sometimes the church is seen, instead, as playing a role in listening to and understanding people's experiences. For instance, in the Faith and Mission Unit report of 1992, rape is mentioned as one of the concerns that motivated a church gathering. The report states, "Increasing church concern about matters related to human sexuality led us to convene a series of meetings to share interests and activities in the area of gender, sexist language, AIDS, rape, abortion, and sexual orientation. Many people suffer extra hurt when Christians do not know how to assist them positively. By sharing insights and resources it is hoped churches can enable one another to be more involved in providing understanding and help."[103] Two things are interesting to note here. First, the issues that are named are seen to be related to "human sexuality." GBV is not understood to be an issue of gender and power. Second, there is a recognition here of the harm that Christians can do when they do not understand how to respond to the issue. But there is not a robust recognition of the church's need to enter into suffering solidarity with the marginalized. At best, churches can offer "understanding and help." This is not a robust theological condemnation of GBV as something that violates women's God-given dignity and something that the church therefore ought to accompany them in and through.

Indeed, while the overall pattern in the SACC's discourse about GBV is to see it as a crime and a violation of human rights that is rooted in economic injustices, sometimes there are hints of a deeper theological engagement with the problem. But these are just that—hints—not a full-fledged theological response that draws on their theological culture to argue for the church's deep engagement with the problem. For instance, in an *Ecunews* issue in 1997, General Secretary Brigalia Bam reflects on the language of the "miracle" of the democracy, and names rape as one of the issues that threatens its vibrancy: "We read about corruption, experience violent crime, learn about the rape of women and the abuse of children, watch a volatile political scene, and hear stories from our past that reveal the sick brutality to be much worse than we had ever feared."[104]

Bam goes on to point to the possibility and challenge of learning how to live well with one another, drawing on the ways the theological culture adapts in the democracy to focus on healing and moving forward as they navigate this time of wilderness wandering. She writes, "We live in an era of different challenges, of learning to live with new neighbors, of discovering each others' [sic] humanity, of finding ways to share the beauty and bounty of the land with one another, and of creating a new society built on respect for each ones dignity. And for those of us who bear the name of Christ, the challenge remains to hear the promises of God and to be faithful to them and to one another. This is the stuff out of which miracles occur."[105] This call to be faithful to the promises of God as the solution to various social problems reflects the path the SACC's theological culture follows in the democracy. Bam recognizes the multitude of issues that are presenting themselves in this time of wilderness, and, without explicitly naming *ubuntu* here, articulates a sensibility around shared humanity and resources. But, again, a crucial element is missing here: there is not a recognition of women as a marginalized group in need of the church's suffering solidarity.

A final illustration will allow us more clearly to see the puzzle that this lack of connection between the SACC's theological culture and GBV presents. In March 1995, General Secretary Bam gave an address entitled "South Africa in Its Regional and Global Perspective: Being the Church Today." Her presentation called attention to the ongoing need for the churches to be an active and vocal presence in the new democracy. The address also includes a section on some of the specific "demands of our region," in which Bam describes the significant influx of refugees, the HIV/AIDS epidemic, and political and criminal violence as pressing issues. As noted in this chapter's introduction, she then states, "The silence of the Church on violence against women and children is deafening. We are prepared to make statements on political violence and criminal violence but not on a violence that brings hurt, humiliation and constant fear to so many."[106] She goes on to note that "this form of violence is on the increase. The numbers of cases are staggering and there is no doubt that much goes undetected behind the walls and fences of suburban homes."[107] She concludes by presenting demographic statistics that reveal how widespread and extreme this form of violence is.

Bam situates her recognition of and concern with violence against women and children in the context of a speech that exemplifies the path the SACC's theological culture follows into the democracy. Indeed, her talk also includes affirmations of African theology's central teaching that "the world was created by God to be good and an important place for people, people who know themselves to be children of God and have a dignity and purpose to life."[108] And, as discussed in chapter 2, she calls on her listeners to embrace the promise that "God has not deserted us," as people "bring from the past not only the legacy of apartheid but also the spirit of the struggle against apartheid."[109]

Bam's speech shows a clear recognition of GBV in the context of a broader quest to adapt the liberation theological culture for the new challenges and opportunities in the democracy. Indeed, women and children are recognized as a group that is experiencing harm. And Bam makes a forceful critique of the church's silence in the face of this staggering violence. The possibility of applying the liberation theological culture to respond to GBV with conviction is clearly evidenced in Bam's speech. And yet, as the previous examples make clear, this possibility is not fully actualized. The patterns I outlined in chapter 2 regarding the adaptation of the liberation theological culture resonate here: GBV is portrayed as one of the many issues that emerge in the time of wilderness wandering, requiring reckoning with economic inequalities in order to find healing and embracing rights in the new democracy. But a strong analysis of gender and power is missing; women experiencing GBV are not seen as a marginalized group requiring the church's suffering solidarity. In chapter 4, I demonstrate that this is due to the ways the liberation theological culture involves tensions and ambivalence around the cultivation of gender justice.

CONCLUSION

I began this chapter by recounting a conversation I had with a journalist about the church's faltering response to GBV. Over the course of our conversation, she not only critiqued the lack of a prophetic voice from the church, she also offered a poignant reflection about how the church can be better prepared to respond to injustice and suffering. She observed, "The prophetic voice, unfortunately, is often only triggered in the face of suffering . . . [but] the suffering is happening as we speak. Do not wait for a disabled young woman to be raped, because they are being raped as we speak. . . . The prophetic voice of the church—of all people, they should give that voice. They should be the voice of those people. . . . I think we come to the same point all the time, that the prophetic voice should not be caught off guard." These prescient observations are still relevant more than a decade later. What does it mean for the prophetic voice not to be caught off guard? And what resources do religious institutions have at their disposal to make sense of, and to be proactive in responding to, GBV?

This chapter demonstrates that theological cultures have a profound impact on the capacity of religious organizations to respond to GBV. Religious beliefs are not cultivated in a vacuum, nor can they be reduced to underlying social structural conditions. They have a distinct power of their own, even as they are also institutionally embedded. This chapter demonstrates that the intersection of theological convictions with social positioning shapes these organizations' responses to GBV. But this happens in different ways for the organizations, sometimes facilitating and sometimes constraining their responses.

PACSA's strong response to GBV demonstrates the power of theological cultures for facilitating the recognition and condemnation of this form of violence. The transformation theological culture proves to be flexible and adept at incorporating additional issues. PACSA authors and leaders draw on their central theological convictions to argue that GBV is an issue that is dealing death but could be transformed, that sexism is a key part of the systems that contribute to GBV, and that it must be transformed through proximity to and solidarity with suffering women. PACSA's social positioning is also consistent here, as they focus attention both on the experiences of women victims of violence and on the men who contribute to the problem. Their theological convictions around the power of God's transforming power intersect with their social positioning of focusing on the marginalized while also attending to the privileged to facilitate a clear and cogent response to GBV.

AE's response shows how theological convictions and social positioning can intersect in ways that constrain responses to GBV. Their portrayal of GBV as both a sign of the need for the Gospel and as an illustration of the power of the Gospel is shaped by their reconciliation theological culture's consistent emphasis on the need for spiritual reconciliation. AE's depiction of the problem as an issue of human sexuality rather than gender reflects the path their theological culture follows in the democracy as they focus on a decline in personal morality, as I discussed in chapter 2. This consistency in theological conviction intersects with a different social positioning for GBV than for racial groups involved in violence and injustice. Rather than focusing on, and sometimes identifying with, members of the group who are causing harm (whether intentionally or more innocently, as is true for their focus on white people, as I showed in chapters 1 and 2), the narratives here center on the possibility of healing for the victim and the power of their stories for the listeners. But a crucial dimension of their theological culture is missing: there is no account of the possibility of social reconciliation between perpetrators and victims, between men and women. Gender itself is unnamed, and there is no hint of awareness of gender inequities as contributing to the problem.

For the SACC, the liberation theological culture is loosely connected to GBV. On the one hand, we see hints of their theological convictions of human dignity and equality. The path their theological culture follows in the democracy, which I demonstrated in chapter 2, shapes their response. GBV is seen as one of the many issues that presents itself in the time of wilderness wandering, and it is attributed especially to economic inequities and injustice. But, on the other hand, a crucial dimension of their theological culture is missing. Women experiencing GBV are not portrayed as a group requiring the church's suffering solidarity. Without a clear posture of concern for women's marginalization, the possibility of a robust theological response is stunted.

What explains these varying responses? This chapter has shown that the most important variation among the organizations is the extent to which they are able to recognize GBV to be an issue of gender justice. Their theological cultures shape these patterns. PACSA contends that GBV is rooted in sexism and gender inequality, and argues that this is a system that needs the Gospel's power of transformation just as much as other unjust systems do. AE does not understand GBV to be rooted in gender inequality or injustice but rather as part of a broader pattern of moral decline and as an issue that can be solved through spiritual conversion, but not through social reconciliation of men and women. The SACC perceives GBV to be gendered, but they see the problem to be rooted in other underlying structural conditions. It is not an issue of systemic gender injustice that requires the church's suffering solidarity with the marginalized. PACSA incorporates GBV and gender justice within their transformation theological culture, AE's reconciliation theological culture constrains a robust response to GBV, and the SACC's liberation theological culture is only loosely applied to GBV.

There are important patterns of connection and disconnection in the theological cultures that are formed to challenge the racial violence and injustice of apartheid, follow a clear path into the democracy, and are tenuous in their application to GBV. I argue that these patterns are rooted in the organizations' varying attention to gender itself. If we are to reckon with the capacity of religion both to be complicit in and to challenge the systems that rely on violence to maintain their power, we need to attend to the ways that gender operates as a central feature of theological cultures. In chapter 4, I argue that these patterns of difference in the organizations' portrayal of GBV as an issue of gender and power are rooted in the ways the theological cultures both facilitate and constrain the development of a conception of gender justice. Attending to these patterns ultimately explains not only the patterns of discourse I have analyzed here, but also their varying actions to respond to GBV, as I discuss in chapter 5.

4 · THEOLOGICAL CULTURES AND THE FRAGILITY OF GENDER JUSTICE

> I think the problem lies mainly with the concept of power. The church reflects too closely the structures of society and the struggle for power in society.... Women do not want to grab power in existing church structures.... We do want to be recognized as co-creators of structures which will reflect the true nature of the church and which will not be conformed to the world as they are at present.
> —Sheena Duncan

In June 1985, member churches of the SACC convened for their annual National Conference. As discussed in chapter 1, the summer of 1985 was a season of intensified political conflict, mass protests, and repressive violence in South Africa. In that context, unsurprisingly, the opening lines of the SACC newsletter that reported on the conference remarked that it was "an echo of the state of affairs in the country." The conference discussions reflected "the deteriorating unrest" in the country and the recent state of emergency that had been declared. The reality of the situation on the ground was seen as "an historical watershed" that would require the churches to make a public and unequivocal response.[1] *The Kairos Document* was published just a few months later, declaring apartheid a heresy. Analyses of the religious and political life of South Africa at this time have rightfully stressed the ways in which this period was indeed a watershed moment for the public witness of the churches against a repressive and violent regime.[2]

But there was an important subplot to the events of that tumultuous summer. As I mentioned in the introduction, this particular SACC National Conference had actually been intended to focus on women, with the theme "Women, a Power for Change." Plans had been in the works for a conference theme on women since at least 1982.[3] Yet, given the political crisis and the escalating violence of the time, the conference newsletter noted, "While the theme of the conference was 'Women a Power for Change' and it was intended that the conference would devote a good deal of its time to this issue, events from outside overruled, and the agenda was radically changed to deal with life and death issues."[4]

From our current historical vantage point, this discursive separation of a focus on women and "life and death issues" is significant, especially given the prevalence of violence against women that intensified in the new democracy, as discussed in chapter 3.[5] And yet, despite the alteration of the intended conference agenda, the special issue of the SACC's newsletter that reported on the 1985 National Conference did still include a reflection on the original conference theme. Their focus on women is not addressed as something separate from the SACC's broader theological convictions. Instead, it is grounded in the SACC's liberation theological culture, which stresses the power of the Gospel to liberate people from oppressive systems. The newsletter asserts that "Jesus still speaks to women through the Gospel today, in new ways, in changing situations, *liberating them* from the burdens of tradition, customs and stereotyped habits which oppress them and prevent them from being a power for change."[6]

On the one hand, this public discourse separates a focus on gender from calls for the churches to be engaged in the social and political context. On the other hand, the attention that is paid to gender draws explicitly on central features of the SACC's theological culture to problematize women's position in society. This tension between segmenting gender from the SACC's broader justice work while at the same time making a powerful application of the liberation theological culture to gender illuminates the central theme and question of this chapter: In what ways do theological cultures shape organizations' capacity to conceptualize and enact gender justice?

The central argument of this chapter is that patterns of institutional attention and inattention to gender emerge through the cultural production of distinct theological claims. I argue that the theological cultures that were cultivated to challenge apartheid are transposed onto gender. In this process, the theological cultures adapt, sometimes facilitating and sometimes constraining the development of a conception of gender justice. That is, based on their theological culture, the organizations vary in their recognition of the ways in which gendered power differences in society present a problem to which they should respond. The distinct theological convictions that they produce in their response to apartheid and that follow a particular path in the transition and early democracy intersect with their posture toward women as a social group to shape this varying attention to gender justice. Put simply, their theological cultures have a profound impact on the organizations' capacity to recognize sexism as a social reality that shapes women's experiences.

To make this argument, I draw on a central insight from gender theory regarding the centrality of cultural beliefs to gendered systems of power.[7] In their efforts to explain persistent gender inequality and stratification in a variety of institutional and everyday contexts, such sociologists as Cecilia Ridgeway and Paula England have argued that cultural beliefs about gender play a key role in legitimizing or challenging inequality.[8] That is, while other social and economic factors also matter, the substance of beliefs about gender has to be reckoned with as a crucial explanation for ongoing gender inequality. Gender essentialist beliefs—that is, beliefs that differences between men and women are intrinsic, inherent, and natural—play a key role in these processes. Surprisingly, while these gender theorists and others who have drawn on their work have examined these patterns in a variety of social institutions, from educational settings to tech industries, few have applied this important theoretical insight to religious cases.[9] Yet, sociologists of religion who study gender have established through an extensive body of empirical work that religion is an important site for the creation and negotiation of gender beliefs.[10]

In addition, while much of the literature on gender and religion has focused on the complex negotiations of gender in everyday life, we also know that religious beliefs about gender equality and gender essentialism are actively produced within institutions and organizations, in ways that reveal the negotiation of gendered power.[11] Some scholars of gender and religion have also shown how the cultural production of religious beliefs about gender and sexuality is connected to broader convictions about, for instance, an intended order for society and the purpose of religious communities' work in the world.[12] Thus, we should attend to the cultural production both of religious beliefs that are specifically about gender and those that may not be directly or explicitly about gender, but which nevertheless shape conceptions of gender justice. Showing these processes at work within each organization, this chapter examines the ways in which religious beliefs are institutionally produced to facilitate and constrain attention to gender.

In the analysis that follows, I demonstrate how the organizations' primary theological convictions shape their posture toward women (and, where applicable, toward men, too) as a social group. I then examine how these theological claims intersect with their posture toward women's experiences in family life and in the structures of the church. Their varying ways of conceptualizing sexism and patriarchy as social realities shaping women's experiences result in very different conceptions of gender justice. These patterns explain the variation in the organizations' depictions of GBV as an issue of gender and power that I showed in chapter 3. In chapter 5, I will explain how these discursive patterns have consequences for their actions concerning gender and GBV.

PIETERMARITZBURG AGENCY FOR CHRISTIAN SOCIAL AWARENESS

Gender and the Transformation Theological Culture

PACSA demonstrates how a theological culture can facilitate the development of a robust conception of gender justice. Their theological convictions center on the belief that God can transform social systems that promote oppression and death into ones that promote justice and life. When it comes to gender, PACSA authors perceive that sexism and gender injustice are distinct components of the death-dealing systems that need to be transformed. These theological convictions intersect with the organization's social positioning. PACSA consistently develops a posture toward various social groups that stresses both the complicity of the privileged and the suffering of the marginalized. This posture is seen with gender and sexism, too.

For instance, as early as 1984 sexism is named as a problem that needs to be addressed by the church. At the end of a discussion of "The Church and the Poor," Joan Kerchhoff focuses not only on the poor in economic terms, but also in relation to a broader conception of justice. She observes that it seems as if the church is no different from the rest of society in its lack of active attention to the lives of the poor, but that, nevertheless, there is a quiet, fragile presence in parts of the church: "There are people who hunger and thirst after righteousness, *who take the side of the poor and oppressed*."[13] She closes with these words: "And as long as they are there, the Church will be part of God's dream and desire and hope. It is the hope of peace on earth; of abundant life for all; of victory over those who are false and powerful and evil; victory over racism, sexism, militarism, greed and exploitation. It is the hope and the dream of a transformed and restored creation."[14]

Kerchhoff names sexism together with these other problems in the context of a discussion of the importance of being part of the group of people who are trying to enact "God's dream and desire and hope" of a "transformed and restored creation." This brief but important mention of sexism during apartheid provides a discursive foundation from which PACSA develops a systematic analysis of gender as equally important to the other forms of injustice that they observe in society. Sexism emerges here as an integral component of the systems that can be transformed.

This conviction is consistent across time. In the Christmas 2001 newsletter, Karen Buckenham draws on U.S. black feminist bell hooks' conception of love, not as "romance, feeling and sentiment" but as rooted in both intent and action.[15] Buckenham observes that "many people believe men can dominate women and children and yet still be loving. Yet, as psychoanalyst Carl Jung wrote, 'where the will to power is paramount, love will be lacking.'"[16] Buckenham draws on PACSA's transformation theological culture to articulate an alternative interpretation of gender and love: "In our transforming country, we work to change structures, rebuild and heal, make justice and envision a whole future. In this enterprise, as hooks says, justice between people is perhaps the most important connection people can have."[17] And this justice that can be pursued between men and women is rooted in Jesus's own transforming love. She concludes, "At this Advent time, we prepare to celebrate the birth of 'God with us,' the revelation of God's love. By learning to consciously and wilfully choose to love in our own lives and in all our relationships, we honour love's promises and can embody love's transforming power."[18] Here, Buckenham contends that the transformation of men's domination over women and children is part and parcel of the ongoing work to change unjust social structures. As they incorporate gender and sexism into their transformation theological culture, PACSA articulates a theological vision of transformed gender relations that are built on God's own incarnational, embodied love.

This theological affirmation of the possibility of seeing sexism transformed along with other systems of oppression, and a vision of a transformed society that is built on love, also intersects with PACSA's social positioning that is oriented toward both the socially privileged and the experience of the marginalized. Thus, PACSA authors sometimes draw on their theological convictions about the possibility of seeing death-dealing systems transformed into life-promoting ones as they also name a posture of privilege that needs to be transformed. For instance, Mike Deeb, a Catholic priest, writes a Christmas reflection for PACSA in 1988, noting the significance of Jesus's incarnation for Christian engagement in the world: "Promoting life inevitably brings with it a lot of pain and suffering—the Cross—as it challenges all our commitments, priorities and lifestyles, such as our hanging on to privileges (as whites, males or educated), or our preoccupation with accumulating money and possessions; it brings on the wrath of the authorities and forces of death. . . . Only when we can let go, and give fully of ourselves, is full life possible."[19] Listing male privilege along with white and educational privilege, Deeb articulates the paradox that resonates across much of PACSA's discourse: entering into suffering—including the suffering of letting go of privilege—allows for the possibility of experiencing fuller life. Their transformation theological culture includes awareness of gender as one of the multiple forms of social statuses and systems of power that are counter to "promoting life." PACSA's theological convictions (an emphasis on suffering being transformed into "full life") intersect with their social positioning (a focus on the privileged needing to relinquish their power) to facilitate a concern with gender justice. PACSA's theological convictions also intersect with their posture of empathy with those who suffer, as I show next. They recognize women to be a distinct social group that is disproportionately burdened because of sexism and patriarchy, and they draw on their distinct theological convictions to problematize women's distinct marginality.

Application of the Transformation Theological Culture: Women as the Marginalized

PACSA's transformation theological culture is applied to women's vulnerability and marginality within unjust systems, especially through their experiences in family life. There are two key messages here. First, PACSA's discourse about women's social roles in the family focuses on the ways their marginalization is due to patriarchy, as well as to other unjust systems. As they ground attention to women in the biblical narratives of Christmas and Easter, PACSA authors both explicitly and implicitly problematize gender injustice. Second, sometimes this discourse also highlights women's marginality to make a broader point about the violence and injustice of the broader systems of which they are a part. I show below that this is an important similarity to the SACC, but the organizations' distinct theological convictions shape the way they articulate this posture toward suffering women in different ways.

PACSA authors perceive that women often bear disproportionate social burdens because of their care work and family responsibilities. Sometimes they include explicit attention to patriarchal social systems that contribute to these burdens. For instance, in Christmas 1998, Gunther Wittenberg reflects on the significance of an image, pictured in the newsletter, that shows Mary holding Jesus, standing in Africa and pointing to the star that guided the wise men to the place where they were. Wittenberg states,

> I find it significant that on the above drawing it is a woman with child who sees the star, not the shepherds, not the three wise men from the East, but a woman from Africa. Women have been the most affected by the crisis in Africa, they have to bear the brunt of the war in many parts of the continent.... Women have had to feed their children in a situation of drought and hunger; women are oppressed by authoritarian and patriarchal societal structures and women most acutely feel the impact of AIDS. They need to see the star rising above Africa to give them new hope, just as Mary, their sister, saw in the birth of her son, the Messiah, the dawning of the new age.[20]

As he reflects on the significance of images that place the biblical figures of Mary and Jesus in Africa, and highlights the impact of an image that portrays Mary seeing the star, instead of focusing on the shepherds or the Three Wise Men, Wittenberg draws attention to the ways in which African women are particularly vulnerable, and in need of hope. This theological parallel between Mary and African women fuels the assertion that women experience a distinct form of marginality as they navigate broader social issues.

PACSA authors sometimes also draw on the Easter narrative to focus on women's marginality and men's complicit ignorance. Graham Lindegger, for instance, reflects in the Easter 2001 newsletter about parallels between the HIV/AIDS crisis and Holy Week. He notes a significant gender difference in perceptions and experiences of HIV/AIDS, especially related to women's caretaking responsibilities and work: "Like the women at the foot of Jesus' cross, in the HIV/AIDS pandemic it is especially women who bear the burden; anxious about partners and families; nursing the pains of illness and death; caring for orphans and anticipating their uncertain future. On the other hand, like Peter in the Gospel accounts, many men continue to deny that they 'know' the reality of HIV/AIDS."[21] As he retells the familiar narrative of Holy Week, which appears frequently in PACSA's newsletters, Lindegger draws particular attention to the disproportionate, gendered burdens of the HIV/AIDS epidemic. In so doing, he situates women's lived experiences of marginality and men's complicity within PACSA's theological culture, emphasizing that patriarchal social forces are in need of transformation.

There are also places where PACSA authors draw attention to the situation and experiences of women not to problematize gender injustice but to make broader points about unjust systems. That is, sometimes authors align women with the marginalized and vulnerable without explicitly developing a concern with gender injustice. In September 1981, for instance, Gunther Wittenberg reflects on the parallels between the experience of forced removals for women and children, and Jesus's apocalyptic words in Matthew 24, which follows his triumphal entry into Jerusalem and concerns the destruction of the temple and signs of the end times. He writes, "Who cannot but think of the women with small children deprived of their miserable shelters in the coldest of Cape winters, when reading verses 19 and 20? 'Alas for women with child in those days, and for those who have children at the breast! Pray that it may not be in winter...' What we have witnessed in recent weeks is the systematic and brutal destruction of family life, because this is what the demolition of squatter huts really means."[22] In making this scriptural allusion, Wittenberg centers the lived experience of women and children who are marginalized and brutalized by these policies to highlight the impact of forced removals on family life.

PACSA authors draw on their central theological conviction about light having more power than darkness, and life having more power than death, to make sense of women's suffering and marginality. For example, the Christmas 1992 newsletter begins with a focus on women returning to their homes after fleeing political violence. Robin Hutt, a member of a group of overseas church delegates for the Ecumenical Monitoring Programme of South Africa, reflects, "They were ordinary people: mothers and grandmothers returning to burnt out houses in a small settlement beyond the Nseleni river. 'Why did they do this to us and our children?' Their cries, which were echoed in Folweni and Mpushini, join the cries of the mothers of Bethlehem as the slaughter of the innocents goes on unabated."[23] Hutt draws a parallel between the lamentation of these women and the biblical narrative in Matthew 2 of King Herod slaughtering all male children under two in Bethlehem, after the Three Wise Men do not return to him to tell him where Jesus is. In so doing, Hutt narrates the plight of these socially marginalized mothers to condemn the political violence in the transition era.

Hutt then draws on PACSA's central theological conviction about light overcoming darkness to make sense of this parallel between mothers mourning for their children in the biblical text and in the contemporary South African context. He notes that even "in the bloody and bewildering mess that life is for so many in Natal, Christ is present. The very name of the province is a constant reminder. In the darkness a light has been born that nothing can put out."[24] Drawing on this theological contrast between darkness and light that consistently characterizes PACSA's discourse, he goes on to write, "The light of Christmas is the reflected light of the resurrection beyond the cross, that light shows us that though sin and pain and death are real enough, they will not have the last word. The last word will be with light and life, with love and goodness and joy—the underlying themes of

Christmas."[25] This reflection draws a connection between women's lived experience and PACSA's theological convictions about the power of resurrection for transforming death and violence. Narratives about women's marginality and vulnerability are interpreted through the lens of their theological convictions to make a broader point about the possibility of transforming death-dealing systems into life-promoting ones.

PACSA's theological culture shapes how they perceive and respond to women's marginality related to their social roles in the family. Their transformation theological culture incorporates attention to women by aligning their experience with that of biblical women, especially in the Christmas and Easter narratives that appear so frequently in their discourse. As these connections are made, the organization sometimes problematizes patriarchy as a system in need of transformation, and sometimes aligns women with populations who are marginalized and vulnerable, more generally. In both cases, PACSA's attention to women's experiences is grounded in the theological narrative of death being transformed into life, of suffering leading to transformation.

Application of the Theological Culture: Patriarchy and the Church

PACSA's theological convictions also intersect with their posture of empathy with the marginalized as they critique the complicity of the church in gender oppression. As with their attention to women's marginality in the family, PACSA authors also contend that the way to address patriarchy in the church is to center the experiences of suffering women. This emphasis on the need to focus attention on the voices of the marginalized is a consistent theme in PACSA's discourse. Their theological culture follows a distinct path across time and from race to gender. In PACSA's case, this process facilitates a robust conceptualization of gender justice.

For instance, in the Christmas 1996 newsletter Janet Trisk invites other women to join a group of women who have felt alienated by the church and have been regularly gathering to do their own liturgy. She describes how these gatherings center on women telling their own stories and holding a eucharist. Trisk notes that "in different ways, we have found the liturgy, teaching or spirituality of the church... to fall short of our needs—perhaps because we have received 'scriptural advice,' rather than empathetic listening from a male minister; perhaps because we were never opened to ways of imaging God, other than 'Father;' perhaps because we have found the institutional church dominated and run by men; perhaps because we have simply not found it a spiritual home."[26] As she depicts the varying ways in which women have experienced alienation in their churches, Trisk points to the possibility of a different kind of church liturgy. She does so by highlighting the various ways that women have experienced sexism in the church, ranging from patriarchal imagery to their exclusion from leadership. PACSA's theological culture incorporates a concern with sexism as they continue to emphasize the importance of listening to those who experience marginalization.

PACSA's focus on women's experiences of marginality within the structures of the church is also evidenced as they center women's narratives in more depth. For instance, they invited Purity Malinga, the fourth woman to be ordained in the Methodist Church of Southern Africa and the first woman bishop of that denomination, to give an address. In her remarks, which are reproduced in PACSA's September 2001 newsletter, Malinga describes the ways that "women in the church have found themselves discriminated against and confined to supportive roles," noting that "the issue of the ordination of women has challenged the churches to deal with sexism in the church and in the society at large."[27] When reflecting on whether there has actually been transformation of sexism now that women are occupying leadership positions, Malinga notes that this struggle is not just about men accepting women's leadership; women also need to recognize the ways they have been socialized into patriarchy. She observes that, for women, "it is much easier to conform than to work for transformation."[28]

And yet, "the church is supposed to bring about transformation. When the church is transformed, only then will it be able to transform the society."[29] Malinga calls on women, in particular, to "commit themselves to transforming the church." She also recognizes the importance of women leaders identifying and working with men "who [also] want to see a transformed society."[30] Indeed, in keeping with PACSA's theological culture that stresses the need for the marginalized to share their stories and the privileged to relinquish their privilege, Malinga contends that, just as both men and women have been socialized not to engage in the transformation of sexism, both men and women are needed to enact such transformation.

How should this process of transformation happen? Malinga concludes by pointing out that "women's experiences and understandings of God have been ignored down the ages but they need to be taken seriously."[31] In addition, churches must "make women leaders visible" and "women leaders need to insist on being themselves," rather than fitting the established confines of expected leadership.[32] By inviting Malinga to share her experience and call for the church to transform patriarchy, PACSA centers a woman church leader's voice. This is a consistent feature of their theological culture, as they focus attention on the experience of the socially marginalized in order to call for the transformation of unjust systems into just and equitable ones instead.

Finally, PACSA not only focuses on women's experiences of marginality within the church. They also draw on women's voices to cast a vision of what a transformed church could be. For instance, in Easter 2000 Reverend Barbel Wartenberg-Potter addressed a PACSA presentation on "Feminist Theology." In this talk, Wartenberg-Potter reflects on the symbolism of the eucharist—that is, the commemoration of the Last Supper, with a focus on bread and wine as the body and blood of Jesus—through the lens of feminist theology. She writes, "Women have always participated in the central sacramental act of the church, a symbol of shared eating. Women were the administrators of food in the house. Bread was predominately in the hands of women."[33]

Perceiving women at the center of this holy ritual, Wartenberg-Potter also considers the practical ramifications of understanding the eucharist in this way, for women specifically. She asserts, "In a world full of denial of women's identity it is good to see the connections between the fertility of the earth, the fertility of women, the work of women, elementary food and bread-sharing. The eucharist is a symbol out of the realm and world of women. There is no better symbol than this table to restore the broken identity of humanity."[34] Wartenberg-Porter reclaims a central Christian symbol as something that connects directly to women's status, including a society that denies their dignity. In so doing, she perceives that transforming sexism, by interpreting the Eucharist through the realm of women, can restore broken humanity.

Working within a given theological culture opens up particular opportunities for imagining the role of the church in the world.[35] In PACSA's case, the transformation theological culture enables a clear and strong conceptualization of gender justice. Their theological convictions concerning the transformation of death-dealing, unjust systems into life-promoting, just ones facilitate their recognition that sexism is a system that needs to be transformed, just as racism and economic injustice need to be transformed. Their social positioning that stresses both the complicity of the privileged and the suffering of the marginalized manifests in their explicit naming of male privilege and centering women's experiences. This pattern of centering women's suffering in their discourse usually, but not always, results in a clear condemnation of patriarchy. But even in cases where the critique of sexism is muted, PACSA still clearly interprets women's experiences through the lens of their central theological convictions. These patterns result in a clear and direct incorporation of gender into the transformation theological culture.

AFRICAN ENTERPRISE

Gender and the Reconciliation Theological Culture: God's Way Is a Gendered Way

AE shows how a theological culture can prevent the conceptualization of gender justice. They do not describe or perceive sexism as a force that shapes social relations the way that they had perceived racism to be such a force. AE's distinct religious convictions intersect with their posture toward women to restrict their capacity to promote gender justice. Their theological culture centers on the theological conviction that there is a distinct Christian way to order society. The Jesus Way is characterized by right relationships, and spiritual reconciliation with God necessitates social reconciliation across groups that are alienated from one another. I argue here that these theological convictions also imply a gendered order. AE's discourse about a Christian way to order society relies on and perpetuates beliefs about God-given social roles for men and women. There are some hints of gender essentialist beliefs that rely on notions of inherent differences between men and women in the other organizations, too. But the other two also make clear affirmations of gender equality. Within AE, by contrast, assumptions of inherent gender difference are untroubled and uncontested—indeed, they are reified throughout their discourse.

Sometimes AE's gendered belief system can be seen when gender is strikingly absent as a relevant social category in their discourse. For instance, founder Michael Cassidy reflects in the November 1997 newsletter that "our age is basically one of deep alienations at almost every level, whether interpersonal, marital, denominational, racial, tribal, class or whatever. How critical, therefore, to remind ourselves... that the Kingdom of God is the Kingdom of right relationships."[36] Drawing on AE's theological concern both with alienations that need to be reconciled and the assertion that God's intention for society is for right relationships across such alienations, this list of multiple forms of social relationships in need of healing does not include gender. "Marital" and "or whatever" are as close as this list comes to an explicit recognition of gender as a relevant social category in the "Kingdom of right relationships." Perhaps "marital" is meant to imply relationships among men and women. But it is not made as explicit as the naming of "racial, tribal, [and] class." And if the intention is to use marriage as the primary instance of gender relations, this precludes AE from recognizing that gender also functions as a social reality outside of marriage.

AE's lack of recognition of gender alienation stems from beliefs in the God-given nature of gendered social roles. For instance, a reflection on various events at a May 1983 mission in a city in the Eastern Cape called Umtata includes a description of a woman offering "a beautiful message on the need for forgiveness and the importance of women in the home today."[37] The wife of the president of the Transkei, the former "homeland" where Umtata is located, hosted the event, and the newsletter reports that she responds to the message by telling the women present: "What we grow up with is what we become. We need to raise our children in the ways of God."[38] The emphasis is on women's unique capacity to be a presence in the home and thereby to change society. Women fulfilling their distinct role in society as mothers will ensure a healthy society, as they model forgiveness and ensure that children are following God's way. AE's theological convictions about following God's way intersect with a posture toward women that stresses their spiritual investment in the home as their key contribution to social life.

This emphasis on mothers playing a crucial role in God's ordained social order remains consistent over time. For instance, the June 2005 newsletter reports on a local conference in Pietermaritzburg that included a talk entitled "Born for a Purpose," an address to women that highlighted the significance of motherhood. The speaker, Phineas Dube, said, "It is mothers who teach their children how to be human beings, and that mothers need to discover their purpose as quickly as possible.... It is their responsibility to impress upon their children the commandment to 'love the Lord your God with all your heart and with all your soul and with all your strength.'"[39] Referencing the distinct "purpose" for which women are born, Dube taught that "mothers are perfect for the purpose for which God has designed them physically, mentally and spiritually. Purpose, he said, was more powerful than plans, and that the only plan that will succeed is God's plan for one's life."[40] Here, biology and destiny are intertwined, and women's unique capacity for mothering is established as an important—perhaps *the* important—purpose for their lives. AE's fundamental theological concern with enacting the Christian way for society intersects with a posture toward women that affirms their primary purpose in forming the spiritual lives of their children, as they teach them to love God. This is women's purpose in life.

AE's theological convictions imply a gendered way for Christians to engage in social life. This belief is not contested, nor is it complicated by the inclusion of alternative views, as we see below with the case of the SACC. This pattern of a consistent, untroubled gender essentialist belief system means that AE is stunted in their capacity to articulate a robust concern with gender injustice. We see this most clearly in an example where AE comes close to problematizing gender oppression but then immediately reaffirms gender difference as a fundamental component of the order of society. In 2003, there was a major event coordinated by AE along with other church leaders to call churches to engage with pressing social issues, similar to the way that the original South African Christian Leadership Assembly (SACLA) gathering had done in 1976. "SACLA 2" was intended to discuss several issues facing South Africa in the democracy, approaching ten years since the first elections. In the February 2003 newsletter that describes preparations for this event, the list of issues to be addressed includes HIV/AIDS, poverty, violence, crime, and racism. It also includes the following: "The Gender issue needs to be addressed by making sure that people are cognizant of the need to right the gender imbalance in South Africa. Not to deny the distinctive roles that males and females have to play within our society but to make sure that sufficient and honorable attention is paid, on a biblical basis, to the richness that our society and our families can attain through the gender roles we are given."[41] This inclusion of gender as a serious contender for attention along with issues of racism and other social issues is a notable exception in AE's discourse. The reference to "the Gender issue" implies that AE understands the need to respond to the broader context, in which gender has become an increasingly salient topic. But this acknowledgment of "the need to right the gender imbalance" also reflects a concern with the idea that addressing gender inequality could result in a problematic denial of distinct gender roles. In fact, the only way gender can make an appearance is with a strong caveat that recognizing inequality is not calling into question "the gender roles we are given"—that is, gender roles that are seen to be ordained by God.

It is also significant that immediately following this statement about gender is a description of the ongoing need to address racism. The newsletter affirms that "racism and reconciliation is [sic] still an issue needing attention in our society today. There are 3 justices. We have achieved political justice but we have to work on economic justice and social justice. Racism is a part of social justice and, in many respects, racism in some quarters in South Africa is as bad as it has ever been. Some of us are still in denial about racism in the nation and, worse still, in the church."[42] This statement about racism demonstrates that AE has the capacity to recognize social justice issues and to name their sources. Why is sexism not considered to also be "a part of social justice," the way that racism is? AE's theological culture relies on an untroubled and uncontested gender essentialist belief, such that gender inequality cannot even be hinted at without an immediate reaffirmation of God-ordained gender roles. Perhaps unsurprisingly, in the SACLA 2 documents, gender is later dropped from the list of issues that need to be addressed in South Africa, with "sexism" making some small appearances and then also slipping by the wayside. AE's distinct religious ideas that enshrine gender essentialism prevent the development of a conception of gender justice.

Application of the Theological Culture: Women's Relational Brokenness and the Healing Power of the Gospel

AE's theological conviction about a gendered social order intersects with their posture toward women. In particular, their theological culture's emphasis on the power of the Gospel for relational and spiritual healing is applied to women. This pattern presents an important tension in AE's discourse. Establishing and reaffirming a theological foundation for a gendered order of society precludes the possibility of cultivating a sense of gender justice. And yet, women are recognized as a group whose experiences of brokenness in their family lives and intimate relationships necessitate healing that the Gospel can provide.

This posture toward women is shaped by the ways that AE's theological culture not only emphasizes a right way to order society, but also stresses the role of experiencing spiritual healing as a pathway to reconciled social relationships. This pattern explains the clear lack of accounting for GBV as an issue of gender and power that I discussed in chapter 3. AE's theological culture facilitates their recognition that women are a social group who need healing from particular forms of pain and brokenness. But, in contrast to their discourse about cross-racial reconciliation, there is no conception of the need for reconciliation among men and women. Instead, women's broken family and intimate relationships are seen as a sign of a deeper spiritual need that can be resolved through faith in Jesus and, sometimes, by fostering connection among fellow women. This lack of institutional imagination for gender reconciliation constrains AE's ability fully to reckon with sexism as a social reality that shapes women's lives.

This pattern emerges early on in AE's discourse. For instance, the May 1983 report from the mission in Umtata described above also included a "ladies tea," at which women members of the AE team shared their testimonies. At this point, "a young woman began weeping, pouring out her fears and the deep needs of her family. Many barriers came tumbling down as different women openly shared their need for Christ and accepted Him as the Healer of their broken lives."[43] In fact, at the evening rally for the mission at least one of the women who was at the tea "took Christ as Lord and Saviour."[44] AE's theological convictions about the power of the Gospel for healing spiritual and emotional needs intersect with a posture toward women that focuses on their brokenness and spiritual needs. As the group listens to the women's testimonies, unspecified "barriers came tumbling down," implying that the women are united with one another through their recognition of their shared spiritual needs. The brokenness that women experience in their family lives is healed through the power of the Gospel and as they encounter one another.

AE's discourse about women often situates their experiences of pain and brokenness specifically within their relational and familial lives. In so doing, they intertwine an affirmation of the importance of women's role in the family with a recognition of the need for healing of broken intimate relationships. For instance, an image of a young woman figures on the front page of the May 1992 *AE Update*, where woman evangelist Dawn Guinness is ministering to a young woman who comes from "a broken home" and who is now living in a children's home to get out of her parents' house.[45] The young woman says, "I've just come out of a terrible relationship with a guy I truly loved. It really broke my heart. Then that very first evening's message [of the mission] was that God is really there when you're in pain."[46] Situating a woman's experience of brokenness in the context of an intimate relationship, the message here draws on AE's theological conviction about the power of the Gospel for healing to address the particular pain that a woman is experiencing. And again, though this is not the focus of the story, a woman evangelist connects with the young woman in order to minister to her in that pain. A frequent motif in AE's discourse is that as people encounter one another, they can find healing across lines of difference. This theme occurs in this narrative, but not through stressing connection between men and women. Encounters that spark spiritual change occur between women, instead.

AE's discourse about women's lived experiences includes recognition of the complexities of broken family life in need of redemptive healing. For instance, the organization sponsored several seminars on divorce. After one such event on "divorce recovery," an article entitled "Finding Hope and Sparkle in Broken Lives" notes that, as the seminar leader described, "we virtually opened the Word and let the redemptive Grace of the Lord work in their lives."[47] The newsletter includes a reflection on the weekend by a woman who "'came from an abusive marriage ... and I think that over the last two years that is what I have actually been dealing with. I hadn't actually dealt with the issue of divorce and come to terms with it.'"[48] She goes on to note that "'God has really spoken to me and I really felt His love and His peace through it all. I feel I can go away and put the whole "sin"—if you can call it that—of divorce behind me and look to tomorrow. I no longer feel guilty. I have been released.'"[49] This woman's account resonates with two other women profiled in this piece, who similarly describe being released from the guilt and fear that come from being divorced. The clear message here is that the power of healing redemption can reach divorced people, even if there is not a social reconciliation that results in a restored marriage. AE acknowledges the reality of divorce—and even abuse—and the power of the Gospel for redeeming women in those situations.

AE's reconciliation theological culture also reifies gender essentialism and constrains the development of gender justice by depicting women as instruments of either sin or salvation, especially through their sexuality and beauty. Spirituality is overlaid with gender essentialist norms about women's sexuality and attractiveness. For instance, a narrative about a woman who had been involved in Satanism intertwines gendered norms with the power of the Gospel for freedom from brokenness: "She . . . lost her virginity at 17. She even prayed for Satan and demons to have sex with her. When she became a student she began to sleep with men on the campus. She tried to steal their intelligence and put curses on them, causing them to become depressed."[50] This girl, possessed by Satan, used her sexuality to deprive men of their mental acuity.[51] The speaker notices she is not looking at him directly, and he commands her to look at him and prays in the name of Jesus for whatever is possessing her to "'come out.'" The girl emerges from something like a trance, the speaker prays, and she is converted. "Susan has been set free," the piece concludes.[52] The dramatic power of the Gospel is evidenced in this conversion of a woman whose demon possession manifested in sexual sin and attempts to assert power over men's emotional and mental stability.

Women's sexuality and attractiveness can also serve as an instrument of salvation. That is, women can use their femininity to bring others to Christ. For instance, a piece entitled "Running into Full-Time Commitment" begins this way: "The young man jogging past a bench on the Sea Point beach did a double-take. The attractive young woman sitting there held something out to him and smiled. He turned, interested, and jogged back to her. And found Christ."[53] This successful evangelism story portrays a beautiful woman as offering the young man not herself, but Jesus, through a leaflet for an AE mission. Playing on gendered norms of women's beauty and men being drawn to that beauty, the story surprises the reader by revealing the man was offered something far more precious than the woman's body—his soul's salvation.

Similarly, in October 2005, the opening to a mission at the University of the Western Cape included "two beautiful local Christians, chosen as 'Miss Connected' and 'First Runner-up' [who] were to be driven right around the campus and then up to the UWC student centre in these luxury cars."[54] This was supposed to happen while others were out advertising the event, but a massive rain storm disrupted their plans. "Team members were discouraged. Beauty queens were freezing."[55] But the ultimate result was a good one, because everyone flooded to the student center to escape the rain. The two beauty queen women then "spoke about how they got connected to Jesus, and the difference He has made in their lives."[56] Here, women's beauty is used to draw people into an event, but their faith in Jesus is the more important message. These examples reflect a gender essentialist framework that portrays women as seductresses and as sexually attractive to men, while also maintaining the theological emphasis in AE's theological culture on the healing power of the Gospel. These various narratives show how AE's theological convictions about the power of the Gospel intersect with their posture toward women's distinct experiences of brokenness in their intimate relationships and families to prevent a conceptualization of gender justice.

Application of the Theological Culture: Social Constraints on Women and Christian Identity

A theological culture also has implications for the organizations' understanding of the church's complicity in patriarchy. Unlike the other two organizations, AE's theologically formed gender essentialist belief system intertwines with a posture toward women that does not perceive gender inequality as part of the constraints women experience. Within their emphasis on a gendered order for society, AE sometimes recognizes that these social roles can be limiting and that women need to be validated and affirmed in their capacities to minister in their homes and churches. But the possibility of attending to sexism as a source of women's struggles is sublimated into a concern that women are prevented from living into their capacity to enact the Gospel by some of the limitations of their social roles.

For instance, AE's May 2002 newsletter describes a "Women of Influence" seminar as "one of the best-attended conferences" sponsored by the organization.[57] The idea for this conference originated with the woman who ran the development office at AE, Sandra Pillay. She states that she was motivated to hold such a conference for pastors' wives "'because often their husbands are so busy looking after the flock that they don't have time to encourage them.'"[58] Pillay goes on to assert, "'I felt a need to empower women to take their rightful place, especially in their homes and ministry. So often women lose their sense of identity.'"[59] Here there is a recognition that women's lost identity is connected to a loss of meaningful place in the social roles they occupy. Women are to influence society from within their homes and their ministry, and to be reminded of their core identity—their faith. Patriarchy is not identified as part of the problem here, the way that it is for both the SACC and PACSA.

In fact, the main speakers at this conference "shared about the need to connect with God, a woman's purpose and responsibilities, and women being special to God."[60] The limitations that prevent women from being empowered to take their place are resolved through reminding women of their distinct and unique capacities. One of the participants notes how effective this was for her, saying, "'I now realize that as a woman I have the power, ability and talent to go out there, be who I am and impact the nation for God.'"[61] As they experience spiritual connection and reminders about their Christian identity and distinct (though, at least here, unspecified) "purpose and responsibilities," women will be able to impact the nation for God.

This sensibility around women's identity sometimes focuses particularly on the role that women play in their churches. But this does not translate into the kind of critique of women's lack of access to leadership positions in churches that we see in both the SACC and PACSA. For instance, after a seminar on effective preaching, which was led by all men, two women's comments are reported in the newsletter. One of them "felt the training would enable her to prepare her talks and preach better in her ministry to women in her church," so the skills she has acquired can allow her to better reach the women in her congregation.[62] And the other was a lay minister in an Anglican church who "had not had any formal training in preaching," but clearly does, or would, preach in her own congregation as she describes how this seminar "'has given me the courage to try new ideas on preaching.'"[63] Here, the fact that women are preaching is unquestioned, perhaps reflecting AE's ecumenism. But neither woman is an ordained pastor; in fact, one focuses specifically on women's ministry, while the other operates as a lay minister. AE does include these women in the preaching training. But, in contrast to the other two organizations, there is no explicit attention to the ways that women who work in and for the church occupy leadership positions and narrate their experiences of the gendered constraints and resistance they experience within those positions.

Indeed, where there is awareness of the constraints that women may experience in church and society, AE's solution is for women to reach for a faith that transcends their social roles. Put simply, the answer is for women to find their identity in Christ, not to have their social marginality recognized and challenged, as both the SACC and PACSA perceive and argue. A retreat in October 1999, for instance, "gave the participants an opportunity to see their value *not only* in their roles as single women or wives and mothers or grandmothers, but also as women fulfilling many different and important roles in the body of Christ."[64] Messages at this retreat drew on the biblical example of Naomi and Ruth to highlight the importance of women's relationships with one another, and suggested practical ways of following God in everyday life. But even here where there is an opportunity to look beyond social roles, women are encouraged to "see their value *not only*" according to their relationship status. This does not translate into a challenge to gendered roles as such, but points to the need for women to be affirmed in their Christian identity more generally.

AE's reconciliation theological culture prevents the development of a conception of gender justice. Their theological culture relies on and perpetuates a gender essentialist set of theological convictions. Authors draw on central elements of the reconciliation theological culture to argue that women are to live into God-ordained roles. Following the Jesus Way means enacting a gendered social order. These convictions intersect with AE's posture toward women. Women are recognized to be a particular group in need of the healing power of the Gospel, and there are sometimes accounts that recognize some of the limitations of their social roles. But, in contrast to the organization's discourse about race and racism, there is no recognition that gendered alienation is rooted in sexism and that cross-gender reconciliation needs to be pursued to address these problems. The social reconciliation that is sometimes at work in the background of the narratives is one that highlights women's connections with other women. AE does not develop a conception of gender justice because their theological culture produces uncontested beliefs that God's design for society includes a gendered social order.

SOUTH AFRICAN COUNCIL OF CHURCHES

Gender and the Liberation Theological Culture

The SACC shows how a theological culture can result in ambivalence around gender justice. The SACC's theological convictions center on the belief that people share an inherent dignity that is violated by systems of oppression, and that, as God takes the side of the socially oppressed and marginalized, so the church should also. These beliefs are transposed onto gender in complex ways, mirroring patterns that are seen in the broader liberation movement in South Africa and in other countries as well.[65] On the one hand, women are clearly seen—and sometimes speak—as a group in need of liberation from oppression. On the other hand, women in the organization had to fight for attention to their concerns, and women's liberation was sometimes seen to be an ancillary concern to the broader liberation movement. Thus, the SACC's liberation theological culture does open up the possibility of articulating a clear theological mandate to promote women's equal dignity. But this conviction intersects with a posture toward women that is ambivalent about whether they constitute a marginalized group who need to be liberated from sexism. As a result of this ambivalence, the predominant message in the SACC is that women should be liberated in order to enact broader social change, not necessarily for their own sake.

Women within the SACC do apply the organization's theological affirmation about all people being created in the image of God to gender, contending that both men and women need to be liberated from the traditions and structures that hinder them. For instance, a Women's Dialogue at the National Conference in 1982 resulted in an explicitly theological affirmation of women's dignity. The report from the dialogue affirms, "Our starting point is not a philosophy but a theology based on the firm conviction that we are created in God's image and that Christ died for us. Because we believe this, we also believe that we have a responsibility to ourselves as women, and to Christ, to fulfill that image both in the church and in society."[66] Distancing themselves from a "philosophy" that would argue for gender equality, the dialogue establishes the theological necessity of recognizing women's equal dignity, while also emphasizing that women have "a responsibility" to enact that dignity in their social and religious contexts. What it means to enact this responsibility is not entirely clear from the report, but the women do state that they need to "disturb the complacency of the women themselves" and help the church to move from affirmations that they are the "'backbone'" of the church in ways that end up relegating them to the "'background.'"[67]

This same 1982 report on the Women's Dialogue also pays particular attention to the cultural factors that constrain gender equality and dignity, and the need to pursue liberation: "We also believe that while we are born into a culture, Christ offers us a new humanity. And, because of Christ's offer, we are called to free ourselves from those cultural traditions that are contrary to Christ's calling for us: this is as true for men as it is for women."[68] Perceiving that cultural traditions contribute to a failure to honor the equal dignity of women alongside men, women in the SACC assert that being theologically grounded in Christ's liberating power also necessitates social liberation from restrictive traditions. Their action plan, then, includes the need to "work out a theology of liberation for women and men."[69] The SACC's liberation theological culture is transposed onto gender as they affirm that both men and women are to be liberated from cultural traditions that impede their ability to embrace the new humanity that is offered through Jesus.

The liberation theological culture also stresses the importance of the role of the church in embodying and enacting God's vision for society. In keeping with this dimension of the organization's theological culture, sometimes women in the SACC argued that the theological principle of their equal dignity with men had ramifications for how they should be included in the structures of the church. For instance, a report by the Christian Women's Movement to the National Conference in 1984 begins by again situating attention to gender in the theological principle of equal dignity: "We believe that we are all, both women and men, created in the image of God and that Jesus Christ died for us. That means we all have intrinsic worth and are equal in the sight of God."[70] The report then again connects this theological principle to the idea that women also "have responsibilities and obligations."[71] In particular, it states, "Part of that responsibility and obligation is to recognize and accept our own intrinsic worth as women and to take up the challenge of calling to the church to recognize and accept that as women, we represent half of God's creation. Without us there can be no 'community of women and men' in the Church."[72] This theological affirmation of equality and dignity simultaneously critiques the church for not fully honoring women's status while also calling women, themselves, to take up the responsibility of realizing their potential and accepting their worth.[73]

These clear theological affirmations of women's equal, inherent dignity are complicated by another key dimension of the SACC's discourse: Sometimes women's liberation is not seen as an integral, constitutive dimension of the quest for justice but as a mechanism to achieve broader liberation. These threads are often interwoven, as in the 1985 National Conference that stressed that women's liberation from social, cultural, and political structures is necessary in order for them to be a "power for change." Intertwining a critique of the forces that prevent women's liberation with a call to women to look for ways that they can change society, the newsletter's presentation of the 1985 conference theme includes an exhortation to women "to be awake to the fact that they should be a power for change because God expects it of them. It has to be admitted that perhaps not all of them are there yet because of all kinds of blockages, cultural, institutional and otherwise. In society the woman has been relegated to the place where she is not to seek power."[74] This discussion of the 1985 conference theme names women's involvement in society as something that God expects them to do. That is, there is a theological mandate for women's social action in the broader liberation struggle. But women are constrained by all sorts of social and cultural "blockages" because of their lesser power position in society.

As noted in the introduction to this chapter, the newsletter then applies the SACC's theological culture of liberation to women by affirming that "Jesus still speaks to women through the Gospel today . . . liberating them from the burdens of tradition, customs and stereotyped habits which oppress them and prevent them from being a power for change."[75] After asserting that Jesus still liberates women today, the statement contends, "If women realise and accept this challenge they cannot but come forth self-confident, self-reliant and with a fresh understanding of their worth as persons, and therefore changed—capable of bringing about change."[76] This discourse situates women's liberation within the broader liberation theological culture as it draws on theological convictions about God-given dignity and Jesus's liberating power from oppressive structures. But the theological culture also adapts as it is applied to gender. Women are to be liberated from what oppresses them not just for their own sake, but also in order to contribute to the broader liberation struggle against apartheid.

This emphasis on women being liberated in order to enact broader political change matters for the SACC's posture toward women's roles in the democracy, too. For instance, at the 1989 Annual General Meeting of Women's Ministries, Brigalia Bam, who went on to become a deputy general secretary and then the first woman general secretary of the SACC, gave the opening address for the meeting. She "addressed the question of sexism and national liberation, stressing that the women's struggle must not be postponed to the Post Apartheid period because if that happens we will not be ready to take up vital roles."[77] Recognizing tensions between the women's movement and the broader liberation movement, Bam notes that delaying women's quest for liberating equality will result in the failure of women to contribute fully to the new democracy.[78] Women are to be liberated in order to fulfill the political roles they are meant to occupy.

As I showed in chapter 2, the SACC's liberation theological culture follows a clear path from challenging the racism of apartheid to pursuing economic justice in the democracy. This path impacts the ways they perceive the role women should play in their efforts to promote development work.[79] For instance, in the 1991 "South African Council of Churches Report on the Programmes of the Council," Bam, as deputy general secretary, includes a section on the recent organizational integration of women's issues into the organization's Department of Development and Training.[80] She notes that "development efforts will fail if women are excluded in defining and implementing development. The central issue is that God grants gifts to every member of Christ's body. As church of Jesus Christ, as ecumenical movement, as member of society, we are the poorer when we do not allow those gifts of God to be fully manifested for the service of all."[81] Calling for women's inclusion in the development work that was central to the SACC's adapting identity in the transition and early democracy, Bam articulates an instrumental vision of both the rationale and the consequences for this work. As God bestows gifts upon all, those gifts are to be enacted "for the service of all." Women have a contribution to make to broader society. This capacity still needs to be fully realized as both a theological and practical imperative.

The SACC's liberation theological culture opens up opportunities for seeing women as a social group whose equality with men needs to be affirmed, and authors critique social and cultural factors that prevent women from living out their dignity. At the same time, this notion of inherent dignity is complicated by a tendency to treat women's liberation as a means to an end. That is, women are to be liberated in order to contribute to broader change, not necessarily because of their inherent dignity. As the next section demonstrates, this instrumental conception of gender justice, rather than seeing it as fully constitutive of an overall quest for justice as PACSA articulated, also has implications for the SACC's perceptions of women's social roles in the family.

Application of the Liberation Theological Culture: Women in Family Life

One of the SACC's central theological convictions is that God has a particular concern for the socially marginalized. This conviction intersects with their posture toward different social groups. As I described in chapter 1, the organization paid particular attention to the plight of the oppressed black population during apartheid and, as I described in chapter 2, this commitment followed a path for their concern with economic marginalization, especially, in the democracy. How do these same convictions apply to women's experiences?

We see a complicated answer to this question when we consider the SACC's discourse about women's roles in the family. The family is seen as a social sphere within which women have particular influence and thus can work to enact broader social change.[82] Acknowledgment of women's influence in the home is sometimes also accompanied by a recognition of women's social marginality and affirmations of God's solidarity with the marginalized, more generally. But the SACC does not clearly critique the way that sexism contributes a distinct social marginalization for women, especially in comparison to PACSA's clear recognition of the ways that women's marginality has been caused by the unjust system of patriarchy. In fact, sometimes a gender essentialist belief system undergirds their discourse in ways that work against a strong conception of gender justice.

We see these patterns in some of the earliest documents concerning the SACC's institutional attention to women. For instance, minutes from the Meetings of the National Committee of Justice and Reconciliation from April 1973 include a discussion of women's work. The woman spearheading these efforts was Shirley Turner, who founded an organization called Church Women Concerned to bring women together across racial divides.[83] Turner raised several points about the importance of church women, in particular, in contributing to broader efforts to enact social change in the midst of the apartheid regime. She begins by simply asserting, "Church women have an important role to play in bringing about justice, reconciliation and unity."[84] In keeping with the ways the SACC's theological culture applies to women, Turner then notes that there are social constraints that prevent church women from enacting their capacities to contribute to social change: "Most church women do not even begin to fill this role because the attitude to herself, prevent[s] her from recognizing either potential or responsibility as an agent of reconciliation."[85]

Despite this situation, Turner notes, "church women can be enabled to play a significant role in promoting justice and reconciliation through a programme of education."[86] A key aspect of this educational program is that church women should be "helped to use the home base as a means of reconciliation."[87] This early attention to women acknowledges both their capacities and the social constraints that prevent them from being agents of change in social life. It also portrays women's role in the family and the home as a specific sphere within which women can exercise their social influence.

In fact, Turner argues that women "have a natural role in reconciliation and an opportunity must therefore be created for them to relate to other women of other cultures and races."[88] Without specifying the particulars of this "natural role," the point is clear: there is a distinct role that women can play in relating to one another across racial divides to prompt social change. While the language of reconciliation here resonates with AE's discourse, there is also an important difference. For the SACC, attention is also drawn to the ways that women are constrained by attitudes that prevent them from "recognizing either [their] potential or responsibility." There is a dual message for the SACC here that is shaped by the theological convictions described in the previous section. One thread relies on a gender essentialist framework about women's natural roles in the family; the other recognizes and problematizes social attitudes that constrain them.

This interweaving of a gender essentialist framework with a recognition of various factors that can constrain women results in ambivalence around whether women constitute a distinct marginalized group that need the church's solidarity. Sometimes authors narrate accounts of women's distinct experiences as mothers to call attention to the consequences of apartheid policies, particularly the disruption of family life through forced removals.[89] The SACC's posture toward women in these narratives does not include a critique of gender injustice. Rather, women's marginality serves as an illustration of the devastation of apartheid on family life. In so doing, the liberation theological culture is applied to women's family roles to attend to social marginalization more generally, rather than the need to also address gender injustice.

For instance, a 1982 "Report on Justice & Society" by the SACC's director of justice and reconciliation, Dr. Wolfram Kistner, reflects on the significance of a gathering of women near Ladysmith that included "a discussion of joint action which could strengthen and give new hope to the community. They were especially concerned about the children growing up in this setting."[90] Emphasizing that women can play a crucial role for their community because of their concern for the children, the SACC's newsletter notes that the meeting concluded with singing the Magnificat: "This biblical hymn of Mary, the mother of Jesus, (Luke 1:46–55) had a special meaning in this setting. It was sung by a group of women who had gone through an extremely hard time when the removal took place and who had lost most of their belongings and savings, and who were now living in an area of economic deprivation. The Magnificat emphasizes God sees the lonely, the humble people, those who are otherwise discarded by society."[91] Kistner's portrayal of this event identifies a parallel between these suffering women and Mary, the mother of Jesus, drawing on the SACC's liberation theological culture that stresses the care of God for those who are marginalized and "discarded." He does so while also stressing the important role that women can play in helping their community and prioritizing their concern for their children.

Here, the SACC's theological concern with social marginalization intersects with a posture toward women that does not problematize their marginality due to sexism but instead focuses attention on their economic position. That is, the liberation theological culture is applied to women in ways that highlight their status as a marginalized group related to their economic and political position vis-à-vis the home. But this does not develop into a concern with gender justice. In fact, the focus in the narrative is on God's solidarity with those who are "discarded" because of the injustice of apartheid policies; women's experiences are incorporated into their broader concept of the poor rather than treated as a distinct form of marginalization.

The SACC's discourse about women in family life provides an important contrast to PACSA's. PACSA consistently affirms the theological belief that light has more power than darkness, and that Christians are to embody hope in the possibility of a new social order. This theological conviction intersects with their focus on women's disproportionate social burdens to critique sexism as a system that needs to be transformed. The SACC consistently grounds their discourse in the theological conviction that God is partial to the poor. But there is more ambivalence in their discourse over whether and how women should be understood as a distinct marginalized group. Instead, women are sometimes counted *among* the poor.

In fact, sometimes SACC leaders align South African women's experience with the mothering role of Mary by relying on gender essentialist norms that reify women's marginalized social position. For instance, in a speech on neighborliness, Desmond Tutu draws on a long-standing comparison in Christian tradition between Eve's responsibility for the fall of humankind into sin and Mary's choice to bear Jesus into the world.[92] He does so in order to highlight women's role in being change-agents, stating, "If it took a woman to get us into trouble, then it took a woman to get us out of trouble. Jesus could not have been born unless a woman had agreed to cooperate with God."[93] Tutu connects this parallel between Eve and Mary to the importance of women's contributions to the liberation movement. He says, "I have said that as a preamble to underline that I believe that you have a tremendous role to play, that you are playing a tremendous role. It is utterly true that behind every successful man there is a woman. Perhaps it should not be *behind* but *beside* (and after all the hand that rocks the cradle, they say, rules the world!)."[94] Here Tutu affirms women's contribution as mothers (rocking the cradle) to point out that women can contribute to the broader struggle through their roles in the family. The discursive shift from "behind" to "beside" is a hint in the direction of affirming women's equality with men, but it is not an explicit call for women's emancipation because of their own oppression. Instead, Tutu also relies on gender essentialist beliefs about women's different status and role from men's due to their mothering. Gender inequality is untroubled here.

Thus, the SACC's discourse about women in the family demonstrates some important tensions in the ways their theological culture shapes their attention to gender. Authors perceive that women have a particular role to play within their families, and they draw on key aspects of their theological convictions to depict some of the social constraints and marginality that women experience. But this application of the liberation theological culture does not translate into a full recognition of the gendered structures that can constrain women's participation in both family and public life. Indeed, sometimes gender essentialist beliefs are cultivated as women are called upon to enact broader social change without an accompanying challenge to the gendered injustices that might prevent them from being able to do so. But, as the next section illuminates, this ambivalence about gender justice is also accompanied by increasingly pointed critiques by women within the SACC of the church's failure to address sexism.

Application of the Liberation Theological Culture: Patriarchy and the Church

One of the most interesting and important features of the SACC's discourse about gender is that it is clear that the pursuit of gender justice was contested within the organization. Sometimes women within the organization clearly speak from a position of marginalization. In the 1980s, especially, they make increasingly pointed critiques of the church's role in fostering patriarchal and sexist attitudes. They assert that the church's own complicity in sexism runs counter to the church's claims that it is working for justice and liberation.

For instance, the 1982 Women's Dialogue that I discussed above names the ways that the broader quest for liberation must affirm gender equality, too, if it is to truly be of God. Calling the church to account for the ways that it is failing to honor the dignity of women, the women's report states, "The Church has rightly taken up the challenge of exposing apartheid and has sought and continues to seek ways to re-educate its members into the new humanity that Christ offers. In the light of this, we need to ask ourselves why the church ... is willing to re-educate its people on every issue except on the issue of the dignity and equality of women."[95] They go on to say, "We believe that women have an important contribution to make in helping the church be faithful to the liberation struggle of all people. We also believe that unless the church is willing to proclaim the liberation of women[,] the church['s] proclamation cannot be about divine liberation."[96] This statement shows both creativity and constraint in the application of the liberation theological culture to gender. The women cannot simply affirm their right to be liberated—they have to also affirm their support of the broader liberation movement. But this is also a clear and direct appeal for women's liberation that is grounded in the same theological convictions that are being mobilized to call for the church's engagement against apartheid.

Similarly, a full report from the 1985 National Conference that was supposed to focus on women, as I described above, also draws directly on central aspects of the SACC's theological convictions concerning liberation and oppression to critique a tendency not to consider gender justice as integral to the cause of justice. The report states that this particular conference was noteworthy in three key respects: "the active presence of Revd Dr Beyers Naude as General Secretary," after being banned by the apartheid regime for the past seven years; "the focus on women, blurred though it was by the incorrigibly masculine composition of the delegations and the loss of workshop time during the emergency visit to Duduza"; and the "heightening of tension with the State."[97] It goes on to note that the first and third issues "clearly hold together. Was the middle one [i.e., the focus on women] a distraction or an integral part of the struggle to seek and serve God's righteousness (justice) in a sub-continent racked with conflict and violence?"[98]

To answer this question, the report draws on the SACC's theological convictions about liberation to focus clear attention on women as the marginalized. It notes that "for most of the women present the three elements do belong together. The Bible bears witness to a partisan God, one who is actively involved in history on the side of the oppressed, seeking their liberation and healing. The Church as the people of God is called to share this mission of God and to reflect in its life the kind of priorities of love and justice, freedom and truth, sharing and servanthood expressed in the earthly life of Jesus Christ our Lord."[99] This is a posture toward women that names and problematizes their own, distinct marginalization. It perceives that the church is required to partner with the God of liberation who takes the side of the oppressed. Gender injustice is not subsumed under other categories of marginality here but is seen to matter in its own right.

Indeed, the report goes on to call the church to account for the inconsistency in its treatment of women in relation to its broader work for justice: "If the Church in South Africa is to become more demonstrably a sign and sacrament (instrument) of union with that God and of the divinely willed community of humankind, it cannot with integrity attack the external oppression of apartheid and ignore the glaring internal contradiction presented by its treatment of women as unequal members of the Body of Christ."[100] This statement draws on the SACC's theological convictions about a "partisan God" to contend that women must be treated as equal members of the church community.

This focus on women's marginality within the church, and the accompanying concern with delaying women's liberation, continues throughout the 1980s. For instance, some women in the SACC participated in a consultation in the United States on the theme "Women and Apartheid" in 1986. In a report back to the SACC about the event, Venita Meyer, the SACC liaison, remarked, "The church was also accused by certain womens [sic] group of being oppressively patriarchal. It was pointed out that while the women struggle with their men for liberation, their efforts often go unrecognized."[101] Meyer then contends that, in fact, women's liberation and the national liberation struggle "should be addressed together."[102] If not, she notes, "I fear that when we finally reach our planned goal of a peaceful and just rule in a country free of racism, the woman [sic] will again be fighting another struggle and the Church will have to deal with another problem."[103]

This statement perceives that, rather than simply calling upon women to participate in the struggle against apartheid, the church needed to recognize that women are *already* participating in the struggle. But patriarchal structures and beliefs within the church were preventing that awareness. Meyer calls for attention to sexism within the movement now, before it is too late. This discourse has some resonance with the instrumental understanding of women's liberation described above, with its focus on the importance of women being liberated to contribute to the broader justice movement. But here, Meyer also critiques women's own, distinct experience of marginalization and a lack of attention to women's contributions to the broader movement for social change because of patriarchy within the church. A stronger sense of gender justice emerges here.

The urgency of addressing women's oppression at the same time as apartheid's other forms of inequality was sometimes also intertwined with a call to the church to empower women rather than reinforce their lower social position. For instance, a 1987 document by the new director of Women's Ministries, Lulama Xingwana, outlines the purposes of their program for women and includes the following statement: "The patriarchal, capitalist and apartheid systems will need to be dismantled before women's liberation is finally achieved. It is part and parcel of the national liberatory struggle."[104] Xingwana goes on to state that this is as much a church problem as a broader system problem, arguing that "the Church should no longer equate servanthood with servitude and 'keep women in their place' but rather enabling [sic] others to become what God means them to be."[105] Here, the church is critiqued for its complicity in promoting religious beliefs that subordinate women, and women's own liberation is seen as a constitutive component of the anti-apartheid struggle. Women are not treated as a means to the end of ushering in broader social change. Instead, in naming women's oppression as a theological problem as much as a systemic one, this statement incorporates a critique of patriarchy alongside other oppressive systems, suggesting that religiously sanctioned gendered beliefs that support women's subordination are not in keeping with God's plan for women.

This theological analysis of gender and critique of the church's complicity resonates across time. Much of the discourse about gender inequality during the apartheid years emerges from and focuses on the experiences of women within the SACC who advocated for attention to gender alongside the struggle against apartheid. But, especially in the new democracy, sometimes men who lead the organization also acknowledge the complicity of the church in failing to promote gender equity and call specifically upon men to address their role in gender injustice. In 1996, for instance, the issue of women's empowerment comes to the fore in the SACC president's address to the Central Committee. The president, Bishop Sigqibo Dwane, first draws on the SACC's central theological conviction of shared human dignity to situate his attention to gender, stating, "I think we owe it to one another as members one of another in the body of Christ, to affirm in one another the common humanity we share as brothers and sisters. I state this theological principle first in order to remind us that this is not an optional extra, but an imperative of the faith which we profess."[106] Seen here to be an essential theological principle, one that is not ancillary but is central to Christian faith, Dwane applies the SACC's central theological convictions to the common humanity of men and women.

The president then also draws an explicit parallel between the ways in which gender oppression and racial oppression operate. Referencing patterns of oppression under apartheid, he calls on his fellow men to stand in solidarity with women now in their quest for justice:

> We, men in the church, have a way of abdicating our responsibility to stand by women and support them in their struggle for equity instead of tokenism. We stand back and watch as if to say it is *their* struggle, *they* must get on with it. And we adopt this position as if *we* are neutral, and the women's struggle has nothing to do with our entrenched position of privilege. But then if we have learnt anything of value from our struggle for liberation, it must surely be that it takes two to make a dance: the oppressor and oppressed. We have to be prepared to relinquish privilege in order that women may regain their dignity, self esteem and rightful place in society.[107]

Here, Dwane calls for attention to gender by drawing on the SACC's long-standing commitment to call on oppressors to relinquish their power and reclaim their own broken humanity. Gendered social problems have to do with unequal power relations, and the way forward is to address these fundamental imbalances of justice, as had been advocated against apartheid. Dwane draws on the liberation theological culture to claim that women's position is a form of oppression that requires men's active and robust contributions, not tokenizing. Men are to let go of privilege and advocate for women's equality to be fully enacted in the democracy. As the church is critiqued for its complicity in gender oppression, the SACC reaffirms theological principles that center on women's dignity to call on men to abdicate their privilege and their role as oppressor.

Thus, the SACC's liberation theological culture results in ambivalence toward gender justice. Women, and sometimes men, within the organization draw on some of the central theological convictions of the liberation theological culture to argue that women have equal dignity. They call for women's liberation from the cultural traditions that constrain them in order for them to enact broader social change. Yet these calls for women to be liberated in order to enact social change sometimes occur without perceiving and critiquing the ways that gendered power differences constrain women from living out that liberated, change-making capacity. At the same time, women within the organization increasingly voice their concerns with their own marginalization and challenge the church's complicity in sexism. For the SACC, the intersection of their theological convictions with their posture toward women both facilitates and constrains their capacity to cultivate a robust conception of gender justice.

CONCLUSION

Each of the three organizations demonstrates how the cultural production of distinct religious justifications for social engagement shapes patterns of attention and inattention to gender. The possibility of developing a conception of gender justice in these organizations is profoundly shaped by their theological cultures. Indeed, the fragility of the development of a conception of gender justice within each organization is the result of the ways in which their distinct theological convictions intersect with a posture toward women that does not always involve the recognition of the realities of sexism and patriarchy that shape their experiences.

For PACSA, the transformation theological culture is transposed onto gender by incorporating a concern with sexism in their account of death-dealing systems that need to be transformed into life-giving ones. PACSA authors sometimes highlight women's experiences to make broader points about social marginalization, violence, and injustice, and they do so in ways that do not always explicitly problematize gender injustice. At the same time, their theological culture also shapes their attention to the complicity of the church in patriarchy and their call for Christian symbols and practices to be reclaimed by women, for women. This marks a subtle, but important, difference from the SACC. For the SACC, there is more ambivalence in the application of the liberation culture to women's experiences of marginalization. For PACSA, the theological culture expands to incorporate attention to women's experiences, and this sometimes develops into a robust critique of sexism as part of the systems that are in need of transformation. In particular, PACSA's emphasis on multiple systems in need of transformation and their frequent discussion of the Christian narratives of Christmas and Easter shape their incorporation of gender justice into their theological culture.

AE's discourse shows most clearly the power of theological cultures for preventing the development a conception of gender justice. But here, too, there are important patterns of both creativity and constraint. On the one hand, a gender essentialist belief system that relies on an understanding of a gendered order for society clearly limits AE's capacity to recognize and problematize gender injustices. Gender is not recognized as a social category in need of reconciliation and justice. On the other hand, there is also a recognition of the particular social burdens that women navigate, particularly in the context of their family and intimate relationships. But because AE's distinct religious ideas that emphasize a God-ordained way for society also imply an untroubled gender order, this awareness does not translate into a robust theological response to gender injustice.

The SACC shows most clearly the tenuousness of efforts to enact gender justice. The liberation theological culture is transposed onto gender to insist on women's equal dignity with men and call for women to be liberated from the cultural and social barriers that confine them. Interestingly, this results in a primarily instrumental, rather than constitutive, understanding of women's liberation. That is, women are to be liberated in order to enact broader social change, not because their own liberation is essential in the quest for justice. The complexity of the SACC's discourse is important here: While there are times when a theological affirmation of women's equal dignity is clearly stated, there is at least an equal, if not stronger, emphasis on the distinct contributions of women to society. Sometimes this discursive emphasis on women's unique capacities does not involve problematizing the structures that are preventing women's liberation. Rather, women's marginality is folded into other forms of marginalization. This results in ambivalence toward gender justice.

These discursive patterns raise the following questions: How do these theologies impact institutional outcomes? Where and how is attention to gender housed organizationally, and what are the consequences of these theologies for practical responses to GBV? In chapter 5, I argue that the patterns we see in this chapter of theological attention and inattention to patriarchy as a system of injustice shape the organizations' varying practical responses to GBV. Where chapter 3 showed how different discursive attention to GBV develops, this chapter points us to consider how the organizations' theological convictions intersect with their posture toward women as a social group more generally. Chapter 5 will show how these patterns of attention to gender shape the organizations' practical responses to GBV.

5 · IMPLICATIONS FOR ACTIONS

> Violence against women raises profound question[s] for Christians. It is about power and control, dignity and personhood, freedom and life, and ultimately mutually respectful and lifegiving relationship for the community. In South Africa, the experience of oppression and political liberation offers unique opportunity for penetrating insight into issues of oppression of women, violence against women, authentic justice, and new visions.
> —Karen Buckenham

In November 1990, South African church leaders from different racial backgrounds and denominations convened in the city of Rustenburg to consider the church's role in a changing sociopolitical environment. As I discussed in chapter 2, this gathering and the resultant Rustenburg Declaration contained significant expressions of confession and complicity in the racism of apartheid. But there was also an important story about gender at the conference—a story that has implications for how we understand the fragility of religious organizations' efforts to enact gender justice.

Sheena Duncan, who led the women's protest organization The Black Sash in the late 1970s and 1980s and served as vice president of the SACC from 1987 to 1990, has described what happened in detail. She recounts how "at a very late stage in the planning of the conference someone realized that women had been excluded from the agenda altogether and it was hastily decided to cobble together a 'women's hour' at 5:30 one afternoon far on in the conference process. Two women were invited to speak and one of the few female representatives was asked to chair the session."[1] Duncan continues, "When we took our places on the platform at the appointed time, a delegate took up the floor microphone and addressed the assembling crowd to the effect that this session was a waste of the time of the conference and not a priority at a gathering such as this one. It was apparent that most of the representatives agreed with him, so we walked out accompanied by most of the women present in the hall."[2] The women's departure was followed by one male delegate chastising the men in the room, and another going into the hallway to implore the women to return, which they did. Duncan describes both the women's decision to participate in the conference at all, given the last-minute addition of programmatic attention to them, and their decision to return to the room after they had walked out as a "mistake."[3]

In the end, the Rustenburg Declaration included not only various expressions of guilt and confession for complicity in the racism of apartheid, as I discussed in chapter 2, but also an acknowledgment by men that they "have often disregarded the human dignity of women and ignored the sexism of many of our church, social, political, economic and family structures. By limiting the role and ministry of women—as was reflected at this Conference—we have impoverished the church."[4] But Duncan notes that "the problem for the women who were there is that there is a question mark as to whether those who adopted the Declaration really understand the difference between confession and repentance."[5] In other words, expressions of remorse are not the same thing as concrete actions to address harm.

In her reflection on what the church can and ought to do with respect to gender justice, Duncan writes, "We who care about the church, women and men, need to cling to our vision of what can be."[6] She then draws on the description of the early church in the biblical text of Acts 2 to cast such a vision, stating, "We must never lose sight of what we believe the church can become—a communion of believers continuing together in close companionship, praising God and enjoying the goodwill of all the people, preserving our sense of awe, and holding all things in common, so that we can distribute to each according to her/his need."[7] Duncan perceives that a theological vision must orient the work of the church in order to implement gender justice.[8]

Duncan's account and interpretation of these events illuminates the tensions and themes taken up in this chapter, as I analyze the ways that theological cultures shape practical responses to GBV as an issue of gender justice. As I discussed in the introduction, the sociological literature on social movements and social change documents a pattern that has existed in multiple empirical contexts across time: tensions sometimes emerge over the inclusion of gender concerns within movements for racial, economic, and political justice.[9] And as I have argued throughout the book, religious organizations play a particularly interesting role in this process because they are key sites for the cultural production of belief systems that can be marshaled to challenge structures that are being targeted for change.[10] Yet these same religious institutions are also part of the environment they seek to change, often mirroring and sometimes exacerbating social inequalities.[11] Consequently, theological convictions can be mobilized in uneven ways to respond to different social issues.

This chapter draws on these insights to examine the ways that the theological cultures of PACSA, AE, and the SACC shape their practical attention to GBV. As I have argued in previous chapters, my central contention is that theologies have consequences for organizations' capacities to respond to social injustice and violence. We need to understand how the substance of theological belief systems shapes identities and actions. At the same time, these theologies do not emerge in an institutional vacuum. How they are articulated and enacted is profoundly shaped by organizational postures toward and identification with various social groups. This is a dynamic process. The theological cultures follow a distinct path that connects across social issues and across time, but it does so in ways that reflect a range of tensions and contingencies.

Duncan's account of the questioning about the inclusion of women's concerns at Rustenburg demonstrates that the convictions that facilitate the recognition of and practical response to some social issues do not necessarily translate to others—at least, not without contestation and resistance. This chapter draws on her insights about the power of theological imaginations for gender justice to ask two questions: What are the practical consequences of varying attention to gender justice within organizations that have recognized and fought to address other dimensions of social injustice? And how do theological convictions intersect with organizations' social positioning to shape their actions to address GBV?

On one level, this chapter simply documents the practical efforts of PACSA, AE, and the SACC to address GBV, providing an account of how their theological convictions intersect with their posture toward women to shape their actions. On another level, the chapter invites us to reflect more deeply on the causes and consequences of commitments to justice, and how those commitments become institutionally embedded in ways that can both facilitate and constrain organizations' actions. I do not believe we can fully understand these organizations' varying attempts to respond to GBV without considering broader questions about the fragility of institutional efforts to pursue full justice. In what follows, I take each organization in turn, demonstrating that PACSA develops a robust response, AE no practical response, and the SACC a partial response to GBV. Throughout, I analyze the ways in which these outcomes are shaped by the organizations' theological cultures. I conclude by offering some reflections on the implications of these patterns for our understanding of the fragility of religious institutions' attention to GBV.

PIETERMARITZBURG AGENCY FOR CHRISTIAN SOCIAL AWARENESS: A ROBUST PRACTICAL RESPONSE

Of the three organizations, PACSA's programmatic response to GBV was the strongest. As I documented in chapter 3, they drew on central features of the transformation theological culture to develop a clear and direct critique of GBV. In particular, PACSA perceived GBV to be rooted in the system of sexism that was dealing death to women. They incorporated concerns about sexism and gender injustice within the transformation theological culture, as I discussed in chapter 4. The intersection of their theological convictions with a posture of empathy toward and solidarity with women and calling on men to forego their complicity in the problem enabled PACSA to channel their discursive concern with GBV into practical action.

While they were aware of the problem before the transition to democracy, PACSA's efforts to address it did not begin until the mid-1990s, as attention to the problem became more widespread. Beginning in 1995, PACSA's actions to address GBV ranged from dissemination of information through factsheets and other publications to workshops with local area churches and schools. They published three factsheets specifically on GBV, focusing on rape; domestic violence; and gender, violence, and HIV/AIDS.[12] Workshops covered various aspects of GBV and occurred in a range of contexts, including church groups, schools, and NGOs.[13]

A major output of PACSA's work on GBV was a manual that Karen Buckenham developed, entitled *Violence against Women: A Resource Manual for the Church in South Africa*, which aimed to equip churches with a range of resources for addressing GBV.[14] The manual includes demographic information and discussions about various forms of GBV, numerous theologically grounded analyses of the problem, and practical resources, such as templates for liturgies and workshops. PACSA also regularly participated in the international 16 Days of Activism campaign to end violence against women, which occurs every year from November 25 (International Day of No Violence Against Women) to December 10 (International Human Rights Day).[15] PACSA's staff developed promotional pamphlets and flyers for churches to distribute in support of the campaign, and they helped develop a liturgy that named the realities of such violence and included expressions of repentance for failing to attend to the problem.[16]

Over time, PACSA's work on GBV expanded from its primary focus on the church's responsibility to attend to women's experiences of violence. First, they incorporated more attention to men's role in both contributing to and ameliorating the problem. From early on in their work on GBV, their staff recognized that only focusing on women would not solve the problem.[17] In 2001, therefore, they launched a pilot research project to get a sense of other organizations' efforts to address men's role in GBV, and they conducted some focus groups with local men to gauge what kinds of programs might be most helpful for PACSA to develop.[18] A range of initiatives emerged from this initial step, including the incorporation of specific content for men in their workshops, as well as attempts to collaborate with other NGOs in the area.[19]

A second expansion of PACSA's work related to the intersection of gender, violence, and HIV/AIDS. As rates of HIV/AIDS skyrocketed, PACSA staff devoted significant attention to the issue, including its intersections with GBV and poverty. The third director of the Gender program, Daniela Gennrich, came to PACSA in February 2003 from an organization that supported people with HIV/AIDS.[20] Under her leadership, PACSA expanded their attention to the intersections of GBV and HIV/AIDS. This included incorporating more content on HIV/AIDS in their workshops; reprinting the factsheet on gender, violence, and HIV/AIDS; and publishing a workbook designed to be used in churches, which examined these intersections in depth.[21]

Thus, through a range of programs, PACSA developed a robust practical response to GBV. My argument is that the clear and direct application of their transformation theological culture to GBV facilitated their development of multiple programmatic efforts to address the problem. Indeed, PACSA's theological culture is clearly evidenced in their programmatic efforts. For instance, the resource manual that Buckenham developed contains numerous affirmations of the Gospel's relevance for suffering women, including "the calling of the gospel to justice-making as a community" and "the call of the gospel to a survivor for healing."[22] Developing both ideas further, she affirms that the Christian community is called "to be in solidarity with those struggling for justice in relationship and society" and to "applaud and support the life of someone who is throwing off the chains of fear and shame, and who is drinking the healing water of love, justice, self-acceptance and honoring of the image of God inside."[23] PACSA's theological convictions around God's transforming power intersect with a posture of solidarity with suffering women in their efforts to address GBV.[24]

This was not an inevitable outcome, however; it was contingent upon women within the organization mobilizing to bring greater attention to gender justice. Through a broader organizational development process that PACSA undertook in 1992, women within the organization came to recognize "that issues of sexism/ gender [had] of late been neglected at PACSA," and they took steps to address this gap.[25] Karen Buckenham began working at PACSA in 1993, leading their Human Rights program, and she described witnessing a troubling contrast between the attention being given to public, political violence and the private, domestic violence that she was encountering through her work.[26] These threads of growing organizational concern with inadequate attention to gender itself, and an awareness of the specific crisis of GBV, intertwined in PACSA's work.

PACSA also developed programs to address gender issues more generally. Documents explaining the background and purpose of PACSA's resultant Gender program state that it emerged from their concern with GBV, in the context of their human rights work.[27] In addition to their work on GBV, they performed a gender audit of the curriculums at local universities and seminaries, and addressed the intersections of poverty, gender, and HIV/AIDS, especially with young people.[28] They produced a periodical entitled *Women in God's Image*, which contained narratives of women's experiences, with topics ranging from leadership in churches to abuse to caring for elderly parents to prayers directed to God.[29] As part of their efforts to address gender more broadly, PACSA ran workshops, developed and disseminated factsheets, and continued to network with other local NGOs. Throughout these materials, the staff articulated a clear critique of sexism as the root cause of gender inequality that needed to be transformed and called on the church to pursue gender justice.[30]

PACSA's efforts were not always uncomplicated or straightforward. Both their internal and public-facing documents demonstrate the fragility of these efforts due to funding and staffing constraints, and they frequently describe the challenges of adapting to an ever-changing social, political, and economic landscape.[31] Discussions of PACSA's community engagement efforts also highlight the challenges they encountered. Practically, although these efforts were led by their Black woman fieldworker, Lihle Dlamini, it was difficult to gain access to the Black African church women's groups, or *manyanos*. Ideologically, PACSA encountered difficult terrain with the conservative gender theology within the groups.[32] The attempt to connect with the *manyanos* was eventually abandoned.[33]

But even though their work was characterized by a tenuous fragility, it is undeniable that, of the three organizations, PACSA's response to GBV was the most robust and comprehensive. I argue that this is due to the ways that their theological convictions about God's transforming power intersect with a posture of solidarity with suffering women. The transformation theological culture incorporates sexism, facilitating a strong practical response to GBV.

AFRICAN ENTERPRISE: NO PRACTICAL RESPONSE

AE is on the other end of the spectrum of practical response. I found no evidence of this organization devoting any practical attention to GBV. As I analyzed in chapter 3, the problem does emerge as a matter of discussion among young people in the context of an existing ministry (the Foxfires program) and in the context of a gathering of Christian leaders that AE convened to discuss the church's role in the face of numerous social challenges around the transition and early years of the democracy. But this awareness of the problem does not result in any specific programs to address it. What explains AE's lack of practical attention to GBV?

On the surface, and as at least one person at the organization suggested to me when I was there, it is plausible that AE perceived that other organizations were better equipped to tackle the problem, and that doing so would also be a departure from their own primary focus on evangelism. There is some validity to this explanation, but the archival evidence shows that there is more to the story. When we look at the kinds of programs that AE did develop to address social issues over time, it is clear that there was a capacity within the organization to pick up new issues that were not obviously connected to their primary mission of evangelism. And there were some programs specifically for women—but they emerged in ways that reflected and reified AE's commitment to the gender essentialist belief system I described in chapter 4. AE's theological convictions about God's intended order for society intersect with a posture toward women that sees their need for healing without problematizing sexism to shape their lack of practical response to GBV.

This pattern becomes clear as we consider the kinds of programs AE did develop to respond to social issues. For instance, AE's commitment to racial reconciliation had practical expression in their Bridge Building Encounters. As I described in chapter 1, this program brought people together across racial differences and facilitated them building relationships with one another. In fact, Bridge Building Encounters grew out of a perceived need to expand AE's work beyond simply preaching the Gospel at missions and to find ways to incorporate the social dimensions of the Gospel.[34] Similarly, the development of the Bonginkosi feeding program in schools emerged from the initiative of two women, one black and one white. They were brought into AE's work as a board member and a team member, respectively, and the program was expanded with the practical support that AE provided through both networking and resources.[35] And, as I discussed in chapter 2, the organization developed a program in Social Empowerment and Development, and an African Leadership Development Institute in the democracy. Both programs aimed to equip people with tangible skills and resources to invest in themselves and their communities.[36]

So, part of AE's story does have to do with decision-making around how to focus on the primary issues of concern to them. But it is also clear from the historical record that, however imperfectly, AE has consistently sought to integrate spiritual and social concerns, and that they have developed specific programs to address new social problems and issues as they emerge.[37] What, then, explains why GBV does not receive the same kind of attention?

My argument is that AE's reconciliation theological culture plays a powerful role in their lack of practical response to GBV. In particular, as I showed in chapter 4, a key feature of their theological convictions is not only that there is an intended order for society that God has ordained, but that this is a gendered order. This theological conviction intersects with the organization's social positioning regarding gender relations. AE's posture toward women is one that recognizes the brokenness women experience as evidence of the need for the Gospel, but they do not perceive a need for social reconciliation among men and women. Where the theological cultures of the other two organizations—however tenuously—did facilitate a conception of gender justice, AE's did not. This lack of a theological imagination for gender inequality had practical consequences for the organization's lack of programmatic attention to GBV.

Two illustrations from the early 2000s will help to illuminate this pattern. One is a newsletter story about a lunch that Carol Cassidy, founder Michael Cassidy's wife, hosted for other wives of AE team members. The newsletter acknowledges a gender imbalance in their work: "While the mostly male AE evangelists are on ministry, both in their own areas as well as throughout Africa, back home it is their womenfolk who are creating the firm foundation for their families."[38] In that context, Carol Cassidy recognizes the need for the wives to connect with each other. She said that "as an AE wife herself, she prayed for all, asking for strength, courage and steadfastness in the faith. She warned that the family will often come under spiritual attack while the men are away, but that the wives should be strong, sharing each other's load and praying for each other at these times."[39] Affirming women's place in the home while their husbands are out doing the work of evangelism, this account stresses the importance of women connecting with other women in order to navigate the spiritual challenges that will come their way.

The newsletter description of this event ends by suggesting that a women's group be formed, based in the acknowledgment of their shared need for domestic support and prayer. In particular, "Ann Hewetson, wife of Canon David Hewetson, chairperson of AE's Support Board in Australia, said that although their environments and daily needs were different, all the women in the group had the same basic need for support within their home, as well as for prayers. They should continue to share and support each other more regularly in the future."[40] While the historical record is unclear about whether such a program was started, it is important to note that this discussion recognizes the reality of the burdens the AE wives experience—but in a way that does not trouble the gendered structure that is relied upon in the work. Unlike in the SACC, in particular, where there is evidence of women within or connected to the organization raising concerns about the assumption that they would primarily play a supportive role to men, here the division of labor is clear and uncontested.

Another program started specifically for women similarly reflects and reinforces AE's theologically buttressed gender essentialist posture toward women, who are to play supportive roles for others. The June 2004 newsletter's opening story is titled "The Vital Role That Women Play in Society." It recounts how "women have consistently played key roles in God's strategies. The Lord has used many women in ministry throughout the ages."[41] But rather than cite biblical examples such as the judge Deborah who led the people of God when a man refused to do so, the story lists biblical women who support others' ministry.[42] This includes how "God sent Elijah to a widow woman in the midst of a terrible famine. Elijah asked her for the last bit of flour that she had, and she gave it to him as he had requested her."[43] Several New Testament examples also appear: "A group of women used their personal resources to support Jesus in ministry," "Mary the mother of Mark fearlessly hosted a large prayer meeting while Herod was shedding Apostolic blood all over town," and "Lydia made her house available to the entire Church at a time of violent opposition."[44] Women's sacrifices for the sake of the broader needs of the community are emphasized here—not women's capacity to lead as they serve the people of God.

Flowing from this particular interpretation of the role of women in the Bible, the newsletter invites its women readers to join a group of women called "Enterprising Women," "who provide special support for the AE Foxfire Youth Teams."[45] These women will not only pray for these AE youth evangelists, they will also do some "practical things like sending that person a 'care parcel' from time to time or a telephone call or letter to encourage them.... These young people are out in ministry and are in the forefront of the battle."[46] This program is the logical consequence of a theological culture that intertwines a theological commitment to gender essentialism with a posture toward women that sees their primary role to be a supportive one.

In addition, as AE's theological culture in the democracy more generally developed a strong concern with a decline in moral values, their leadership also adopted a conservative approach to gender and sexuality issues. For instance, as I noted in chapter 4, while there was the possibility of programmatic attention to sexism at the second SACLA conference in the early 2000s, this did not develop into a concern with gender justice. Instead, AE tended to direct their attention toward a reclamation of traditional values with respect to gender and sexuality. As I mentioned in chapter 2, in 2004 Cassidy led an initiative called the Marriage Alliance of South Africa, which sought to challenge constitutional support for same-sex marriage.[47] And he also participated in and expressed support of both the Promise Keepers movement in the United States in the 1990s and the Mighty Men movement in South Africa in the 2000s, men's movements that reassert a traditionalist masculinity as they advocate for racial reconciliation.[48] While AE's public affirmations of Cassidy's participation in such movements is not the same thing as a specific program run by AE, it does signal an uncontested and untroubled commitment to a gendered order for society that has been an implicit feature of the organization's identity throughout its history. These actions are rooted in AE's theological convictions, which center on their interpretation of God's design for society. In the democracy especially, this theological conviction is mobilized around the organization's increasing concern over decline in the realm of personal morality, specifically with regard to sexuality.

There are organizational features that also matter. For instance, AE's leadership has remained almost exclusively male. The board has had female members, and at least one woman, Esme Bowers, has served as its chairperson.[49] But there has never been a woman "Team Leader," as the head of the organization is called, and women have been significantly under-represented in their top leadership positions. Again, this is a contrast to the other two organizations. Women have served in key leadership positions in PACSA's organizational structure from the beginning, and two women have served as the director of the organization after leading their Gender program. And while women within the SACC clearly had to struggle for their inclusion within the organization, it is also the case that women have served in executive positions, including as vice presidents and general secretaries.

An interesting puzzle also emerged as I was analyzing the public discourse of AE and PACSA. Several of PACSA's annual reports actually mention holding events related to GBV at AE, at least one of which was under the auspices of AE's Social Empowerment and Development program.[50] But I found no mention of these events in AE's public discourse. On one level, this exclusion of the events in AE's documents can serve as a caution against inferring too much from the organization's public discourse. Perhaps there were activities and events that occurred at the organization that did not, then, make it into the final cut of a newsletter with its limited space to report on the various actions of the organization.

But on another level, this lack of inclusion about events related to GBV in AE's public discourse implies that these events were not deemed noteworthy enough to include in the reporting of activities at the organization. As I argued in chapter 4, it was entirely possible for AE to develop a stronger consciousness around gender, given the fact that they clearly perceived women as a group who faced particular challenges. Here, we see evidence that there was also the potential for the organization to couple their discursive attention to GBV with practical attention to it. AE could have partnered with PACSA more fully to address GBV and acknowledged that partnership publicly. But the fact that these events are not acknowledged in their public discourse shows that their flickering awareness of the issue did not translate into robust attention and action.[51]

As with the other two organizations, then, it is clear that AE's internal structure and their practical commitments significantly influence their ability to develop programmatic attention to GBV, whether or not women and their interests are represented in the organization's leadership. These are important structural factors that help explain AE's proclivity not to perceive gender oppression and justice as contributing to GBV, but rather to see GBV as an issue that shows the need for spiritual reconciliation and healing, as I described in chapter 3. But these factors provide only a partial explanation for AE's lack of programmatic attention to GBV. Beyond this, we see a similar pattern with AE to what sociologist Paul Lichterman describes in his analysis of religious organizations' attempts to enact social change: if an issue is not discursively on the table, action does not happen.[52] While GBV itself receives plenty of discursive attention, AE's reconciliation theological culture also contains assumptions of inherent gender difference that have not been contested. Therefore, AE does not perceive GBV in terms of its connection to gender oppression. This lack of a conception of gender justice explains why AE perceives GBV as an issue that could be changed as a result of the work they are already doing as they preach the Gospel, but not as an issue that requires its own programmatic action.

SOUTH AFRICAN COUNCIL OF CHURCHES: A PARTIAL PRACTICAL RESPONSE

The SACC's recognition of GBV in the early 1990s resulted in some programmatic action, especially through their provincial offices and under the auspices of their broader work on human rights and development. But these efforts were not located in a distinct gender program, nor were they grounded in a robust theological account of the church's need to engage in solidarity with suffering women. The SACC also did not develop the same degree of programmatic response as PACSA. I argue that this partial practical response is rooted in the ways that the liberation theological culture results in ambivalence around gender justice, as I described in chapter 4.

Most of the SACC's practical attention to GBV in the 1990s and early 2000s occurred through their provincial offices. This included marches and protests, as well as educational workshops and conferences. The accounts of these events often include discussion of their connection to human rights, stressing the importance of informing women about their rights so they could advocate for themselves.

This is shaped by the way the SACC's theological culture follows a particular path from their opposition to the apartheid regime to their critical solidarity with the state, as I described in chapter 2.

A Women's Service in 1997, for instance, included a presentation from someone from the South African Human Rights Commission who talked about violence against women as a violation of human rights, stressing "the need to promote a culture of human rights as well as arming women with information so they could concretize the imperatives in the Bill of Rights."[53] This same Annual Report that describes the service also notes that a number of "educational workshops focusing on women, children and the Bill of Rights were held in almost all of the provinces" and that "violence against women and children" was one of the major issues discussed.[54]

The SACC's approach to GBV also tended to focus on networking and partnering with existing programs, rather than coming up with their own unique programmatic efforts. Descriptions of these workshops and events noted that part of the aim was to empower women to seek help from existing organizations that could provide them with practical support.[55] Sometimes they mobilized to lobby the government to act. For instance, the 1996 Women's Ecumenical Conference names GBV as a violation of human rights, under a discussion of crime and violence more generally, and commits to "send[ing] a memorandum to the Minister of Justice concerning violence against women."[56]

Activities varied by province. Some provinces do not report any programs related to GBV. But the Gauteng provincial office, for instance, received government funding to start a "one stop center for abused women and children in Soweto."[57] Sometimes seminars and other programs were directed at both women and men, though I did not find evidence of significant programs for men, compared to PACSA's. But there is a recognition within the programmatic work that including discussions with men is important.[58]

In short, the SACC develops some practical attention to GBV, but it is not as robust as PACSA's. What explains this pattern? In chapter 4, I demonstrated that the liberation theological culture facilitates the recognition of women as a group in need of liberation, but there was also organizational ambivalence around the cultivation of gender justice. My argument is that this tension had practical implications for the SACC's response to GBV. In fact, the historical record shows a particular pattern of faltering inclusion of women's concerns within the organization's work. This pattern is inextricably linked to the ways that the theological convictions that consistently motivate the organization's actions intersect with a posture of ambivalence toward women's distinct experiences of marginalization. This concretizing of tensions around gender justice explains why the SACC develops a partial response to GBV.

This pattern is clearly seen in the history of the SACC's programmatic attention to gender. The first mention that I found of a possible program to address women's issues and concerns was in meeting minutes of the Justice and Reconciliation Division in 1973. The two women members of this division, Shirley Turner and

Sally Motlana, were tasked with envisioning and working to possibly establish a new Women's Work program, which would incorporate and expand an existing program for domestic workers.[59] By 1976, a Women's Division had been created, headed by Deborah Mabiletsa.[60] Their programs focused especially on the status of black women as domestic workers and on the legal status of black women. For reasons that are unclear from the historical record, this division was suspended in 1981, and attention to women's issues was incorporated into the Home and Family Life Division.[61]

Meanwhile, women both within and outside of the organization mobilized to garner greater attention to gender issues. As discussed in chapter 4, the 1982 National Conference resolved to focus on women in the 1985 National Conference, which led to the theme "Women, a Power for Change." In the early 1980s, the SACC sponsored a gathering of women that resulted in the formation of a Christian Women's Movement.[62] This group insisted on the importance of churches sending women delegates to the SACC's National Conference and noted with concern when this intention was not actualized. The 1985 National Conference passed a resolution that stipulated that, in future, delegates to the National Conference should be 50/50 male and female. When the 1986 National Conference failed to actualize this resolution, a group of women who had gathered ahead of the event "decided that some of the women must remain and attend the National Conference as a sign of protest."[63]

In a sign of the effectiveness of these efforts to mobilize greater attention to gender, which manifested in the increasingly sharp critique of sexism and patriarchy that I analyzed in chapter 4, the Women's Ministries program was formally established as its own unit again in 1987, headed by Lulama Xingwana. But, during the transition and immediately following the democratic elections, the SACC's organizational structure underwent a significant change, as discussed in chapter 2. This included a massive decline in funding from overseas, the movement of their personnel into the government (including not only General Secretary Frank Chikane, but also Xingwana), and a restructuring of the organization to focus on the provincial offices.

The Women's Ministries program, specifically, "ceased to exist as an autonomous department" in 1990, and was instead "attached to the Development Ministries" program.[64] Through the transition and early years of the democracy, programmatic attention to gender, including GBV, was sometimes housed in the SACC's work on human rights and development work, and sometimes housed in the General Secretariat.[65] In the midst of significant organizational change, the tendency to portray GBV as a problem rooted in economic and other systems, rather than in sexism and patriarchy, which I demonstrated in chapter 3, was concretized organizationally. That is, the SACC tended to locate their work on gender under the umbrella of economic justice issues.

The lack of strong programmatic attention to GBV is surely shaped by the broader contextual factors the SACC was navigating as levels of GBV were reaching crisis levels. At the same time that PACSA was developing its gender consciousness through its work on GBV and finding ways to gain external funding to support those programs, the SACC was clearly struggling for its survival as an organization.

But this is not the only thing that explains the SACC's faltering response to GBV. Throughout the archival materials, there is also evidence that the women within and related to the organization raised concerns with the leadership that their requests for greater attention to women's issues and gender justice were not being heeded. For instance, a memo from the Christian Women's Movement after the 1985 National Conference not only expressed "disappointment that the SACC has not published the report that has been compiled and edited by Dr Margaret Nash of the 1985 National Conference," but also noted their "regret that the SACC and its member Churches have once again dealt with initiatives from women as though they are of no importance."[66] And in 1989, Xingwana sent a memo to General Secretary Chikane, asking him to explain his apparent remarks that "the setting up of this department [i.e., the Women's Ministries program] was an error and by implication therefore not necessary," and notes with concern that he had "decided to postpone the Church Leader's [sic] Consultation for which the women had so well prepared. They felt that this was once again another blow to an issue of great importance to them."[67]

These internal tensions over the cultivation of gender justice mattered for the SACC's subsequent response to GBV. And the organization's liberation theological culture played a crucial role in this process. In particular, the question of whether women's liberation was of equal importance in the struggle for justice was a live and contested one. Were women, too, part of the suffering population with whom the church was to enter into solidarity? The answer to this question was unclear. The SACC's theological convictions about a liberating God intersect with a posture of ambivalence toward women as a distinct marginalized group. These patterns of tension around gender justice, in turn, had consequences for their fragile attempts practically to address GBV.

CONCLUSION

What do these patterns of varying practical attention to GBV show us about the power of theological cultures for religious organizations' social engagement around gender justice? As Sheena Duncan observed, recognizing a challenge or problem is not enough to confront it with concrete actions. I show in this chapter that theological convictions intersect with postures toward suffering women to shape particular actions. PACSA's strong response, AE's lack of response, and the SACC's partial response to GBV are the result of the varying ways that their theological cultures incorporate a concern with gender justice.

On first glance, it may seem as though the SACC's partial response to GBV is due primarily to structural conditions that constrained the organization's work in the early democracy overall, especially their struggle for funding and the movement of key leaders into the government. There is certainly some truth to this. But when we compare the SACC's response to PACSA's, it becomes clear that the theological culture of the organization plays a central role. PACSA, too, had to navigate structural constraints, including leadership disruptions, appeal for resources, and the tumult of the sociopolitical situation. There are some variations in organizational structure that likely make a difference, including the SACC's high national and international profile in the liberation movement compared to PACSA's local embedding, and the SACC's shift to working primarily through their provincial offices.

But I contend that, while these other factors do matter for the organizations' actions, they are not the primary explanation for these different programmatic outcomes. Rather, their different theological cultures are the primary driver of their actions. Both the SACC's faltering attempts to carve out a distinct programmatic space for gender justice and PACSA's more robust development of a Gender Desk in the democracy are concrete expressions of the ways the organizations' theological commitments intersect with their posture toward women.

For the SACC, the tensions in their liberation theological culture between women's liberation for its own sake versus their participation in the broader struggle have practical implications for their ability to concretize efforts to address gendered issues and concerns. As I showed in chapter 3, the key tenet in the SACC's theological culture of the importance of Christians entering into suffering solidarity with the marginalized does not appear in their discourse about GBV. This lack of theological framing of the issue as one that requires identification with the marginalized stunts their capacity to develop a robust programmatic response to the problem. Instead, attention to GBV is housed in human rights and development programs, and the SACC struggles to develop and maintain programming to address gender in its own right.

PACSA's transformation theological culture proves to be more conducive to incorporating sexism and patriarchy, in ways that facilitate their ability to develop a robust response to GBV. The theological narrative of death being transformed into life, and their call to Christians to enter into suffering solidarity with the marginalized is transposed onto GBV. These convictions are remarkably consistent over time for PACSA. Their transformation theological culture forges a path that facilitates their capacity to develop a strong social analysis of gender. In turn, the organization establishes a powerful programmatic response to GBV. For PACSA, the initial attention to GBV as a violation of human rights results in the development of extensive programming around gender justice.

We can also see the significance of theological cultures for shaping organizations' actions when we consider AE's lack of programmatic response to GBV. Part of the difference between AE and the other two organizations does have to do with the structure of their leadership. In contrast to both the SACC and PACSA, the leadership of AE has been male-dominated. By contrast, women served in significant leadership positions in both of the other organizations. Of course, having women in leadership positions does not automatically lead to greater attention to gender issues. But the lack of gender representation among AE's leadership does seem to have constrained their ability to take action on GBV, especially in contrast to both the SACC and PACSA.

At the same time, these organizational characteristics and positionings cannot be divorced from the theological convictions that ground the organizations' mission and actions. AE's reconciliation theological culture centers on the conviction that God ordains a particular order for society. God's intention for society was violated by apartheid, and the pathway to overcome the division and hostility that such a violation of God's order entailed was both spiritual and social reconciliation. But, as I analyzed in chapter 4, this theological culture does not translate to gender. Instead, it follows a path that is shaped by an untroubled presumption of inherent sex difference and gender roles. These gender essentialist beliefs are rooted in the theological culture's emphasis on God's ordained structure for society, and, in contrast to the SACC especially, I found no evidence of internal challenges to or contestation over the role of women in AE. This uncontested reliance on gender essentialist beliefs is organizationally concretized. AE is therefore stunted in its capacity to respond practically to GBV.

The organizations' theological cultures are the primary driver of their discourse and actions around GBV. The particular theological convictions that each organization cultivates intersect with their varying postures toward women in ways that have a profound impact on their actions. The organizations' different pathways of incorporating gender justice in their theological cultures explain their varying practical responses to GBV.

CONCLUSION

> Reconciliation without lament cheapens hope. We must refuse the consolations of cheap hope.
>
> —Emmanuel Katongole and Chris Rice

In 1989, Ghanaian theologian Mercy Oduyoye gathered a group of women theologians from across the continent of Africa to launch a group that became known as the Circle of Concerned African Women Theologians. Frustrated both by limitations of Western theologies and the gendered constraints they experienced within their own churches, Oduyoye and other African women theologians perceived a need to gather, to reflect, and to share their research and insights about African women's experiences in the church.[1] Over a decade after the launch of this group, Oduyoye reflected on the ways she has "called the church to put its house in order, and I have called my sisters to stand together to enhance our being as women.... My call to my sisters tells of my dream; it is a plea for solidarity and a cry to be free of imposed subordination."[2] She then observes, "We all remain free to tell of our dreams if we do not allow our imagination to be captive."[3]

What are the sources of this captivity, and how can it be challenged? Oduyoye goes on to offer a profound sociological insight: "We must recognise that social structures are created by human beings and, therefore, may be scrambled, reorganised, or discarded, if they have become dysfunctional. No culture is fixed."[4] Change is possible. Freedom is possible. The pursuit of a more just world is difficult work, and yet, social structures and cultures are malleable, not fixed.

Oduyoye's use of "if" is also significant. We are free to dream and to share those dreams "*if* we do not allow our imagination to be captive." We can change social structures "*if* they have become dysfunctional." What does it take to resist powers that seek to hold our imaginations captive? And how, then, might we not only recognize where and how our social structures are failing us, but also take courageous action to address their dysfunctions? These are the questions at the heart of this book. The answers that the SACC, AE, and PACSA offer us show the fragility of efforts to envision and enact full justice. They also invite us to try anyway.

THE FRAGILITY OF JUSTICE FOR RACE AND GENDER

The three organizations profiled in this book illuminate the dynamic processes that shape religious institutions' efforts to dream and enact changed social structures. My central argument is that theological convictions have a profound impact on the ways that religious organizations both understand and enact their mission. We cannot reduce religion to other, underlying factors. At the same time, the beliefs that shape religious organizations' actions are also institutionally embedded, in ways that both reflect and perpetuate racial and gender positioning. The organizations adopt different postures to particular social groups. Their beliefs and social positioning intersect to shape their actions.

These theological cultures follow a distinct path over time and across different issues. In each case, the theological cultures that were cultivated to respond to the racial violence and injustice of apartheid have a profound impact on their responses to GBV. This is a dynamic process, not a static or deterministic outcome. And it is a process that sometimes facilitates and sometimes constrains their responses.

PACSA shows us most clearly the possibility of cultivating institutionally embedded theological convictions to facilitate a robust response to both racial and gendered violence. The central theological narrative that grounds their discourse of death-dealing systems being transformed into life-affirming ones is remarkably consistent across time and across social issues. The organization's social positioning with respect to both racial and gender groups is one that focuses attention both on the experience of those who are marginalized and on those who are complicit in that marginalization. This clear connection across racial and gendered issues does not happen automatically or inevitably, but it is facilitated by the theological narrative that powerfully anchors PACSA's identity across time. GBV is incorporated into the transformation theological culture in ways that facilitate their extensive response to the problem.

The SACC shows us most clearly how the theological convictions that mobilize attention to racial violence and injustice can be loosely connected to gender. For the SACC, there was a tenuous, even organizationally fraught, theological recognition of women's marginalization as part and parcel of the quest for liberation from oppression. This mattered for the organization's subsequent attention to GBV. While they drew on some of the features of their theological culture to respond to GBV, the SACC did not perceive women victims of violence to be a marginalized group with whom the church ought to engage in suffering solidarity. The path that their theological culture follows across time meant that they were more likely to perceive the issue as one that was rooted in racial and economic injustice, rather than sexism. This was not inevitable. But the pattern of institutional ambivalence around centering women's voices and concerns within the organization had a lasting impact.

AE shows most clearly the ways that institutionally embedded theological convictions can hinder the recognition of gender injustice altogether. While their depiction of the possibility of racial reconciliation was predicated on the theological conviction that God's reconciliation with humanity has social implications, their theological culture also rests on an untroubled presumption of a gendered order for society. The Jesus Way is a gendered way. AE thus sees GBV as evidence of their broader concern with eroding personal morality in relation to sexuality, especially, and as a sign of the need for and power of the Gospel for changed lives. But this does not translate into calls for the reconciliation of men and women. AE's lack of programmatic response to GBV is the result of the ways their theological culture stunts their capacity to recognize sexism the way they had recognized racism.

Comparisons across the organizations also reveal the significance of these processes. The SACC and PACSA share the theological conviction that the church must reckon with social inequality and strive to upend power imbalances by accompanying the socially marginalized. But these theological convictions are concretized institutionally in different ways, based on a variety of factors. For instance, at the same time that PACSA was drawing on its local connections in communities near Pietermaritzburg to apply their theological culture to GBV, the SACC was struggling for organizational survival. This struggle was partly due to the organizations' different social positioning with respect to race. The SACC's close alignment with the liberation movement and radical opposition to the government resulted in a more dramatic shift in their identity and work in the transition and new democracy than PACSA's, as I discussed in chapter 2.

The difference in the organizations' posture toward the state also intersects with their theological convictions in different ways to shape their responses to GBV. The SACC's opposition to the apartheid regime turns into critical solidarity with the new government. But their theological convictions are continuous: the church's obligation is to maintain its solidarity with the marginalized, and the new government ought to enshrine rights and implement policies that will improve the lot of the disadvantaged. While they do not draw on their theological convictions around solidarity with the marginalized to respond to GBV, they do perceive it to be linked to unjust economic and historically exclusionary systems. The SACC's practical work on GBV, then, tends to be housed in programs for democratic and human rights and sometimes with funding support from the government. This is a contrast to AE. In fact, part of AE's consistency in both conviction and posture is their critique both of the apartheid regime *and* of the new democracy. For AE, neither regime was following the Jesus Way, though for different reasons and in different ways. They are concerned that the opening of new opportunities is coinciding with a decline in the realm of personal morality, especially for sexuality. GBV is, thus, a sign of that broader trend of moral decline.

A comparison of AE and PACSA shows us how a similar racial positioning can be expressed differently based on distinct theological convictions, as well as how a particular racial position manifests differently for gender. Both organizations focus on and sometimes identify with a collective white experience. But this positioning is articulated and enacted differently because of their different theological convictions. PACSA's analysis of power differences that need to be transformed manifests in a focus on white complicity and the need for white people to go to the places of pain and brokenness. AE's theological affirmation of reconciliation manifests in a focus on a more innocent white ignorance, and on the initiative that black people can take in leaving their townships and then encountering and forgiving white people.

These intersections of racial positioning with theological convictions matter in interesting ways for GBV. PACSA's response to GBV is similar to their response to racism and racial violence, highlighting not only the ways that women's experiences of violence need to be heard but also the ways that men need to be educated and relinquish their privilege. There is a disconnect for AE: Their strong emphasis on cross-racial reconciliation does not have a corresponding imagination for cross-gender reconciliation. This is due to the ways that their theological culture also enshrines their belief in a God-ordained gendered order for society. In all these ways, we see the power of the distinct paths that the theological cultures follow for the organizations' responses to racial and gender violence.

THE FRAGILITY OF JUSTICE FOR THE PRESENT

As I was completing the book, I realized it had been more than a decade since I first began this project. What were the organizations up to now, I wondered? At the time I write this, the SACC's work continues, and they have developed a new program on "Patriarchy and Society" that aims to address GBV.[5] AE is also still in existence. The home page of their website highlights a new book by Michael Cassidy, and their relatively new team leader references the U.S. theologian Wayne Grudem, who was instrumental in creating the gender ideology of "complementarianism."[6] PACSA closed in 2021, due to misappropriation of funds and fraud by their finance manager.[7] Journalistic reports hint at a possible breakdown of communication between the board and the staff as they were investigating the issues, and letters to the local newspaper showed signs of potential efforts to try to reimagine the organization.[8] But as of now, the organization appears to have permanently closed.

The pursuit of justice is fragile, indeed. PACSA's closure highlights the role of social structural contingencies that shape the pathways that each of the three of the organizations have followed across time and issues. People, money, and politics, among other factors, can alter an organization's path in significant ways. This is why my argument is anti-deterministic. The theological convictions of each organization do intersect with their social positioning in ways that shape their actions in the specific way that I have shown throughout the book. But the dynamic process that is at work in these interconnections is flexible and malleable.

The SACC's renewed attempts to address GBV and patriarchy shows the importance of recognizing contingencies and flexibility, as well. The path the SACC followed in their initial, partial response to GBV was not inevitable. In fact, their programmatic response now highlights the fact that they have had the capacity to do so all along. A simple glance at AE's website confirms a pattern of attempting to pass leadership on to the next generation, while also remaining firmly committed to Cassidy's legacy. The organization's continued reliance on Cassidy's voice, and the mention of a U.S. theologian who promotes a view of gender that enshrines gender essentialism shows that their theological culture persists to the present day.

THE FRAGILITY OF JUSTICE FOR THE FUTURE

Finally, where do we go from here? My primary aim in this book is to provide a robust sociological analysis of the institutional processes that link theological convictions with social positioning to shape organizations' actions. There are also undeniable practical and moral implications of this argument, for people across different faith traditions and life experiences. The stakes of this argument seem particularly relevant today. Our contemporary life is saturated with stories of religious denominations and faith-based organizations that have not only failed to protect people from various forms of abuse and injustice, but have also failed to hold those responsible accountable, especially concerning sexual abuse. In the United States, we have seen this pattern in responses to documentation of widespread abuse in the largest Protestant denomination in the United States, the Southern Baptist Convention, as well as the U.S. Catholic Bishops Conference.[9] Survivors and advocates who speak out can be vilified as troublemakers and choose to leave their religious communities over the lack of accountability and protection for survivors and others who are vulnerable. This has been the case with prominent figures such as Beth Moore, who left the Southern Baptist Convention at least in part over its treatment of sexual abuse. Rachael Denhollendar, who has been outspoken not only about her own abuse by USA Gymnastics doctor Larry Nassar, but also about her concern with protecting vulnerable people in churches from abuse, also left her church.[10]

Maybe we have been asking the wrong questions. Maybe, as Oduyoye observed, our imaginations are held captive, and we need actively to resist that captivity in order to dream new dreams and reimagine and enact different social structures. Maybe part of what we need to resist is the fear that telling the truth and accepting its consequences will prevent us from doing the good work we want to do in the world. We need to center the voices and experiences of those who have been harmed, and act with compassionate knowledge that aims to repair harm while also addressing its sources. As we do this, we must resist the temptation to dehumanize perpetrators of violence while also finding just practices that hold them accountable for their actions. As my colleague Sameer Yadav said in a public forum on the origins of race, what would it look like to orient our attention not around questions of blame or debating the veracity of claims of hurt, but around the questions "Who has been harmed?" and "What does repair look like?"[11]

This call to center the voices of those who have experienced harm finds deep resonance within the global movement to address intersectional violence.[12] When she started the #MeToo movement in 2006, Tarana Burke, a Black woman social worker, did so in order to build solidarity and connection across survivors.[13] Centering the voices and lived experiences of those who had experienced violence, Burke has consistently called for an approach that honors the dignity of those who have been harmed. Recent analyses of GBV in South Africa similarly note the importance of implementing practices that center the voices and experiences of survivors.[14]

One possible pathway to address some of the moral and practical implications of this work is to reflect on where and how we might adopt practices of lament. Another African theologian, Emmanuel Katongole, writes with Chris Rice, "To learn to lament is to become people who stay near to the wounds of the world, singing over them and washing them, allowing the unsettling cry of pain to be heard."[15] We cannot lament if we do not tell the truth. And the truth is that there is much to lament in our world today about the complicity of religious institutions in various forms of violence and injustice. Staying "near to the wounds of the world" may not sound like a particularly compelling call to action. But it is an essential step in the process of resisting the captivity of our imaginations and bodies to systems that dehumanize and exploit.

At the end of the day, the organizations I profile in this book show us that efforts to address injustice and violence are fragile. And yet, people can and do sometimes develop and employ theological convictions in ways that mobilize their efforts to challenge social structural barriers. This sometimes has unintended consequences, sometimes involves the perpetuation of further blinders and barriers, and sometimes involves actions that can spark transformation. In some ways, this is not a very optimistic story. The evidence here all points to the tenuousness of efforts to respond to social issues, based on the ways that theological cultures both open and close particular possibilities for imagining and enacting a more just world. Full, deep justice remains an elusive goal. But the stories of each of these organizations show that there are social and cultural processes that *do* allow people to challenge the systems and norms that perpetuate injustice and violence. We would do well to listen to their voices, and attend to their calls, fragile as they are, for justice.

APPENDIX A
Key Features of the Theological Cultures

	SACC	PACSA	AE
Theological culture	Liberation	Transformation	Reconciliation
Theological convictions	God's liberating power	God's transforming power	God's reconciling power
	God on the side of the marginalized	God brings life out of death	God's way for society
Social positioning	Suffering of the oppressed; solidarity with the marginalized	Complicity of the privileged and suffering of the marginalized	Equality of need across different experience
Posture toward race	Black dignity and marginality	White complicity and black suffering	Black forgiveness of whites
Posture toward gender	Ambivalence about women as a marginalized group	Women a suffering group in need of church's solidarity	No attention to cross-gender reconciliation
Implications for GBV	Partial response	Robust response	No response

APPENDIX B
Sources, Case Selection, and Standpoint

SOURCES

The introduction mentions that I collected historical data from a number of sites. Here are a few more details about those locations:

Historical Papers Library, University of the Witwatersrand, Johannesburg, South Africa (SACC internal documents: divisional reports, National Conference materials, Women's Ministries program materials)

Divinity Library Special Collections, Yale University, New Haven, CT (SACC newsletters)

Special Collections Library, Wheaton College, Wheaton, IL (AE newsletters)

African Enterprise, Pietermaritzburg, South Africa (AE newsletters; other internal documents such as SACLA materials, Cassidy's radio addresses, and book manuscripts)

Pietermaritzburg Agency for Christian Social Awareness, Pietermaritzburg, South Africa (PACSA newsletters; other internal documents such as Gender Programme Reports and Annual Reports)

Alan Paton Centre, University of KwaZulu Natal, Pietermaritzburg, South Africa (additional PACSA materials that filled gaps in newsletters)

CASE SELECTION

As I mentioned in the introduction, I originally thought that this project would focus on groups that were known to be most effective and active in responding to GBV. This would likely have meant a combination of groups that had started post-apartheid (e.g., the Sonke Gender Justice Network), as well as possibly some that had existed during apartheid (e.g., Rape Crisis Cape Town Trust), and it would have included a combination of religious and nonreligious NGOs. But as I read about different organizations and then met with different contacts in South Africa in 2012, I could not shake the sense that there was a different question that needed puzzling through. I was not so interested in understanding what made for the most effective response. I was more interested in understanding the varying pathways that religious organizations took from responding to one form of social inequality and violence to another.

This led me to the SACC as the first obvious choice of an empirical case to include. Their story has been told by other scholars, and some of their leaders are still internationally recognized as being among the most important prophetic Christian leaders of the twentieth- and twenty-first centuries. The other two organizations were less well-known, but as I started to look into their histories, I was intrigued—particularly by AE's insistence on reconciliation and their "behind-the-scenes" work to promote social change, and PACSA's insistence on the need to work with white people in order to challenge apartheid. After I made contact with staff at these two organizations and gathered some preliminary historical data, I knew I wanted to include both of them.

In fact, I considered centering this project on a two-case comparison of AE and PACSA. In many ways, this would have been ideal: I had established contact with both and could easily have done extensive interviews with former and current staff of each organization. They were in the same geographic area, and their theologies varied in interesting and important ways. But had I done this, I would not have been able fully to tell the story about race that the inclusion of the SACC allows me to tell. Nor would I have been able to include the gender story of the SACC—a story that, to my knowledge, has not been the subject of any extensive scholarly attention.

This three-case comparison does come with an important trade-off. The reader will astutely observe that the data I use in this book is entirely text-based. Prior to going to South Africa in 2012, I obtained approval from the University of Notre Dame's Institutional Review Board to conduct qualitative interviews. Over the course of a few trips to South Africa in 2012 and 2013, I conducted interviews with approximately fifty people, including some current and former staff of AE and PACSA, as well as experts on gender and anti-apartheid activism. I initially thought that I would do a mixed-methods study that would include qualitative and oral history interviews as well as published texts, and thus started to interview people at both AE and PACSA. But, unfortunately, I was unable to interview people at the SACC. At the time of my initial research, the organization was in a period of significant decline, and I was navigating some personal health challenges that restricted my capacity to persist as long as I wish I could have. I did not end up establishing contact with them.

While this was initially a setback, it also allowed me to hone in more closely on the key question that is at the heart of this book: How are public, institutional expressions of religious belief concretized organizationally? It would, of course, have been fascinating to also include more context and background from people at the organizations. I lament, in particular, that this shift in focus meant that I did not interview the women of the SACC who fought for their voices to be heard. But I immersed myself in textual data that afforded more than enough information to construct a deep and wide analysis. In fact, it still amazes me that we can learn as much as we can from institutional documents. They leave a clearly marked trail, if we are observant enough to follow it.

STANDPOINT

Whenever I have presented on various aspects of the argument of this book, at least one person asks me to evaluate the organizations. These questions have varied from "What do *you* think about these organizations' responses?" to "Is one of these theologies inherently more conducive to pursuing justice?" to the universalizing "So, what's your answer? Can religious organizations do good in the world, or is it only bad?" My first response is always, "Well, the main contribution I can make is an empirical one, not a moral one. What does the data suggest?" As a social scientist, I am committed to examining patterns and processes in the empirical world carefully and thoroughly. Following Max Weber, I believe that while we are all standing somewhere as we ask our questions and interpret the answers, and that our own presuppositions and evaluations shape the way we do this, our accounts of the world are not hopelessly subjective.[1] It is also not the job of a social scientist to prescribe what *ought to be* based on our empirically robust descriptions and accounts of what *is*—much less to offer our own opinions based on what we might personally wish were true.

At the same time, Patricia Hill Collins and other intersectional theorists I draw on to frame the argument of this book have made very clear that our own knowledge is not produced outside of the contexts and social systems that shape us.[2] The story I tell here is conditioned by my own social position as a white, middle-class, educated woman from the Northeastern United States who grew up as a pastor's kid. It is also conditioned by particular features of my own family's story of encountering violence. This includes both the hidden, domestic violence that one of my grandmothers and great-grandmothers experienced, and the more recent murder of a family member that was caused by many things, one of which is misogyny. And it is conditioned by my experience as a college student when, during an internship, I met several women who had left their abusive husbands for various reasons, but who all had one thing in common: their churches did not believe them.

These experiences and my own position in interlocking systems of race, class, gender, and religion undoubtedly shape the things I see and the way I tell the story. They have certainly motivated me to want to use my knowledge and skills to shed light on patterns and processes that we might find difficult to attend to. And they have heightened my awareness of the deeply personal implications of institutional attention and inattention to complex human experiences.

So, what do I make of these organizations' responses? My main answer to this question is to acknowledge the worries I have about how readers might interpret my analysis. I recognize that it is possible to read this book primarily as a critique, especially of AE. The irony is that I spent the most time with AE when I was there, even staying at their Conference Center. This project would not have been possible without the deep hospitality and generosity I experienced from the staff of the organization. While I do think the account I offer here of the ways AE's theological culture constrains their capacity to respond to GBV is true, I also think that this was not inevitable.

Inversely, it is possible to read this book as a ringing endorsement of PACSA's theology and positioning. But this, too, would be a mistake. It is the case that PACSA deployed their theology in the ways they did to effectively respond to GBV. But they also had plenty of their own internal struggles, including the eventual breakdown that led to the closure of the organization in 2021. As with the other two organizations, none of their work was inevitable. Whether the transformation theological culture is inherently more conducive to facilitating robust response to pressing social problems than the others I describe here could be an interesting question for theologians to weigh in on. It is beyond the scope of my own knowledge and position to make such a claim.

And finally, it is possible to read this book as a white woman outsider's critique of a black-led organization that was on the front lines of the anti-apartheid struggle, at great cost. While I am sure there are ways in which my own position as a white woman outsider does limit my understanding of the SACC, I also found myself compelled to include the organization in this book because I found evidence of a story about women within the organization that I had not yet seen acknowledged. I still remember the day I was sitting in Wits University's Historical Papers Library and found the memo of Lulu Xingwana asking Frank Chikane to explain why the women's concerns were being ignored. It was paper-clipped to another document. I could easily have missed it. But I didn't. And I think their story warrants our attention.

At the end of the day, I hope that, rather than interpret the main story of this book as a critique or endorsement of particular organizations or theologies, readers will instead choose to ask questions about where they, themselves, are standing as they develop convictions about their own actions in the world. I hope that readers will pay attention to the discourse and actions of the institutions that have formed them, and of which they are a part. And I hope that they will have the courage—as the people within all three of these organizations did, albeit with the blind spots that all of us are prone to—to grow, to change, and to choose hope.

For as careful, thorough, and truthful as I have tried to be here, there are sure to be things I have missed and additional complexities that could be accounted for. And there are surely more stories to be told about the ways that these and other religious organizations perceive their mission and do their work in the world. I hope that others will also seek to deepen our knowledge of the way that religious institutions can both be complicit in and challenge inequality and violence. And I hope that, as they do, they will be as humbled and inspired as I have been through the course of researching and writing this book to try to enact a more just and loving world.

ACKNOWLEDGMENTS

There are many people whose attentiveness and generosity have made this book possible.

I can trace the beginnings of this book all the way back to my experience as a college student at Gordon College, when I was fortunate to be mentored by a number of faculty and staff who saw my potential, and who encouraged my interests in South Africa and gender. Thanks especially to Gregor Thuswaldner, Elaine Phillips, Dan Johnson, Jennifer Hevelone-Harper, Lawrence Holcomb, and Greg and Laura Carmer. I owe a particular debt of gratitude to Ivy George for first taking me to South Africa.

The community I found at the University of Notre Dame nurtured me intellectually as I worked on the dissertation that formed the basis for this book. I am grateful to the participants of the Culture and Religion workshops in the Department of Sociology, especially to Daniel Escher, Ann Mische, and Ana Velitchkova. Shanna Corner, Karen Hooge Michalka, and Megan Rogers were faithful companions throughout the dissertation process. The members of my dissertation committee were the epitome of generosity, kindness, and helpfulness. Thanks to Robert Fishman, Paul Kollman, Lyn Spillman, and Christian Smith. Your investment in me continues to resonate in my work and life, and I am deeply grateful.

Thank you to Lisa Weaver Swartz and Abi Ocobock, who have journeyed with me from the days of writing at coffee shops through the book production process. Thank you for reading and providing feedback on chapters, sharing insights about the process, and providing encouragement whenever it was needed.

This work would not have been possible without the financial support of multiple entities. Thanks especially to the Kellogg Institute for International Studies at the University of Notre Dame for funding both research costs and a dissertation fellowship, and to the Global Religion Research Initiative for providing a writing fellowship. I am also grateful to the Graduate School, the Institute for Scholarship in the Liberal Arts, and the Center for the Study of Religion and Society at the University of Notre Dame for their support of the initial research. The Provost's Office at Westmont College provided generous financial support to collect additional archival data and to take the sabbatical that allowed me to finalize the manuscript.

I have been fortunate to find intellectual companions along the way who offered incisive insight in the formulation of this project, including Derek Peterson, Alice Wiemers, Rick Elphick, and Paul Ocobock. And thanks also to the people I met in South Africa who helped me to hone in on the questions that needed answering, including Mike Deeb, Peter-John Pearson, and Susan Rakoczy. The hospitality I experienced in South Africa was unparalleled; thanks to the staff at AE and PACSA for their generosity and care for me as I spent time with them, and to the Holy Family Sisters of Corrie for welcoming me on multiple occasions. Particular thanks are due to Mervyn Abrahams, Daniela Gennrich, Miles Giljam, and Michael Cassidy for their openness and encouragement as I pursued this project. And I am deeply grateful to the people who generously shared their insights with me through interviews.

On one of my trips to South Africa, photographer Meghan Kirkwood and I happened to cross paths in Cape Town. One day, as we hiked Lion's Head, Meghan took the stunning photograph that appears on the cover of this book. I am deeply grateful for the ways we shared the natural beauty of South Africa together, and for her permission to use the photograph.

Thanks to the archivists and librarians who facilitated my access to the documents that I analyze in the book, especially Michele Pickover at the Historical Papers Library at the University of the Witswatersrand, Jillian Clark at the Alan Paton Centre at the University of KwaZulu Natal, Sarah Stanley at Wheaton College, and Sara Azam at Yale University. And thank you to Katherine Goodwin and Nina Whitnah for their assistance in collecting archival data.

At Westmont College, a vibrant community of colleagues and students shaped the direction of the book. Particular thanks are due to Sameer Yadav and Felicia Song for many conversations, strategy sessions, incisive feedback, and encouragement. Thanks to Helen Rhee for helpful feedback and for always being in my corner. Thank you to my gender studies and ethnic studies colleagues, especially Caryn Reeder, Cheri Larsen Hoeckley, Dinora Cardoso, Jason Cha, Kya Mangrum, Blake Thomas, Tom Knecht, and Aaron Sizer, for their interest and support. I am also grateful to my students, especially those who have taken my seminars on race, gender, and religion, and to the ethnic and gender studies students. Teaching you has allowed me to sharpen my own ability to grapple with sociological insights, and your questions often helped me to reflect in deep ways on the implications of this way of understanding the world. Thank you to the students who provided research assistance, including Kyra Coleman, Joy Han, Siena Keck, and Bryanna Rivera. I am particularly indebted to Mackinzie Warne-McGraw for the many hours she spent indexing archival documents, literature searching, and note formatting.

Thank you to Christopher Rios-Sueverkruebbe and to Carah Naseem at Rutgers University Press for their advocacy of the project and their prompt attentiveness, to the marketing and production teams at Rutgers University Press for bringing the book into the wider world, and to Jordan Beltran Gonzales for constructing the index.

Many friends have come alongside me with good humor, encouragement, playground time, coffee, long beach walks, and many other forms of care, including the Sparkman Zylstra, Eyer-Delevett, O'Hara, Currie, Powlison-Belkovic, Nelson, Kotulski, Gray, Harper, Swartz, Toms Smedley, Huff, Song, McNamara, Sizer-Foell, and Yadav families. Thanks to Mary Petersen for writing retreats by the water; Anne Blackwill for hospitality, conviction, and encouragement; Julie Brazzi for steadfast championing; and Frances Shavers for insisting that balance was necessary. Thanks to Aimee and Gerry Doran for a real vacation in a beautiful place, many conversations about the implications of the book, and to Gerry for reading the whole book and providing incisive feedback.

As I note in appendix B, my work to complete this book coincided with the traumatic loss of a family member. My heartfelt thanks go to the Poetry Group with the Hospice Center of Santa Barbara, who accompanied me through that difficult time. Writing poetry every week not only helped me to process my grief, but it also unlocked more creativity and courage than I had previously found in the process of writing. I am deeply grateful.

My family has provided immeasurable support. I owe particular thanks to Tom and Barbara Evans, Chuck and Cheryl Rynd, Diane Rynd, Michael Rynd and Julie Thorne, and Gretchen and Doug Sassi for their steadfast interest and encouragement. Lauren, Michael, and Joanna Whitnah have offered humor and conviction. Charles and Annalie Whitnah provide ceaseless inspiration and opportunity to affirm what's most important. Chris Slone came along at just the right time, and his advocacy and attentiveness mean the world to me. Thank you for reading the whole thing, and for being with me as it launches.

Finally, this book is dedicated to the three people whose love made its completion possible. My dad, John Whitnah, inspires me by his integrity and his commitment to bring everyone to the table and my mom, Nina Whitnah, by her conviction that love is not a duty but an expression of grace. Mary Ellen Konieczny was a consummate mentor and advocate. She believed in me when I didn't know how to believe in myself, and never failed in her championing of me as a scholar and as a person. I lament that she is not here to see the fruit of this labor, but I hope and trust that she would be proud.

NOTES

INTRODUCTION

Epigraph: Tutu and Tutu (2014, 24).

1. Tutu (1996, 2000, 2011).
2. *Ecunews*, special issue, August 1985, 3.
3. Abrahams et al. (2012); DuToit (2014); Jewkes and Abrahams (2002); Jewkes et al. (2002); Mathewes et al. (2004); Naidoo and Buiten (2022); Vetten (2007); L. Walker (2005).
4. As I describe in more detail in chapter 3, the origins of this phrase are debated. Some attribute it to a Human Rights Watch Report in 1995 (for instance, Jewkes and Abrahams 2000). Others have attributed it to Interpol (for instance, "Every 26 Seconds," CBS News, February 1, 2000, https://www.cbsnews.com/news/every-26-seconds/). Please see chapter 3 for more discussion.
5. In 2012, PACSA changed its name to the Pietermaritzburg Agency for Community Social Action. This reflects a change in strategy to deepen partnerships with community-based organizations. Since the analysis here is primarily historical, I use the name that was employed in the past.
6. Examples of this abound in our contemporary discourse. For instance, the Intersectionality Research Institute at George Washington University defines intersectionality as "the concept that all oppression is linked and people are often disadvantaged by multiple sources of oppression: their race, class, gender identity, sexual orientation, and religion, just to name a few. So for a Black woman, Intersectionality recognizes that your identity as a 'woman' and as 'black' do not exist independently of each other." See "About," Intersectionality Research Institute, accessed March 30, 2024, https://intersectionality.gwu.edu/about. The Office of Equity, Diversity, and Inclusion of the U.S. National Institutes of Health starts its description of intersectionality in this way: "How would you describe the different facets of your identity? Do you identify as Hispanic and/or Latinx? A trans-man? A federal employee? A nurse? These aspects of our lives make up our identities and shape how we perceive the world, and in return, how the world perceives us as individuals." See "Intersectionality Part One: Intersectionality Defined," Office of Equity, Diversity, and Inclusion, accessed March 30, 2024, https://www.edi.nih.gov/blog/communities/intersectionality-part-one-intersectionality-defined. The Kroc Institute for International Peace Studies at the University of Notre Dame notes the need for increased attention to intersectionality in peace studies, and defines the framework in this way: "The term intersectionality has become a key conceptual framework and method of identifying the complex overlap of various social identities, such as race, gender, sexuality, and class, and the ways systemic oppression and discrimination are experienced by individuals." See "Intersectionality and Justice," Kroc Institute for International Peace Studies, accessed March 30, 2024, https://kroc.nd.edu/research/intersectionality/. My point is not that there is anything wrong with focusing on how intersecting systems shape individual experience, but that we need to not lose the emphasis in intersectional theory on the power of institutions to support intersecting systems of power.
7. Crenshaw (1991).
8. Collins (1998).
9. Choo and Ferree (2010).
10. See, for example, Browne (1999); Lerner (1998); and Yellin and Van Horne (1994). In their compilation of an extensive range of documents from this time period, Maureen Moynagh and

Nancy Forestell (2012) point out that, as they title the first volume of their work, "transnational collaborations and crosscurrents" were also an important feature of the movement. They also highlight how various forms of social privilege were at work in these connections, as international travel was a feature of elite white women's experience that was not possible for others (xxii).

11. Kimberlé Crenshaw (2010) revisits this history in an analysis of the 2008 Democratic nomination contest between Hillary Clinton and Barack Obama.

12. Cott (1987); Evans (1979); Nicholson (1997); Roth (2004). See also Verta Taylor's (1989, 761) famous argument that the second-wave feminist movement can not only be traced to the U.S. civil rights movement, but also be seen as a "resurgent challenge with roots in an earlier cycle of feminist activism." Taylor argues that in the 1940s and 1950s the feminist movement experienced a time of "abeyance," and was then reactivated in the 1960s.

13. Barnett (1993); Robnett (1997). For additional analysis of the gendered dynamics of the civil rights movement, see McAdam (1992).

14. See, for example, Ferree and Tripp (2006); Jaquette (1989, 1994); Molyneux (1998, 2001); Ray and Korteweg (1999); and Tripp et al. (2009). Differences in geography and status make a difference here. Where feminists in Western Europe and the United States have focused more on issues of reproductive rights, what Molyneux (1985, 232–233) has described as "strategic" issues, women in various parts of the majority world have tended to advocate more for necessities, or "practical" issues, like access to clean water.

15. Block (2006); Feinstein (2018). This narrative has also been complicated by some historical analyses; see, for example, Somerville (2004).

16. Branche and Virgili (2012); Fitzpatrick (2016); E. J. Wood (2018).

17. See Weldon (2006) for a particularly helpful overview.

18. At the time I was completing this manuscript, we saw this pattern play out in the reporting of—and debates over the veracity of accounts of—sexual violence in the October 7, 2023, attack by Hamas on Israel. A front-page *New York Times* piece contended that sexual violence was a key feature of the violence; see Jeffrey Gettleman, Anat Schwartz, and Adam Sella, "'Screams Without Words': How Hamas Weaponized Sexual Violence on Oct. 7," *New York Times*, December 28, 2023, https://www.nytimes.com/2023/12/28/world/middleeast/oct-7-attacks-hamas-israel-sexual-violence.html. But at least one account the story relied upon had some gaps, and the *Times* staff experienced significant internal conflict over the publication of the story; see David Folkenflik, "Newsroom at 'New York Times' Fractures over Story on Hamas Attacks," NPR, March 6, 2024, https://www.npr.org/2024/03/06/1236130609/new-york-times-hamas-attacks-israel-palestine. A UN official has since confirmed that there was evidence of sexual violence; see United Nations, "Reasonable Grounds to Believe Conflict-Related Sexual Violence Occurred in Israel during 7 October Attacks, Senior UN Official Tells Security Council," press release, March 11, 2024, https://press.un.org/en/2024/sc15621.doc.htm.

19. Collins (1998, 922).

20. Collins (1998, 922).

21. Some of the recent works making this point have focused especially on the case of U.S. white evangelicalism; see, for example, Bjork-James (2021); DuMez (2020); and Weaver Swartz (2023).

22. Wilde (2018a); Wilde and Glassman (2016); Wilde and Danielsen (2014). See also the various articles in Wilde (2018b).

23. Wilde (2019).

24. Against Marx's materialist theory of history, for instance, in *The Protestant Ethic and Spirit of Capitalism*, Weber (1904/2002, 125) argued that a particular set of religious convictions shaped the later development of the industrial capitalist system. But he also argued that economic systems can shape religious ones.

25. Appleby (1999).

26. See, for example, Asbridge (2004) on historical patterns. For analyses of more recent acts and trends, see Iannacconne and Berman (2006); Jurgensmeyer (2008); and Gorski and Turkmen-Dervisoglu (2013).
27. See, for example, Morris (1984); Christian Smith (1996a); and Walzer (1965).
28. Hadjar (2003); Nepstad (2004a, 2004b).
29. Christian Smith (1996b).
30. Sophie Bjork-James's (2021) ethnography of U.S. evangelicalism is an exception to this, as she analyzes the ways that discourse about the family is shaped by race and sexuality. But even here, the point is about the intertwining of these social realities, and not as much about the ways they also operate as distinct axes of power. And while scholars such as Du Mez (2020) and Weaver Swartz (2022) have made invaluable contributions, their analysis foregrounds gender as it intersects with religion. On the other hand, scholars such as Anthea Butler (2021) offer incisive accounts of the centrality of racism to U.S. evangelicalism, and sometimes discuss patriarchy, too, but it is not the central story.
31. Kaufman (2004).
32. Mahoney (2000, 507, 510–512). See also Mahoney and Thelen (2009); and Sewell (1996a, 1996b).
33. For instance, Mahoney (2000) stresses determinism because he finds Sewell's (1996b) description too fluid and open-ended. While taking to heart Mahoney's caution that we be more specific in using the term, it is also clear that, in the quest to specify what is meant when we describe the particular pathways that organizations take, we need to acknowledge the contingencies that shape particular outcomes.
34. Comaroff and Comaroff (1991); DeGruchy and DeGruchy (2004); Elphick and Davenport (1997).
35. Elphick (2012); see also DeGruchy and DeGruchy (2004, 13).
36. Dubow (2014); Fredrickson (2002); Worden (2011).
37. Dubow (2014, 18–22); Renick (1991).
38. Dubow (2014, 3).
39. Dubow (2014, 179–180).
40. Walshe (1983, 1991).
41. Borer (1998); DeGruchy and DeGruchy (2004).
42. Borer (1998); Walshe (1991).
43. See, for example, DeGruchy and DeGruchy (2004, 79).
44. Jubber (1985).
45. Cassidy (1989). See also Renick (1991).
46. Compare Gaitskill (1979, 1997, 2000).
47. Cock (1989); Hassim (2006).
48. Hassim (2006); Meintjes et al. (1993); Patel (1988); Seidman (1993, 1999); C. Walker (1982/1991).
49. Ginwala (1991); Hassim (2006).
50. Basu (1995); Kaplan (1997); Mahonty (2003); Molyneux (2001); Ray and Korteweg (1999).
51. Ferree and Tripp (2006); Jaquette (1994); Tripp et al. (2009).
52. Compare Jeffery and Basu (1998).
53. Rakoczy (2000, 2004).
54. Ackermann et al. (1991); DeGruchy and DeGruchy (2004); Göranzon (2010).
55. See, for example, DeGruchy and DeGruchy (2004). Walshe (1991) also briefly names sexism at the end of this discussion of prophetic Christianity.
56. Weldon (2006, 65–66) outlines a clear timeline of growing awareness and mobilization to confront the problem.

57. For an internal history of the organization, see "Who We Are," Rape Crisis Cape Town Trust, accessed March 30, 2024, https://rapecrisis.org.za/who-we-are/.
58. DuToit (2014); Vetten (2007).
59. See Britton (2020); and West (2019). I discuss these patterns, including the way they mirror empirical findings in other contexts, in more depth in chapter 3.
60. Hassim (2006, 52).
61. See, for example, Borer (2009); Goldblatt (2006); and Ross (2003, 2010).
62. Regarding the TRC, for instance, Tutu wore his clerical robes and opened the sessions each day with prayer (Krog 1998; Philpott 2012). Religion's presence was also seen in the TRC process as various denominations submitted reports about their own complicity in apartheid. In the context of broader discussions about how to rectify the injustices in the past and move forward, the church's role in actively and subtly supporting apartheid was publicly acknowledged by a variety of denominations. See TRC of South Africa (1998, 4:59–92).
63. For an internal history of the organization, see "History," SACC, accessed July 5, 2024, http://sacc.org.za/history/.
64. For the full list, see "Members," SACC, accessed July 5, 2024, http://sacc.org.za/members/.
65. This information is taken from SACC, *The Constitution of the South African Council of Churches 2017 Edition*, June 2017, http://sacc.org.za/wp-content/uploads/2020/12/SACC-Constitution.pdf.
66. An internal history of AE was written by Anne Coomes (2002), and founder Michael Cassidy describes it especially in *The Passing Summer* (1989).
67. PACSA has also produced internal histories that shed light on their interpretation of their origins, including *Journeying for Justice* (2009) and *Hope beyond Apartheid* (2002).

CHAPTER 1   RACIAL POSITIONING AND THEOLOGICAL CULTURES IN THE FIGHT AGAINST APARTHEID

Epigraph: The Kairos Theologians (1985, chap. 1).

1. The Kairos Theologians (1985).
2. Concerned Evangelicals (1986).
3. Ntlha (1994).
4. Mabuza (2009, 92). See also Beyerhaus (1987), cited in Mabuza (2009, 95).
5. Mabuza (2009, 100).
6. Borer (1998, 112–113); DeGruchy and DeGruchy (2004, 199).
7. This sociological insight can be traced back to some of the earliest sociological thinkers in Europe, with Karl Marx (1843/1978) and Max Weber (1904/2002) posing different answers to the question of both the source and influence of religion's impact on other aspects of society. More recent work has taken up this insight and question as there has been renewed interest in the sociological significance of religion. See, for instance, Asbridge (2004); Jurgensmeyer (2008); Morris (1984); Nepstad (2004a, 2004b, 2008); and R. L. Wood (2002).
8. As I noted in the introduction, Melissa Wilde, in particular, has taken up this point with her recent work on "complex religion"; see Wilde (2018a, 2018b, 2019); Wilde and Danielsen (2014); and Wilde and Glassman (2016). A large number of studies have examined the connections between race and religion, specifically; see, for example, Butler (2021); Edwards (2008, 2019); Emerson et al. (2015); Emerson and Smith (2000); and Patillo-McCoy (1998).
9. This insight can be traced back to Weber (1904/2002), in particular. See also Riesebrodt (1993, 2010); and Christian Smith (2017).
10. Omi and Winant (2015). There is some debate among scholars of race concerning the extent to which racial formation is essentially a flexible and dynamic process versus something

that is more powerfully shaped by white supremacy. See, for example, the symposium on Omi and Winant's work with Feagin and Elias's critical engagement with this question in *Ethnic and Racial Studies* 36(6) (2013). See also Patricia Hill Collins's (2015) work on the usefulness of racial formation theory for intersectionality.

11. Omi and Winant (2015).
12. Walshe (1991).
13. Analysis of the SACC's role in the struggle against apartheid has been a significant component of several works on the role of religion in South Africa already (Borer 1998; DeGruchy and DeGruchy 2004; Walshe 1991). These other texts have tended to examine how the SACC came to denounce the apartheid state and what institutional and ideological resources they mustered to do so. I draw on and extend these previous studies in subsequent chapters by showing how threads of discourse regarding the racial inequality of apartheid were carried through for gender.
14. Tristan Borer (1998) helpfully analyzes and defines contextual theology in her account of the radicalization of the SACC, comparing it to the Southern African Catholic Bishops' Conference. She defines the key features of contextual theology in South Africa as centering on "the responsibility of churches to work for social justice and the need for Christians to engage their social environment." And she notes that, by the 1980s, these ideas had coalesced into a "religious subculture" that promoted "overt political activity" (84).
15. The Black Consciousness Movement was initiated by Steve Biko and cultivated especially among university students (Biko 1978/2002; see also Fatton 1986; Gerhart 1978; Hirschmann 1990; Magaziner 2010). The United Democratic Front was an explicitly nonracial, grassroots coalition of organizations that aimed to bring down apartheid; see, for example, Borer (1998, 48–49); and Dubow (2014, 207–210).
16. This included, for instance, describing how the Presbyterian Church sought to allow multiracial marriages and how the white Dutch Reformed Church could not be a member church of the SACC until it denounced apartheid. See, for example, *Ecunews*, October 30, 1981, February 5, 1982, and February 19, 1982.
17. See, for example, Borer (1998, 131); and DeGruchy and DeGruchy (2004, 188). In fact, Borer (1998, 130–131) notes that the differences between the leadership and the member churches were related to the SACC's dual organizational role as both a representative body of denominations in South Africa and as an independent organization that had progressive people working in its headquarters.
18. Borer (1998, 146); DeGruchy and DeGruchy (2004, 113).
19. DeGruchy and DeGruchy (2004, 190).
20. Borer (1998, 89–91); DeGruchy and DeGruchy (2004, 102).
21. Borer (1998, 64, 66); Chikane (1988/2010); DeGruchy and DeGruchy (2004, 197).
22. Borer (1998); DeGruchy and DeGruchy (2004).
23. Borer (1998, 56–58); DeGruchy and DeGruchy (2004, 189).
24. The Eloff Commission ended up finding no evidence of the SACC engaging in illegal activities. But this signaled intensified state scrutiny and attempts to delegitimize the SACC's work. Borer (1998, 56–58) notes that this was a key episode that radicalized the SACC. See also DeGruchy and DeGruchy (2004, 189–190).
25. Borer (1998, 206).
26. Borer (1998, 162).
27. Desmond Tutu, "Liberation," SACC National Conference, 1976, 3.
28. Tutu, 1976, 3.
29. Desmond Tutu, *Ecunews*, September 1982, 8.
30. Lubbe (1983); *Ecunews*, November 1983, 3.
31. Desmond Tutu, "Sermon Preached at St. Mary's Cathedral—Healing Service" [on Genesis 3], 1979?

32. Beyers Naudé, "South Africa: The Current Situation and the Challenge Facing the Churches in Their Search for Justice and Peace," *Ecunews*, June 1987, 12.
33. Naudé, June 1987, 12.
34. Naudé, June 1987, 10.
35. Borer (1998); DeGruchy and DeGruchy (2004). This appeal to engage in suffering solidarity with the marginalized resonates with liberation theology in Latin America (Boff and Boff 1987; Gutiérrez 1973) and black theology in the United States (Cone 1970).
36. Frank Chikane, *Ecunews*, August 1988, 3.
37. Desmond Tutu, "Report to the SACC's Executive Committee," 1984, 23.
38. Tutu, 1984, 23.
39. Tutu, 1984, 23.
40. Desmond Tutu, *Ecunews*, February 1982, 7.
41. *Ecunews*, September 1982, 14.
42. *Ecunews*, September 1982, 15.
43. *Ecunews*, September 1982, 16.
44. Tutu, February 1982, 24.
45. Desmond Tutu, *Ecunews*, June 1983, 27.
46. Desmond Tutu, *Ecunews*, September 1983, 10.
47. *Ecunews*, March 1984, 8.
48. Tutu, 1984; *Ecunews*, May–June 1984, 27.
49. The Lausanne Congress was sponsored by evangelical leaders Billy Graham and John Stott. The intent of the conference was to bring worldwide evangelical leaders together to discuss the needs and vision of evangelistic ministry in a changing world. At the convention, one of the stirring topics was whether, and how, the mission of saving souls fit with the social needs of those whose souls were seen to be at stake (Tizon 2008; Yates 1996). Evangelicals from non-Western contexts pushed back against the assumptions of those who had advocated for the primacy of preaching conversion, and who were concerned that the push to address social issues would lead to the neglect of preaching salvation (Costas 1990; Swartz 2012; Tizon 2008). The Lausanne Covenant, which was published after this congress, reflects a shift in perspective, one that asserts the necessity of social concern as a component of the preaching of the Gospel, not a separate and unrelated issue that can be bracketed (Gill 1975; Padilla 1975). For the full text of the Covenant, see "The Lausanne Covenant," Lausanne Movement, accessed October 6, 2024, https://lausanne.org/statement/lausanne-covenant.
50. This is described in depth in AE's internal history by Anne Coomes (2002), as well as Cassidy's (1989) spiritual autobiography, *The Passing Summer*.
51. Cassidy (1989).
52. Cassidy (1989, 117–119); Coomes (2002, 115–119).
53. Coomes (2002, 392–402).
54. Coomes (2002, 405).
55. Interpretations of the impact of this event vary. AE's internal history and newsletters stress the significance of having, for instance, both Pentecostal and Dutch Reformed Church leaders at the event (Coomes 2002, 402–409), while external accounts note that while the sheer number of people gathered was unprecedented, the volume and the reality of ongoing racial divides also meant that it was difficult to achieve concrete outcomes from the event (DeGruchy and DeGruchy 2004, 190–191).
56. Coomes (2002, 451–454).
57. Coomes (2002, 455).
58. Cassidy (1989); Coomes (2002, 452–455).
59. Coomes (2002, 455).
60. Coomes (2002, 377).

61. Cassidy (1989); Coomes (2002, 375–381).
62. Coomes (2002, 415–416).
63. John Smyth, *AE Update*, April 1985, 3.
64. Smyth, April 1985, 3.
65. Smyth, April 1985, 3.
66. *AE Update*, January 1986, 1.
67. Michael Cassidy, *AE Update*, August 1985.
68. Cassidy, August 1985.
69. *AE Update*, April 1988, 2.
70. Michael Cassidy, *AE Update*, October 1989, 3.
71. Cassidy, October 1989, 3.
72. *AE Witness*, March–April 1985, 3.
73. *AE Witness*, March–April 1985, 3.
74. Michael Cassidy, *AE Update*, September 1985, 1.
75. Cassidy, September 1985, 1.
76. Cassidy, September 1985, 1.
77. Cassidy, September 1985, 2.
78. Cassidy, September 1985, 2.
79. *AE Update*, October 1985, 1, emphasis in original.
80. *AE Update*, December 1985, 1.
81. *AE Update*, December 1985, 2.
82. *AE Update*, December 1985, 2.
83. *AE Update*, September 1986, 3.
84. Cassidy, September 1985, 3.
85. Cassidy, September 1985, 3.
86. Cassidy, September 1985, 3.
87. Cassidy, September 1985, 3.
88. Biko (1978/2002); Fatton (1986); Gerhart (1978); Hirschmann (1990); Magaziner (2010). See also DeGruchy and DeGruchy (2004, 146–164) for the ways in which black theology was formed in relation to the Black Consciousness Movement.
89. PACSA (2009, 10–13).
90. PACSA (2009, 12).
91. See, for example, Nuttall in Levine (2002, 17) for a discussion of the significance of these gatherings.
92. Nuttall in Levine (2002, 20–21); PACSA (2009, 30–31).
93. PACSA (2009).
94. This constitutional configuration was orchestrated by President P. W. Botha to give political representation to Indian and coloured constituents, while still excluding black Africans. Saul Dubow (2014, 205) discusses how this political reform prompted both a right-wing exodus from Botha's supporters and the emergence of the United Democratic Front. See also Worden (2000, 140–141); and Nuttall in Levine (2002) for a discussion of this shift for PACSA.
95. Worden (2000, 150–152).
96. PACSA (2009, 40).
97. Levine (2002, 113–144); PACSA (2009, 40–41).
98. John Aitchison, *PACSA Newsletter*, March 1980.
99. Aitchison, March 1980.
100. Joan Kerchhoff, *PACSA Newsletter*, August 1982, 1.
101. Graham Lindegger, *PACSA Newsletter*, April 1982, 1.
102. Lindegger, April 1982, 1.
103. Lindegger, April 1982, 1.

104. Lindegger, April 1982, 1.
105. John Aitchison, *PACSA Newsletter*, April 1984, 1.
106. Neville Richardson, *PACSA Newsletter*, March 1983, 1, emphasis in original.
107. Alex Bhiman, *PACSA Newsletter*, December 1985.
108. Bhiman, December 1985.
109. Theo Kneifel, *PACSA Newsletter*, Easter 1986.
110. Kneifel, Easter 1986.
111. Kneifel, Easter 1986.
112. Kneifel, Easter 1986.
113. James Massey, *PACSA Newsletter*, March 1979.
114. Colin Gardner, *PACSA Newsletter*, December 1981, 1.
115. Gardner, December 1981, 1.
116. Peter Kerchhoff, *PACSA Newsletter*, December 1981, 2.
117. Kerchhoff, December 1981, 2.
118. Gunther Wittenberg, *PACSA Newsletter*, June 1983.
119. Wittenberg, June 1983.
120. *PACSA Newsletter*, June 1986, 1.
121. *PACSA Newsletter*, June 1986, 1.
122. Mark Butler, *PACSA Newsletter*, March 1988, 3.
123. Butler, March 1988, 3.
124. James Hlongwa, *PACSA Newsletter*, March 1988, 4.
125. Hlongwa, March 1988, 4.

CHAPTER 2 CONTINUITY OF THEOLOGICAL CULTURES IN AN EMERGING DEMOCRACY

Epigraph: Alberts and Chikane (1991, sec. 2.2).

1. Considered the "broadest range of black and white church leaders ever to convene in South Africa," this gathering of 230 people represented eighty denominations and forty organizations (Borer 1998, 186).
2. The text of his statement can be read in Alberts and Chikane (1991).
3. See DeGruchy and DeGruchy (2004, 211) for a discussion of the mixed responses to Jonker's speech.
4. Rustenburg Declaration, sec. 2, "Confession," in Alberts and Chikane (1991).
5. Rustenburg Declaration, sec. 4, "Affirmation," in Alberts and Chikane (1991).
6. See Borer (1998, 186–187).
7. My emphasis here is on the process of political transition from the apartheid regime to a democratic regime. But it is important to note that one of the key questions facing the "prophetic" church voice, in particular, also concerned how to navigate a changing *religious* context. For instance, the growth of megachurches, particularly in the Pentecostal tradition, meant that the role of the organizations was also changing in relation to the religious ecology of the time. See, for example, A. Anderson (2005); Gifford (2004); Hefner (2013); B. Meyer (2004); and Miller et al. (2013) for further context. I am grateful to Paul Kollman for honing in on this question. In addition, as political opportunities were expanding with the transition from apartheid to democracy, this prompted debates about the proper relation of church and state, the role of church ideology in instilling social values in citizens, and the obligation of the church to be a moral conscience for the nation (DeGruchy and DeGruchy 2004; Villa-Vicencio 1992).
8. The work of William Sewell (1996a) on the significance of events is particularly illuminating in this respect. In his discussion of the significance of the taking of the Bastille for the French

Revolution, Sewell describes historical events as "dislocations and transformative rearticulations of structures" (861). For Sewell, social structures are "multiple, overlapping, and relatively autonomous" (842). This means that disruption or dislocation of one structure can influence another one, and it is not the case that all structures cohere into a "unified totality of some kind" (842). Cultural schemas are a central component of structures, along with resources and modes of power that regulate action (842). Thus, as they dislocate structures, events "introduce new conceptions of what really exists . . . of what is good . . . and of what is possible" (861). Discursive transformation is central to this account of the power of events for changing social structures. The process of new articulation is marked by uncertainty and "produces in actors a deep sense of insecurity," but for Sewell such uncertainty also prompts "collective creativity" (867). This way of thinking about the significance of events can illuminate patterns that we see in South Africa: the events of the transition dislocated the racial and economic structures of apartheid. The result of this was that people were cultivating more expansive imagined possibilities of how society could be structured.

9. See, for example, Fishman (2011); Huber et al. (1997); O'Donnell (1996); and Rueschemeyer (2004). The distinction in political sociology between the transition to democracy and the consolidation of democracy is also helpful here (see, e.g., Linz and Stepan 1995; O'Donnell 1996). This scholarship reveals some important tensions between seeing consolidation simply as the successful institutionalization of democracy—that is, "becoming the only game in town" (Linz and Stepan 1995, 5)—and efforts to problematize such a conceptualization because it can fail to consider the actual quality of social life assumed to be ushered in with democracy (O'Donnell 1996; see also Dahl 1998). See Huber and Stephens (2012) for an in-depth discussion of social inequality and social policy; and Fishman (2017) for an account of the vital role civil society plays in democratization.

10. Dubow (2014, 268) notes, in particular, that the number of people killed in this period was three times greater than those who had died from political violence in the previous six years.

11. See Dubow (2014, 268–272) for a description and analysis of the violence.

12. See Ebrahim (1999); Gloppen (1997/2020); and Klug (2010) on the process of creating the Constitution.

13. See, for example, Gibson (2006); and Philpott (2012).

14. These social imaginaries were articulated by such leaders as Nelson Mandela (1995) and Desmond Tutu (1996, 2000). For how these ideas resonate with broader, global cultural imaginaries around human rights, see, for example, Dubow (2012); and Risse-Kappen et al. (1999).

15. The country has consistently had one of the highest Gini coefficients (a measure of how wealth is distributed in a society) in the world. For documentation of these trends, see "Six Charts Explain South Africa's Inequality," International Monetary Fund, January 30, 2020, https://www.imf.org/en/News/Articles/2020/01/29/na012820six-charts-on-south-africas-persistent-and-multi-faceted-inequality; and World Bank, *Inequality in Southern Africa: An Assessment of the Southern African Customs Union*, 2022, https://documents1.worldbank.org/curated/en/099125303072236903/pdf/P1649270c02a1f06b0a3ae02e57eadd7a82.pdf. See also, for example, Alexander (2003); Langford et al. (2013); Nattrass and Seekings (2001); and Tshitereke (2006).

16. See, for example, Gibson (2006); Gibson and Gouws (2005); Mamdani (2002); C. Moon (2008); and Wilson (2001). Existing scholarship on post-conflict areas more generally has highlighted the fragility of the process of truth-telling, acknowledging the limits that such work has for truly healing societies ripped apart by conflict, inequality, and violence (Lambourne 2009; Minow 1998).

17. Campbell (1997); Decoteau (2013); Hunter (2010); Jewkes (2010). See also Baxen and Breidlid (2009).

18. For crime trends in the first decade of the democracy, see, for example, Berg and Scharf (2004); Louw (1997); and Schönteich and Louw (2001). News stories about South Africa's

high crime rates have appeared as recently as 2024; see Associated Press, "As Police Lose the War on Crime in South Africa, Private Security Companies Step In," NPR, January 7, 2024, https://www.npr.org/2024/01/07/1223358578/as-police-lose-the-war-on-crime-in-south-africa-private-security-companies-step-#:~:text=Violent%20crime%20in%20South%20Africa%20has%20spiked%20over%20the%20past,with%2016%2C213%20in%202012%2D2013. On corruption, including its connections to the apartheid regime, see, for example, Hyslop (2005); and Lodge (1998). See also the more recent accounts of "state capture" in former president Jacob Zuma's administration in Chipkin and Swilling (2018).

19. As noted in the introduction, the concept of "path dependency" has been a subject of considerable scholarly discussion and debate, particularly among historical sociologists. See, for example, Sewell (1996a, 1996b); Mahoney (2000); and Mahoney and Thelen (2009).
20. *Ecunews*, December 1991, 3.
21. *Ecunews*, December 1991, 3.
22. Borer (1998, 200). The SACC navigated some internal challenges related to finances, too. For example, *Ecunews*, 1996(1), 6, documents patterns of financial problems in the Western Cape.
23. Borer (1998, 201) describes how this was a change from the past, in which the regional offices were given autonomy in order to avoid financial scrutiny by the state.
24. See Borer (1998, 198–203); DeGruchy and DeGruchy (2004, 208); and Göranzon (2010) for further discussions of the SACC's changing structure in the transition and early democracy.
25. Brigalia Bam, who became general secretary after Chikane, articulates this challenge and renewed commitment in *Ecunews*, 1996(3), 15. Borer (1998, 200–201) describes this, too, pointing to the strategic decision to refocus attention on member churches in order to navigate the financial strain.
26. Kuperus (1999). The conference is also discussed in *Ecunews*, 1996(3).
27. Kuperus (1999, 659); see also chap. 7 of Borer (1998).
28. There are interesting descriptions of this work in newsletters. *Ecunews*, 1997(1), 7, for example, includes the leader of their Development Ministries program, Mongezi Guma, describing the need not just to fund projects, but also to engage in both "facilitation" and "capacity building"—helping people to become self-reliant and grow in skills they would need to achieve economic stability.
29. *Ecunews*, November 1992, 4; Mongezi Guma, "Into 1996," *Ecunews*, 1995, 13.
30. These are described in various newsletters; see, for example, *Ecunews*, 1997(1), 14.
31. See, for example, *Ecunews*, 1997(1).
32. *Ecunews*, 1996(3), 18.
33. 2000 Annual Report, 32.
34. SACC and WCC, "International Conference Statement on Reconstructing and Renewing the Church in South Africa," 1995, 2.
35. SACC and WCC 1995, 2.
36. SACC and WCC 1995, 2.
37. The concept of *ubuntu* has been the subject of a range of both popular and scholarly discussion. See, for example, Cornell (2014); Metz (2007); and Schutte (2001). Desmond Tutu famously drew on the concept in interviews and other public venues; see, for example, Tutu (2011).
38. Brigalia Bam, *Ecunews*, 1996(1), 3.
39. Bam, 1996(1), 3.
40. Bam, 1996(1), 3.
41. Bernard Spong, *Ecunews*, 1997(1), 2.
42. *Ecunews*, 1996(3), 23.

43. Brigalia Bam, "South Africa in Its Regional and Global Perspective: Being the Church Today," March 1995, 2.
44. SACC and WCC, 1995, 3.
45. *Ecunews*, December 1991, 11.
46. *Ecunews*, December 1991, 11.
47. Frank Chikane, *Ecunews*, March 1992, 11.
48. *Ecunews*, January–February 1992, 8.
49. *Ecunews*, January–February 1992, 8.
50. Frank Chikane, "Address by the General Secretary to the 26th National Conference of the South African Council of Churches," July 1994, 8.
51. Eddie Makue, "Into 1996," *Ecunews*, 1995, 5.
52. Makue, 1995, 5.
53. Molefe Tsele, "The General Secretariat Report," 2001, 6, emphasis in original.
54. Tsele, 2001, 6.
55. Michael Cassidy, *AE Update*, June 1991, 1.
56. Cassidy, June 1991, 1.
57. This was especially noticeable with the appointment of Mark Manley, who served for under two years. He started in January 2002, and the November 2003 newsletter notes that he had been released from his position.
58. While the Marriage Alliance was formed in the early 2000s, there were quite a few earlier signs of concerns about "biblical sexuality" in AE's newsletters. For instance, biblical sexuality was a theme of discussion at a KwaZulu Natal Christian Leaders Assembly (*AE Update*, April 1996, 1). The April 1996 *AE Update* also highlights a talk Cassidy gave on the future of marriage, including discussion of homosexuality (2). The October 1996 *AE Update* names another talk Cassidy gave on homosexuality (as well as his and others' concerns with abortion) (2). The Marriage Alliance itself is described in AE's biography of Cassidy on its website and discussed in at least one newsletter; see "Michael Cassidy," AE, accessed February 28, 2023, https://africanenterprise.org/our-team/michael-cassidy; and *AE Update*, January 2006, 2.
59. On political violence, see Dubow (2014, 268–272). Schuld (2013) documents the high prevalence of political violence in KwaZulu Natal and provides an interesting analysis of the tendency to separate "political violence" from "crime" in ways that obscure important dynamics of the role of violence in post-conflict situations. Regarding the high rate of HIV/AIDS, see, for example, Zuma et al. (2016); and Zuma et al. (2022).
60. Cassidy (1995).
61. Similarly to the SACC's development programs, AE also founded a program aimed at empowering people with practical skills and knowledge in their communities: a certificate program in Social Empowerment and Development. Newsletters highlight "a thriving fabric-painting business" (*AE Update*, September 1996, 3); describe one of the founders of the program who also facilitated it, Marit Garratt, taking the program to a township in Pretoria (*AE Update*, May 1997, 3); and stress the ways that the program "should be part of every mission undertaken by AE in an effort to be truly contextual in today's Africa" (*AE Update*, August 1997, 3). The African Leadership Development Institute was launched in 1997. The July 1997 *AE Update* highlights its launch, and subsequent ones highlight how the program instills Christian and biblical values into leadership training (e.g., *AE Update*, October 1997, 3) while also being culturally sensitive (e.g., *AE Update*, January 1998, 1).
62. This program is ongoing; for more information, see "Foxfires," AE, accessed February 28, 2023, https://africanenterprise.org/foxfires/. It is also frequently mentioned in newsletters during the 1990s and early 2000s, especially highlighting the various youth participants who have joined the program.
63. Michael Cassidy, *AE Update*, July 1993, 1.

64. Michael Cassidy, *AE Update*, February 1994, 2.
65. Cassidy, February 1994, 2.
66. Michael Cassidy, *AE Update*, April 1995, 2.
67. Cassidy, April 1995, 2.
68. Soh Chye Ann, *AE Update*, November 1995, 2.
69. Soh, November 1995, 2.
70. Mike Odell, *AE Update*, August–September 2000, 2.
71. Odell, August–September 2000, 2.
72. Mark Manley, *AE Update*, April 2003, 2.
73. Michael Cassidy, *AE Update*, July 1992, 2.
74. Thanks to Lisa Weaver Swartz for this analytic observation.
75. Michael Cassidy, *AE Update*, March 1993, 2.
76. Cassidy, March 1993, 2.
77. Michael Cassidy, *AE Update*, August 1993, 1.
78. Michael Cassidy, *AE Update*, November 1992, 2.
79. Cassidy, November 1992, 2. Andries Treurnicht was a minister in the Dutch Reformed Church and a key architect of apartheid policies, most notably insisting that children be taught in Afrikaans, which led to the Soweto uprisings in 1976 (Dubow 2014, 179–180). He then led a far-right wing to break away from the National Party and formed the Conservative Party, which remained committed to policies of separate governance and development.
80. Cassidy, November 1992, 2.
81. Cassidy, November 1992, 2.
82. Cassidy, November 1992, 2.
83. *AE Update*, October 2002, 7.
84. Levine (2002, 56).
85. Neville Richardson, *PACSA Newsletter*, April 1992, 1.
86. Richardson, April 1992, 1.
87. Richardson, April 1992, 1.
88. Different accounts render slightly different figures. The TRC of South Africa (1998) reports that "over 100 people were killed, some 3,000 homes were destroyed by fire, and approximately 30,000 people fled their homes because of the violence" (2:475–476). It also records that "over seven days, 200 residents in the lower valley were killed, hundreds of houses looted and burnt down and as many as 20,000 people forced to flee for their lives" (3:259). PACSA's (2009, 41) internal history reports that twenty thousand people were displaced.
89. PACSA (2009, 55).
90. Levine (2002, 46).
91. Levine (2002, 72).
92. Initially, Gennrich and another staff member, Samuel Chingondole, were co-directors. But Gennrich writes as director in PACSA's Annual Reports for 2003–2005, which suggests the organization simplified this structure after only a short amount of time.
93. Levine (2002, 41, 73). PACSA's Annual Reports document some of the sources of its income. For example, the 1999 Annual Report expresses the support that their funding partners gave during the transition to Karen Buckenham's leadership after Peter Kerchhoff's unexpected death (7); and the 2002 Gender Programme Report notes that visitors from Norwegian Church Aid visited its program on Poverty, Women, and HIV/AIDS.
94. See Levine (2002, 45–79) for detailed descriptions of these various efforts.
95. See, for example, *PACSA Newsletter*, Christmas 2004. PACSA also published several factsheets that discussed the problem, including one on "Challenges Facing Young People" (Factsheet #48, November 2000) and one on "Gender, Poverty and HIV/AIDS: What Ordinary People Living with HIV/AIDS Want Decisionmakers to Know" (Factsheet #52, August 2004). See chapter 5 for further discussion of their practical efforts to address the issue.

96. Factsheets covered a variety of topics, from economic injustice to abandoned children to capital punishment; see Levine (2000, 76) for a list.
97. *PACSA Newsletter*, July 1992, 4.
98. 1999 Annual Report, 1, 6–7; *PACSA Newsletter*, July 2000, 9.
99. Levine (2002, 108–109).
100. Robin Hutt, *PACSA Newsletter*, December 1992, 2.
101. Hutt, December 1992, 2.
102. Karen Buckenham, *PACSA Newsletter*, Easter 1996, 1.
103. Buckenham, Easter 1996, 1.
104. Buckenham, Easter 1996, 1.
105. Tim Nuttall, *PACSA Newsletter*, Easter 1997, 1.
106. Nuttall, Easter 1997, 1.
107. Nuttall, Easter 1997, 1.
108. Livingstone Ngewu, *PACSA Newsletter*, Easter 2003, 1.
109. Ngewu, Easter 2003, 1.
110. Sid Luckett, *PACSA Newsletter*, August 1991, 1.
111. Luckett, August 1991, 1.
112. John Aitchison, *PACSA Newsletter*, October 1994, 2.
113. Moshe Rajuili, *PACSA Newsletter*, October 1994, 1.
114. Rajuili, October 1994, 1.
115. Mzwandili Rodrigo Nunes, *PACSA Newsletter*, Easter 1995, 1.
116. Nunes, Easter 1995, 1.
117. Beverley Haddad, *PACSA Newsletter*, July 1996, 1.
118. Haddad, July 1996, 1.
119. Renate Cochrane, *PACSA Newsletter*, Christmas 1996, 1.
120. Cochrane, Christmas 1996, 2.
121. Cochrane, Christmas 1996, 2.
122. *PACSA Newsletter*, Easter 2000, 1.
123. *PACSA Newsletter*, Easter 2000, 1.

CHAPTER 3   THEOLOGICAL CULTURES AND GENDER-BASED VIOLENCE

Epigraph: Phiri (2002, 20).

1. Human Rights Watch, *Violence against Women in South Africa: State Response to Domestic Violence and Rape*, November 1, 1995, https://www.hrw.org/legacy/reports/1995/Safricawm-02.htm. The origins and the accuracy of the phrase "rape capital of the world" have been debated publicly. In one of the most frequently cited studies of the prevalence of rape in South Africa, medical researchers Rachel Jewkes and Naeema Abrahams credited the Human Rights Watch report itself with the phrase, but I could not find the phrase in the original report (Jewkes and Abrahams 2002). Various news sources have credited Interpol with using the phrase, but according to at least one South African newspaper, Interpol denied using it. See "Why It Is Wrong to Call SA (or Any Country) the 'Rape Capital of the World,'" *Mail & Guardian*, January 29, 2014, https://mg.co.za/article/2014-01-29-why-it-is-wrong-to-call-sa-or-any-country-the-rape-capital-of-the-world/. Whether just a catchy sound bite or accurate description, the phrase has certainly drawn attention to the high rates of violence against women.
2. Charlene Smith (2001).
3. Helen Moffett (2006, 133) provides a helpful summary of the events and interaction between the two figures.

4. For a detailed timeline of these events, see "Timeline of the Jacob Zuma Rape Trial," *Mail & Guardian*, March 21, 2006, https://mg.co.za/article/2006-03-21-timeline-of-the-jacob-zuma-rape-trial/.
5. Pistorius was initially found guilty of manslaughter, not murder, and sentenced to five years in prison. An appeals court overturned that decision, finding that he was guilty of murder, but sentenced him to only six years in prison. Prosecutors appealed this sentence, which was overturned by the Supreme Court of Appeals, and he was sentenced to thirteen years and five months in prison. For a timeline of these events, see Gerald Imlay, "Track Star, Convicted Killer, Now Parolee. A Timeline of Oscar Pistorius's Life," AP News, January 5, 2024, https://apnews.com/article/oscar-pistorius-parole-murder-reeva-steenkamp-8223c09a76e2e5deca052 71eb65c26b2).
6. For an analysis of some of these dynamics, see, for example, Britton (2020); Hassim (2009); Langa et al. (2018); Moffett (2006); and Robins (2008).
7. Some of the important works to document the high prevalence of GBV initially include Jewkes and Abrahams (2002); Jewkes et al. (2002); Mathewes et al. (2004); Vetten (2007); and Walker (2005). This pattern of high levels of GBV has continued; see Abrahams et al. (2012). Even more recently, political scientist Amanda Gouws, who has written extensively about these topics, published a thought piece; see Amanda Gouws, "Violence against Women Is Staggeringly High in South Africa—a Different Way of Thinking about It Is Needed," *The Conversation*, November 30, 2022, https://theconversation.com/violence-against-women-is-staggeringly-high-in-south-africa-a-different-way-of-thinking-about-it-is-needed-195053. She documents the persistence of these high rates of GBV and suggests several avenues for addressing it. See also Govender (2023).
8. See Britton (2020) for a helpful overview of various policies and other efforts to address the problem.
9. Brigalia Bam, "South Africa in Its Regional and Global Perspective: Being the Church Today," March 1995, 10.
10. See, for example, Jankowski et al. (2018); Levitt and Ware (2006); Nason-Clark (1997); Nason-Clark et al. (2018); and Sharp (2009). In some of my other work, I have also documented how institutional debates about gender ideology shape religious organizations' discursive responses to the problem, highlighting how adopting a defensive posture regarding gender beliefs results in pivoting away from abused women's experiences (Whitnah 2022).
11. See, for example, Brusco (1995); Cunradi et al. (2002); Ellison and Anderson (2001); Ellison et al. (1999); Griffith (2000); and Wilcox (2004).
12. Hannah Britton's (2020, 76) work highlights, for instance, the ways in which pastors can play a crucial role in naming the reality of domestic violence and challenging social norms that can justify violence against women. But she also makes clear that these efforts can be "regressive" in actually preventing violence in the first place, given the role of religion in perpetuating women's subordinate status to men. In chap. 6 of *Solidarity and Defiant Spirituality: Africana Lessons on Religion, Racism, and Ending Gender Violence*, Traci West (2019) discusses the role that collective rituals can play in forming solidarity regarding violence against LGBT people, the importance of recognizing that there are a range of spiritual resources to draw on in responding to and healing from such violence, and the fraught nature of Christian activists entering spaces where those who have experienced violence view Christian leaders and institutions with skepticism because of the unhelpful, harmful, complicit role they have played regarding homophobia and sexism.
13. This insight has been central to the work of two of the early and consistent writers on intersectionality, Patricia Hill Collins (1998, 2017) and Kimberlé Crenshaw (1991). See also E. A. Anderson et al. (2018); and Whittier (2016).
14. Collins (1998, 922).

15. Moffett (2006, 143). Lisa Vetten, who was the Gender program manager for the Centre for the Study of Violence and Reconciliation at the time, makes a similar point in an op-ed she wrote concerning the public debate between Charlene Smith and Thabo Mbeki. She notes Smith's lack of accuracy in some of the statistics she presents, and Mbeki's problematic deflection away from the gendered nature of the problem. Vetten writes: "We need to understand the complex interplay between race, class and gender in a more subtle way if we are to address the causes of rape, and challenge societal responses to the problem. This cannot be done in any meaningful way when gender is erased from the discussion." Lisa Vetten, "Mbeki and Smith Both Got It Wrong," *Mail and Guardian*, November 2, 2004, https://mg.co.za/article/2004-11-02-mbeki-and-smith-both-got-it-wrong/.
16. The image is included as part of a flyer for a Good Friday service sponsored by the Diakonia Council of Churches in Durban. Dina Cormick, a Durban-based artist, is credited with the image; see *PACSA Newsletter*, Easter 2001, 1.
17. Susan Rakoczy, *PACSA Newsletter*, Easter 2001, 2.
18. Rakoczy, Easter 2001, 2.
19. Rakoczy, Easter 2001, 2.
20. Rakoczy, Easter 2001, 2.
21. Rakoczy, Easter 2001, 2. Here, Rakoczy refers to the resurrection narrative in John 20.
22. Rakoczy, Easter 2001, 2.
23. Rakoczy, Easter 2001, 2.
24. Peter Kerchhoff, *PACSA Newsletter*, June 1985.
25. Kerchhoff, June 1985.
26. Kerchhoff, June 1985.
27. Kerchhoff, June 1985.
28. Kerchhoff, June 1985.
29. Kerchhoff, June 1985.
30. Kerchhoff, June 1985.
31. Kerchhoff, June 1985. Kerchhoff notes that he draws these four steps from the work of J. Holland and P. Henriot regarding "'the faith that does justice.'" This is likely a reference to Holland and Henriot's (1983) book, *Social Analysis: Linking Faith and Justice*.
32. Kerchhoff, June 1985.
33. Kerchhoff, June 1985.
34. See the introduction for more on this history, as well as the ways in which this pattern of awareness of the problem emerging through local-level organizations before becoming a more public concern also mirrors the global movement to end violence against women.
35. Kerchhoff, June 1985.
36. Karen Buckenham, *PACSA Newsletter*, October 1994, 5.
37. Buckenham, October 1994, 5.
38. Buckenham, October 1994, 5.
39. Buckenham, October 1994, 5.
40. Buckenham, October 1994, 5.
41. Buckenham, October 1994, 5.
42. Buckenham, October 1994, 5.
43. Buckenham, October 1994, 5.
44. Karen Buckenham, *PACSA Newsletter*, Easter 1999, 8.
45. Buckenham, Easter 1999, 8.
46. Buckenham, Easter 1999, 8.
47. Buckenham, Easter 1999, 8.
48. Buckenham, Easter 1999, 8.
49. Karen Buckenham, *PACSA Newsletter*, September 1999, 13.

50. Buckenham, September 1999, 13.
51. Buckenham, September 1999, 14.
52. Buckenham, September 1999, 14.
53. Beverley Haddad, *PACSA Newsletter*, September 2001, 1. This international campaign runs from November 25 (an International Day for the Elimination of Violence against Women) through December 10 (International Human Rights Day). According to the UN Women's program, "The campaign was started by activists at the inauguration of the Women's Global Leadership Institute in 1991. It is used as an organizing strategy by individuals and organizations around the world to call for the prevention and elimination of violence against women and girls." "16 Days of Activism against Gender-Based Violence," UN Women, accessed November 13, 2023, https://www.unwomen.org/en/what-we-do/ending-violence-against-women/unite/16-days-of-activism.
54. Haddad, September 2001, 1.
55. Haddad, September 2001, 1.
56. Kesavan Kisten, *PACSA Newsletter*, September 2001, 3.
57. Kisten, September 2001, 3.
58. Kisten, September 2001, 3.
59. Kisten, September 2001, 3.
60. The genocide began on April 7, 1994, and lasted one hundred days. Estimates of the human toll vary, but up to one million Rwandans may have been killed, primarily members of the Tutsi minority group at the hands of the Hutu majority. For detailed accounts see, for example, Jessee (2017); Mamdani (2001); and C. C. Taylor (1999/2020). For an account of the role of religion in the genocide and a theological articulation of its theological implications, see Katongole (2009). The United Nations also provides a timeline about the event in their program to prevent future genocides; see "Historical Background," United Nations, accessed February 27, 2024, https://www.un.org/en/preventgenocide/rwanda/historical-background.shtml.
61. Ralph Jarvis, *AE Update*, September 1995, 1.
62. Jarvis, September 1995, 1.
63. Jarvis, September 1995, 1.
64. Jarvis, September 1995, 1.
65. Abiel Thipanyane, *AE Update*, April 1999, 2.
66. Thipanyane, April 1999, 2.
67. Thipanyane, April 1999, 2.
68. Greg Smerdon, *AE Update*, January 2007, 1.
69. *AE Update*, April 2001, 1.
70. This narrative does contain indicators of the importance of other lines of difference: the newsletter story reports that Christians in the community were able to put aside "doctrinal differences" they had with one another in order to come together and minister to the suffering people (*AE Update*, April 2001, 1). I mention this because it is important to attend to the ways that AE's discourse does have the potential—in multiple respects—to facilitate their recognition of GBV as a gendered issue, along with the other lines of difference (racial, cultural, denominational) that they are much more poised to recognize.
71. *AE Update*, October 2002, 5.
72. *AE Update*, October 2002, 5.
73. *AE Update*, October 2002, 5.
74. *AE Update*, April 2001, 3.
75. *AE Update*, April 2001, 3.
76. *AE Update*, April 2001, 3.
77. *AE Update*, April 2003, 2.
78. *AE Update*, April 2003, 2.

79. *AE Update*, September 2002, 4.
80. *AE Update*, August 1990, 4.
81. *AE Update*, August 1990, 4.
82. *AE Update*, August 1990, 4.
83. *AE Update*, August 1990, 4.
84. *AE Update*, December 1995, 3.
85. *AE Update*, December 1995, 3.
86. The WCC's website includes a reflection by one of the key women who initiated this program; see "A Look Back: The Founding of the Ecumenical Decade of Churches in Solidarity with Women," WCC, October 2, 2018, https://www.oikoumene.org/news/a-look-back-the-founding-of-the-ecumenical-decade-of-churches-in-solidarity-with-women.
87. Sigqibo Dwane, "SACC Central Committee Meeting: 11–12 March 1997, the President's Address," March 1997, 2.
88. Dwane, March 1997, 2.
89. Dwane, March 1997, 3.
90. Dwane, March 1997, 3.
91. Dwane, March 1997, 3.
92. Dwane, March 1997, 3.
93. Mbulelo Linda, *Ecunews*, November 1989, 8.
94. Linda, November 1989, 8.
95. Linda, November 1989, 8.
96. Linda, November 1989, 8.
97. 1999 Annual Report, 1.
98. 1999 Annual Report, 1.
99. 1999 Annual Report, 1.
100. 2001 Annual Report, 31–32.
101. 2001 Annual Report, 2001, 32.
102. 2003 Annual Report, 54.
103. Faith and Mission Unit Report, 1992, 3.
104. Brigalia Bam, *Ecunews*, 1997, 3.
105. Bam, 1997, 3.
106. Bam, March 1995, 10.
107. Bam, March 1995, 11.
108. Bam, March 1995, 6.
109. Bam, March 1995, 2.

CHAPTER 4 THEOLOGICAL CULTURES AND THE FRAGILITY OF GENDER JUSTICE

Epigraph: Duncan in Margaret Nash, ed., "Women, a Power for Change: SACC Conference Report," 1985, 25.

1. *Ecunews*, special issue, August 1985, 3.
2. As discussed in chapter 1, there have been some important analyses of the significance of this period for the churches' witness against apartheid, as well as variations in how that witness was expressed and demonstrated. See, for example, Borer (1998); Walshe (1991); and DeGruchy and DeGruchy (2004).
3. A particular resolution at the 1982 National Conference (Resolution #18) is referenced in a letter from Virginia Gcabashe to the General Secretary in April 1984. The specific theme, "Women, a Power for Change," was approved at the 1984 National Conference (*Ecunews*, June–July 1985, 3).

Importantly, this theme emerged in the context of some tensions within the organization about whether women's voices and experiences were adequately recognized. See chapter 5 for an analysis of the processes that led to different organizational spaces for addressing gender issues.

4. *Ecunews*, special issue, August 1985, 3.

5. Of course, there certainly were significant life and death issues in this tumultuous and violent time. Thus, my point is not to detract from the real and urgent concerns with the sociopolitical context. Rather, it is to note the discursive separation made between attention to women and attention to political upheaval. This is important both for the SACC's application of the liberation theological culture to women, as analyzed in this chapter, and for their organizational attention to GBV, as discussed in chapter 5.

6. *Ecunews*, special issue, August 1985, 4, emphasis added.

7. See, for example, Ridgeway (2011); and Ridgeway and Correll (2004).

8. Both authors have devoted significant attention to these patterns; see, especially, England (2010); and Ridgeway (2011).

9. These scholars' work has been applied in a significant range of empirical cases. In addition to their own empirical research (e.g., England 2010; Ridgeway 2001, 2011; Ridgeway and Balkwell 1997), studies have applied these insights about the role of cultural beliefs about gender to a range of empirical cases, from funeral home directors (Donley and Baird 2017) to the gendered negotiation of domestic tasks (e.g., Cooke and Hook 2018; Doan and Quadlin 2019) to work-family programs (Briscoe and Kellogg 2011). See also the 2011 "England Symposium" in *Gender and Society* 25(1), which includes critical engagement with England's (2010) article.

10. There is an extensive literature on the intersections of gender and religion, and particularly the social significance of gendered religious belief systems. See, for example, Ammerman (1987); Avishai (2008); Avishai et al. (2015); Bartkowski (1997, 2001); Chong (2008); Darwin (2018); Davidman (1991); Gallagher (2003); Gerber (2015); Heath (2003); Ingersoll (2003); Irby (2014); Leamaster and Einwohner (2018); Mahmood (2005); Rao (2015); Rinaldo (2019); and Wilcox (2004). But, as Avishai and Irby (2017) also note, despite the clear empirical evidence of connections between gender and religion, religion scholars have not always adequately theorized and documented the centrality of gender for religion, and gender scholars have not always adequately theorized and documented the centrality of religion for gender. Recent work that documents patterns of attention and inattention to gender by religion scholars and to religion by gender scholars helps to illuminate the importance of addressing these "bifurcated conversations." See also Charlton (2015).

11. See, for example, Weaver-Swartz (2022); and Whitnah (2022).

12. Dawne Moon (2004) provides a particularly compelling analysis of these kinds of patterns in relation to Methodist churches' understandings of homosexuality.

13. Joan Kerchhoff, "The Church and the Poor," October 1984, 1, emphasis in original.

14. Kerchhoff, October 1984, 1.

15. Karen Buckenham, "All about Love," *PACSA Newsletter*, Christmas 2001, 1. Buckenham is referring to bell hooks's (1999) book *All about Love*.

16. Buckenham, Christmas 2001, 2.

17. Buckenham, Christmas 2001, 2.

18. Buckenham, Christmas 2001, 2.

19. Mike Deeb, *PACSA Newsletter*, December 1988, 1.

20. Gunther Wittenberg, *PACSA Newsletter*, December 1998, 2.

21. Graham Lindegger, *PACSA Newsletter*, Easter 2001, 4.

22. Gunther Wittenberg, *PACSA Newsletter*, September 1981, 1.

23. Robin Hutt, *PACSA Newsletter*, December 1992, 1.

24. Hutt, December 1992, 1.

25. Hutt, December 1992, 1.

26. Janet Trisk, *PACSA Newsletter*, December 1996, 11.
27. Purity Malinga, "Women in Church Leadership: Co-Option or Transformation?," *PACSA Newsletter*, September 2001, 4.
28. Malinga, September 2001, 5.
29. Malinga, September 2001, 5.
30. Malinga, September 2001, 5.
31. Malinga, September 2001, 6.
32. Malinga, September 2001, 6.
33. Barbel Wartenberg-Potter, "Feminist Theology," *PACSA Newsletter*, Easter 2000, 10.
34. Wartenberg-Potter, Easter 2000, 10.
35. Thanks to Felicia Song for helping me make this analytic observation.
36. Michael Cassidy, *AE Update*, November 1997, 2.
37. *AE Update*, May 1983, 2.
38. *AE Update*, May 1983, 2. See Dubow (2014) and Worden (2000) on the significance of the formation of Bantustans. The terminology for describing the ruler of the Transkei Bantustan varies; "President" is what is used in the AE newsletter and is thus used here.
39. Phineas Dube, *AE Update*, June 2005, 4.
40. Dube, June 2005, 4.
41. *AE Update*, February 2003, 1.
42. *AE Update*, February 2003.
43. *AE Update*, May 1983, 2.
44. *AE Update*, May 1983, 2.
45. *AE Update*, May 1992, 2.
46. *AE Update*, May 1992, 2.
47. *AE Update*, March 1998, 3.
48. *AE Update*, March 1998, 3.
49. *AE Update*, March 1998, 3.
50. *AE Update*, October 2005, 4.
51. In addition to making for a dramatic conversion story, this narrative reflects a long-standing historical pattern in Christianity that associates women's sexuality with sinfulness. This association has been traced through early Christian thinking regarding the entrance of sin into the world through the figure of Eve, who then enticed Adam into sin (Fiorenza 1983/1994; Pagels 1989). This reference to the woman seductress resonates through other historical periods, including the Protestant Reformation (Lemmond 2009; Moxey 1989) and in relation to contemporary visions of womanhood as well (Riesebrodt 1993). Another biblical woman often associated with sexual sin is the Samaritan woman whom Jesus meets and interacts with at a well, as narrated in John 4. See Reeder (2022) for both an analysis of historical and contemporary Christian thought on this association and an alternative interpretation.
52. *AE Update*, October 2005, 4.
53. *AE Update*, June 1993, 5.
54. *AE Update*, October 2005, 1.
55. *AE Update*, October 2005, 1.
56. *AE Update*, October 2005, 1.
57. *AE Update*, May 2002, 4.
58. *AE Update*, May 2002, 4.
59. *AE Update*, May 2002, 4.
60. *AE Update*, May 2002, 4.
61. *AE Update*, May 2002, 4.
62. *AE Update*, August–September 2000, 11.
63. *AE Update*, August–September 2000, 11.

64. *AE Update*, February 2000, 8, emphasis added.

65. These dynamics within the SACC mirrored some tensions within the broader liberation movement concerning the inclusion of women in the struggle for justice, and the work of women within the broader movement to call attention to the gendered dimensions of the apartheid regime. See, for example, Hassim (2006); Meintjes et al. (1993); Patel (1988); Seidman (1993); and C. Walker (1982/1991). In fact, women's involvement in the struggle against apartheid and the development of concern for women's rights in South Africa mirrors a trend that has been established in recent years by scholars of women's movements, particularly in "Third World" countries (Molyneux 2001; Ray and Korteweg 1999). We know from these studies that women are involved in liberation movements in a variety of ways, and that there are often tensions that exist between such movements and the explicitly stated needs and demands of women (Ferree and Tripp 2006; Jaquette 1994; Tripp et al. 2009). These studies have illuminated the importance of understanding the multivalent dimensions of women's participation in the civil sphere.

66. "Women's Dialogue: National Conference 1982—48 Hour Women's Dialogue Report," *Ecunews*, December 1982, 17.

67. "Women's Dialogue," December 1982, 17.

68. "Women's Dialogue," December 1982, 17.

69. "Women's Dialogue," December 1982, 17.

70. "SACC National Conference: A Report to the SACC Conference, 25–29 June 1984, from the Christian Women's Movement," *Ecunews*, June–July 1984, 35.

71. "SACC National Conference," June–July 1984, 35.

72. "SACC National Conference," June–July 1984, 35.

73. Here, the women make a similar argument to what the organization contended about the need to help black people recognize and embrace their dignity as a key component of their liberation. These ideas resonated with the Black Consciousness Movement, black theology in the United States, and contextual theology in South Africa, as I discuss in chapter 1. See Biko (1978/2002); Fatton (1986); Gerhart (1978); Hirschmann (1990); and Magaziner (2010) on the Black Consciousness Movement. See DeGruchy and DeGruchy (2004, 146–164) for the ways in which black theology was formed in relation to the Black Consciousness Movement.

74. "Women, a Power for Change: SACC Conference Report," *Ecunews*, August 1985, 4.

75. "Women, a Power for Change," August 1985, 4.

76. "Women, a Power for Change," August 1985, 4.

77. Brigalia Bam, "Being a Woman," Annual General Meeting of the Women's Ministries Division, March 1989, 2.

78. This, too, mirrored concerns in the broader liberation movement; see Hassim (2006); and Seidman (1993, 1999). As the transition to democracy became more imminent, the tensions continue between recognizing women's contributions and their need for liberation from structures that prevent their full contributions to society.

79. See chapter 2 for a discussion of this shift in the organization's identity and practices. See also Borer (1999); and DeGruchy and DeGruchy (2004).

80. See chapter 5 for additional analysis of these organizational processes for a more in-depth analysis of the SACC's approach to gender.

81. Brigalia Bam, "South African Council of Churches Report on the Programmes of the Council," National Conference of the SACC, 1991, 12.

82. This theme, too, presents an important resonance with the broader liberation struggle. See, for example, Hassim (2006, 76–81) for discussion of the relation of "motherism" to the development of nonracialism in the broader liberation movement.

83. See Gaitskell (2002, 381) for brief discussion of Turner and her organization.

84. Shirley Turner, "Women's Work," Meetings of the National Committee of Justice and Reconciliation, April 1973, 4.

85. Turner, 1973, 4.
86. Turner, 1973, 4.
87. Turner, 1973, 5.
88. Turner, 1973, 5.
89. As discussed in chapter 1, the SACC devoted considerable attention to the apartheid policies that forcibly removed black people from their homes and to the Bantustans. See, for example, Dubow (2014, 112–117); and Worden (2000, 125–126) on the significance of forced removals for the apartheid regime.
90. Wolfram Kistner, "Report of the Division of Justice and Reconciliation for the National Conference of the SACC, June 1982," reprinted in *Ecunews*, November 1982, 26.
91. Kistner, 1982, 26.
92. See, for example, Bullough (2000); Petrou (2002); Ramos (2008); Rhee (2020); and Weyerman (2002).
93. Desmond Tutu, "Love Reveals My Neighbor, My Responsibility," 1981.
94. Tutu, 1981, emphasis in original.
95. *Ecunews*, December 1982, 17.
96. *Ecunews*, December 1982, 18.
97. Margaret Nash, ed., "Women, a Power for Change: SACC Conference Report," 1985, 2.
98. Nash, 1985, 2.
99. Nash, 1985, 2.
100. Nash, 1985, 2–3.
101. Venita Meyer, "Report on Women and Apartheid Conference," 1986, 3.
102. Meyer, 1986, 3.
103. Meyer, 1986, 3.
104. Lulama Xingwana, "Women's Division," 1987, 2.
105. Xingwana, 1987, 2.
106. Sigqibo Dwane, "SACC President's Address to the Central Committee," July 1996.
107. Dwane 1996, emphasis in original.

CHAPTER 5 IMPLICATIONS FOR ACTIONS

Epigraph: Buckenham (1999, 10).

1. Duncan (1991, 386).
2. Duncan (1991, 386).
3. Duncan (1991, 386–387).
4. Duncan (1991, 387) quotes this part of the declaration, and it can also be found in Alberts and Chikane (1991).
5. Duncan (1991, 387).
6. Duncan (1991, 390).
7. Duncan (1991, 390).
8. This phrasing draws on the book of Acts 2:44–47, which describes key features of the early church: "All who believed were together and had all things in common; they would sell their possessions and goods and distribute the proceeds to all, as any had need. Day by day, they spent much time together in the temple, they broke bread at home and ate their food with glad and generous hearts, praising God and having the goodwill of all the people" (New Revised Standard Version).
9. See, for example, Barnett (1993); Browne (1999); Cott (1987); Crenshaw (2010); Evans (1979); Ferree and Roth (1998); Ferree and Tripp (2006); Hurwitz and Crossley (2019); Jaquette (1989, 1994); Kuumba (2002); Lerner (1998); McAdam (1992); D. Meyer and Whittier (1994);

Molyneux (1998, 2001); Moynagh and Forestell (2012); Nicholson (1997); Ray and Korteweg (1999); Robnett (1997); Roth (2004); Tripp et al. (2009); Yellin and Van Horne (1994).

10. See especially the opening section of chapter 1 on race and the opening section of chapter 4 on gender.

11. As I discussed in the introduction, the intersection of religion with social inequality has been the subject of a broad range of empirical work. Melissa Wilde's concept of "complex religion" is particularly helpful for capturing this important reality; see Wilde (2018a, 2018b, 2019); and Wilde and Glassman (2016).

12. "Rape," PACSA Factsheet #44, June 1998; "Domestic Violence Part 1—Wife Abuse," PACSA Factsheet #45, November 1998. While the factsheet on domestic violence was titled "Part 1," I did not find or see references to subsequent parts. Also, multiple documents reference a factsheet that was also published in 1998 on "Gender, Violence and HIV/AIDS," but I could not find an original copy (it is referenced in a *Gender, Violence and HIV/AIDS* workbook, in Factsheet #52 on "Gender/Poverty/HIV/AIDS," and in reports from the Gender program). While it is difficult to gauge their impact, various reports indicate that the factsheets were reprinted multiple times and that they were published in both English and Zulu (e.g., the Six-Month Report of the Gender Programme, January–June 2001, notes that they reprinted 2,000 Zulu copies of the "Domestic Violence" factsheet, 4,000 English copies of the "Rape" factsheet, and 2,000 Zulu copies of the "Rape" factsheet (8). Factsheets on other topics sometimes also included attention to domestic and sexual violence, including one on children at risk and another on gender, poverty, and HIV/AIDS ("Children at Risk," PACSA Factsheet #40, March 1995; and "Gender, Poverty and HIV/AIDS: What Ordinary People Living with HIV/AIDS Want Decisionmakers to Know," PACSA Factsheet #52, August 2004).

13. These efforts are described, for instance, in the 1998 Annual Report (11–17) and the 1999 Annual Report (14).

14. Buckenham (1999).

15. This campaign was begun in 1991 by the Women's Global Leadership Institute. It is now also supported by the United Nations. For its history and additional details, see "16 Days of Activism against Gender-Based Violence," UN Women, accessed March 12, 2024, https://www.unwomen.org/en/what-we-do/ending-violence-against-women/unite/16-days-of-activism.

16. The liturgy is included in a pamphlet entitled "No Violence against Women and Children: 16 Days of Activism 25 November—10 December: Prayers and Readings to Be Used in Services."

17. For instance, Buckenham recounts in the 1996 Annual Report that a common question she is asked is, "'How do we reach the men? How do we stop the men from doing this?'" (10–11). She describes presenting on GBV to gender-mixed groups (e.g., in the 1997 Annual Report) and addressing men's gender socialization (1999 Annual Report, 14).

18. 2001 Annual Report, 15–16.

19. As noted in the 2007 Gender Programme Report, this included both the regional office of the SACC, the KwaZulu Natal Council of Churches, and Ujaama, an organization working to end GBV. Descriptions of these initiatives can be seen in the various reports of the Gender program, and the history summarized in the 2007 Gender Programme Report. This commitment to attending to men as part of the gender work was consistently affirmed, but the practical work on this project experienced some setbacks as the organization navigated staffing challenges. These included the departure of the initial worker, Wayne Alexander, for a full-time position elsewhere. And there was a conflict between Beverley Haddad and Lihle Dlamini over death-threat emails Haddad had received that appeared as though they might be coming from Lihle's husband. Failure to resolve this situation resulted in both staff being released from PACSA in 2002 (both the 2002 Annual Report and Gender Programme Reports from this time document these situations).

20. The 2002 Gender Programme Final Report notes that Gennrich had worked at uMgeni AIDS Center in Hilton (17).
21. 2004 Annual Report.
22. Buckenham (1999, 117).
23. Buckenham (1999, 119).
24. There are numerous instances of this, in addition to the excerpt from the resource manual. Multiple documents describe "spiritual abuse" as a crucial part of the problem. As Buckenham writes in the resource manual, "This is when a woman's faith is used to keep her from finding help, or leaving an abusive situation, by telling her that she must endure, submit, return and make sure she doesn't do anything to upset her husband, etc. She is led to believe the abuse is her fault, and that if she seeks to leave, she is unChristian, and will be condemned by God. The Bible is quoted to her literally, particularly passages that serve to 'put her in her place,' condemn divorce, or glorify suffering" (Buckenham 1999, 51). This inclusion of spiritual violence as an important dimension of GBV resonates in other documents, including the PACSA workbook on *Gender, Violence, and HIV & AIDS* (5). This explicitly theological grounding of the problem is buttressed also by scriptural references. The text of John 10:10 appears in multiple documents, in which Jesus states, "The thief comes only to steal and kill and destroy. I came that they may have life, and have it abundantly" (e.g., "Domestic Violence" factsheet, 1). The Old Testament story of David's daughter Tamar being raped by her brother Amnon also makes multiple appearances, including in the resource manual (Buckenham 1999, 116) and in the "Rape" factsheet (1).
25. *PACSA Newsletter*, October 1992, 8. This reemergence of a gender concern mirrors the discourse in the broader social context, as the democratic transition included explicit discussions of the need to incorporate women's rights in the constitution. PACSA's own internal process thus reflects the growing awareness in the broader social context of the need to attend to gender issues—something the secular feminist movement had been advocating for years and was working to mobilize into a concrete (constitutional) reality (Hassim 2006).
26. She describes this, for instance, in the 1995 Annual Report (10).
27. The 2000 Annual Report (13) and the Gender Programme Six-Month Report, January–June 2001 (1) both narrate this history.
28. These activities are described in detail in Gender Programme Reports (e.g., Gender Programme Final Report, January–December 2002) and Annual Reports (e.g., 2001, 2002, and 2003). I was given access to several internal reports of these programs, as well. These include a report of the gender audit (Beverley Haddad, "Gender and Theological Institutions of the Cluster Final Report, September 2002") and an undated report of the HIV/AIDS and poverty project (Daniela Gennrich, with Thembela Njenga, "Final Report on the Gender, Poverty and HIV/AIDS Research Project").
29. These topics are presented across *Women in God's Image* issues, including in April 2002, August 2007, and November 2009.
30. There are many instances of this throughout PACSA's documents. For instance, Beverley Haddad's report on the gender audit project for the local theological institutions opens with these lines: "Christianity plays a crucial role in the lives of a large percentage of South Africans and acts as a powerful social force in shaping attitudes and behaviour. Patriarchy dominates all the major religions practised in South Africa which are deeply influenced by a variety of cultural practices which also inhibit attempts at gender equality. At this juncture in our history it is important that theological institutions take seriously questions of gender equality" (Haddad, 2002, 1).
31. This included the volatile political scene, as discussed in chapter 2, and factors such as the situation with fieldworker Lihle Dlamini and Gender Desk coordinator Beverley Haddad (see note 19 above). In terms of funding and the broader landscape, for example, the 2004 Annual

Report notes the challenge of finding donors and the need to "professionalize" in order to satisfy donor demands (3).

32. Efforts to address the *manyanos* are described in a range of materials, including the Annual Reports for 1997, 1998, 1999, and 2000 (13–14), as well as the Six-Month Report of the Gender Programme, January–June 2001 (7–8).

33. The Final Report of the Gender Programme, January–December 2002, states that "this stream of work was redirected" (6) due to the various challenges that the organization (fieldworker Lihle Dlamini, in particular, who had led this effort) had faced in attempting to work with these groups.

34. See chapter 1, as well as Coomes (2002, 415–416).

35. Coomes (2002, 375–384). This program lasted until August 1996, according to the December 1996 *AE Update*, which notes that it had "to a large extent been taken over by the government's Reconstruction and Development Programme" (3).

36. The Social Empowerment and Development program was developed by Marilee James and Marit Garratt (Coomes 2002, 383–384), and the African Leadership Development Institute was started by Zimbabwean Phineas Dube (Coomes 2002, 422); see chapter 2 for further details.

37. There have certainly been tensions within the organization over the prioritization of spiritual and social concerns. For instance, Coomes's (2002, 496–501) internal history of AE recounts conflicts between Cassidy and the leader of AE East Africa, Anglican bishop Festo Kivengere from Uganda, that were, at least in part, over these priorities.

38. *AE Update*, November 2002, 4.

39. *AE Update*, November 2002, 4.

40. *AE Update*, November 2002, 4. It is, of course, possible that such a program was started, but I did not find any documentation of it.

41. *AE Update*, June 2004, 1.

42. Deborah's story appears in the book of Judges 4–5.

43. *AE Update*, June 2004, 1.

44. *AE Update*, June 2004, 1.

45. *AE Update*, June 2004, 1.

46. *AE Update*, June 2004, 1.

47. A history of the initiative can be found in Sistig and Nadar (2009). The Marriage Alliance is also referenced in biographical accounts of Cassidy's work; see "History of Michael Cassidy," Michael Cassidy and Friends Legacy Foundation, accessed February 2, 2024, https://michaelcassidyandfriends.org/2018/03/28/history-of-michael-cassidy/; and "Michael Cassidy," AE, accessed February 2, 2024, https://africanenterprise.org/our-team/michael-cassidy/.

48. Cassidy narrates his own experience of participating in the Promise Keepers movement in the October 1996 *AE Update* . He also wrote an op-ed in support of Angus Bachun's Mighty Men movement; see Michael Cassidy, "Oh to Be a Mighty Man," *The Witness*, May 6, 2009, https://witness.co.za/archive/2009/05/06/oh-to-be-a-mighty-man-20150430/. See, for example, Heath (2003) and Bartkowski (2003) for scholarly analyses of the Promise Keepers movement and Nadar (2009) for scholarly analysis of the Mighty Men movement. For a comparison of the two movements, see Dube (2016).

49. Bowers was chairperson during the brief tenure of Mark Manley as team leader and wrote a short piece in the November 2003 *AE Update* naming the board's decision to release Manley from his leadership position (2).

50. For instance, PACSA's 1997 Annual Report mentions holding a "workshop/seminar" for AE's Diploma in Social Empowerment and Development program on "Religion, the Church and Domestic Violence as a Theological and Development Priority" (12). And PACSA's 1999

Annual Report includes Lihle Dlamini mentioning that AE invited her to speak with fifteen students about domestic violence (21).

51. One of the striking features of AE's newsletters, overall, is that they often include a small text box or section that lists the events or workshops that occurred at the Conference Center, or have small paragraphs devoted to a workshop or event. This structural feature of the newsletters makes it all the more puzzling and significant that these events are not documented in AE's discourse.

52. Lichterman (2005, 261–262).

53. 1997 Justice Ministries Department/Human Rights Programme Annual Report, 6.

54. 1997 Justice Ministries Department/Human Rights Programme Annual Report, 7.

55. For example, the 1997 Justice Ministries Department/Human Rights Programme Annual Report notes that some of the workshops' purpose is "to encourage women to act by referring victims of violence to the appropriate agencies for intervention" (10).

56. "SACC Women's Ecumenical Conference in Johannesburg, 3–4 October 1995," 8.

57. 1999 Annual Report, 17. This program is also discussed in the 1999 Report of the Ecumenical Women's Conference.

58. For example, the 2003 Annual Report states that "the program coordinator attended the Sunday service at the above church [i.e., Central Lutheran Church in Soweto] in order to talk about Domestic Violence and Abuse to the congregation. The aim was to address men and women because we usually talk to women alone" (49).

59. 1973 Division of Justice and Reconciliation Report to the Executive Committee; 1974 Report of the General Secretary to the Executive Committee.

60. 1976 Report of the General Secretary.

61. 1981 Women's Desk Report to the SACC National Conference. The reasons for the suspension of the work are unclear—the report states that there has been a "restructuring of the division into Clusters" (3) and that "the counseling services of domestic workers," in particular, have "been handed over to the Witwatersrand Council of Churches as the body that handles local issues in every field" (4). This is because "it intends [to] concentrat[e] on the area of women per se," but further explanation of what this means is not provided in the report (4).

62. Some of this history is documented in the "Christian Women's Movement" files in the SACC's archives. For instance, a 1984 letter from Virginia Gcabashe to the General Secretary states that the movement started from a "48 Hour Women's Dialogue" (date not given, and I could not find documentary evidence to confirm the date, but it was likely in 1982 or 1983). Gcabashe reports on her use of some funding already granted by the SACC, and requests additional funding to support another Women's Dialogue that was being planned for right before the National Conference.

63. 1987 Women's Ministries Divisional Report, 1.

64. 1996 Annual Report, 25.

65. These various structural placements of work on gender are noted, for example, in the 1995 Annual Report (1), the 1996 Annual Report (25), the 1998 Annual Report (33), and the Half-Yearly Report, April–June 1999 (1).

66. The memo is undated, but based on context, it was likely written in early 1986 ("Christian Women's Movement" files).

67. Lulu Xingwana, memo to the General Secretary, August 9, 1989. While I did not find Chikane's response to this memo, he did explicitly call on churches to participate in the Ecumenical Decade of Solidarity with Women in 1990, noting that "it is a program of *Churches* and not a program of women alone. We ask you to demonstrate your solidarity in actions as well as in word." Frank Chikane, "Message to the Churches," National Conference of the SACC, 1990, 1.

CONCLUSION

Epigraph: Katongole and Rice (2004, 95).

1. For more information, see "History of the Circle," Circle of Concerned African Women Theologians, accessed March 29, 2024, https://circle.org.za/about-us/history-of-the-circle/.
2. Oduyoye (2004, 105).
3. Oduyoye (2004, 105).
4. Oduyoye (2004, 107).
5. See "Patriarchy in Society," SACC, accessed October 4, 2024, http://sacc.org.za/patriarchy-in-society/.
6. AE's homepage has since been updated, but there is an archived copy dated February 27, 2024, at the Wayback Machine: https://web.archive.org/web/20240227043746/https://southafrica.africanenterprise.com/.
7. See Lorna Charles, "PMB NGO Shut after R3m Fraud Uncovered," *The Mercury*, February 11, 2021, https://www.iol.co.za/mercury/news/pmb-ngo-shut-after-r3m-fraud-uncovered-1ad6a7e3-1eab-41f3-b678-e23b755d86ce.
8. See Gita Dickinson, letter to the editor, *The Witness*, February 17, 2021, https://witness.co.za/opinion/2021/02/17/letters-pacsa-what-happens-now-20210217/; and Joan Kerchhoff, letter to the editor, *The Witness*, February 23, 2021. https://witness.co.za/opinion/2021/02/23/letters-pacsa-working-to-recover-20210223/.
9. The *Houston Chronicle* broke the story of the prevalence of abuse in the Southern Baptist Convention; see Robert Downen, Lise Olsen, and John Tedesco, "20 Years, 700 Victims: Southern Baptist Sexual Abuse Spreads as Leaders Resist Reforms," *Houston Chronicle*, February 10, 2019, https://www.houstonchronicle.com/news/investigations/article/Southern-Baptist-sexual-abuse-spreads-as-leaders-13588038.php. See also the *Christianity Today* coverage of this story: Kate Shellnutt, "After Major Investigation, Southern Baptists Confront the Abuse Crisis They Knew Was Coming," *Christianity Today*, February 11, 2019, https://www.christianitytoday.com/news/2019/february/southern-baptist-abuse-investigation-houston-chronicle-sbc.html. With regard to the Catholic Church, the *Boston Globe* was one of the first to break the story back in 2002, for which it won a Pulitzer Prize; see Michael Rezendes, "Church Allowed Abuse by Priest for Years," *Boston Globe*, January 6, 2002, https://www.bostonglobe.com/news/special-reports/2002/01/06/church-allowed-abuse-priest-for-years/cSHfGkTIrAT25qKGvBuDNM/story.html. This appears to be part of a global issue; the Catholic Church in Spain recently also received the report of an independent commission that documented a pervasive pattern of abuse. See, for example, Kathyrn Armstrong, "Spanish Church Sexual Abuse Affected 200,000 Children, Commission Finds," BBC, October 28, 2023, https://www.bbc.com/news/world-europe-67238572#; and "Spain's Catholic Bishops Apologise after Report of 200,000 Abused," *Barron's*, October 30, 2023, https://www.barrons.com/news/spain-s-catholic-bishops-apologise-after-report-of-200-000-abused-8b990a01.
10. Beth Moore (2023) recounts her experience in depth in her recent memoir. Denhollander alluded to losing her church in her victim impact statement in Nassar's sentencing hearing in 2018. Full text available at "Read Rachael Denhollander's Full Victim Impact Statement about Larry Nassar," CNN, January 30, 2018, https://www.cnn.com/2018/01/24/us/rachael-denhollander-full-statement/index.html.
11. Yadav (2021). Yadav's particular focus was on the role of religion in perpetuating racism, and he takes this to be the central motivating questions of anti-racist projects. This insight and framing of the core questions seems applicable to many forms of injustice and violence.
12. See, for example, Alcoff (2018); Bourke (2022); DuToit (2014, 119–120).
13. For Burke's background and her motives for starting #MeToo, see Tarana Burke, "Me Too Is a Movement Not a Moment," TED Talks, November 2018, https://www.ted.com/talks

/tarana_burke_me_too_is_a_movement_not_a_moment; and her memoir, *Unbound* (Burke 2021).
14. DuToit (2014); Naidoo and Buiten (2022).
15. Katongole and Rice (2008, 94).

APPENDIX B

1. Weber (1904/1994, 259).
2. Collins (1990).

REFERENCES

Abrahams, Neemah, Shanaaz Mathews, Rachel Jewkes, Lorna J. Martin, and Carl Lombard. 2012. "Every Eight Hours: Intimate Femicide in South Africa 10 Years Later!" South African Medical Research Council Research Brief, August 2012.

Ackermann, Denise, Jonathan A. Draper, and Emma Mashinini. 1991. *Women Hold Up Half the Sky: Women in the Church in Southern Africa*. Pietermaritzburg, South Africa: Cluster Publications.

Alberts, Louw, and Frank Chikane, eds. 1991. *The Road to Rustenburg: The Church Looking Forward to a New South Africa*. Cape Town: Struik Christian Books.

Alcoff, Linda Martin. 2018. *Rape and Resistance: Understanding the Complexities of Sexual Violation*. Cambridge: Polity Press.

Alexander, Neville. 2003. *An Ordinary Country: Issues in the Transition from Apartheid to Democracy in South Africa*. New York: Berghahn Books.

Ammerman, Nancy. 1987. *Bible Believers: Fundamentalists in the Modern World*. New Brunswick, NJ: Rutgers University Press.

Anderson, Allan. 2005. "New African Initiated Pentecostalism and Charismatics in South Africa." *Journal of Religion in Africa* 35(1): 66–92.

Anderson, Elizabeth A., Miriam Gleckman-Krut, and Lanora Johnson. 2018. "Silence, Power, and Inequality: An Intersectional Approach to Sexual Violence" *Annual Review of Sociology* 44: 99–122.

Appleby, R. Scott. 1999. *The Ambivalence of the Sacred: Religion, Violence, and Reconciliation*. Lanham, MD: Rowman and Littlefield.

Asbridge, Thomas S. 2004. *The First Crusade: A New History*. New York: Oxford University Press.

Avishai, Orit. 2008. "'Doing Religion' in a Secular World: Women in Conservative Religions and the Question of Agency." *Gender & Society* 22(4): 409–433.

Avishai, Orit, and Courtney Irby. 2017. "Bifurcated Conversations in Sociological Studies of Religion and Gender." *Gender & Society* 31(5): 647–676.

Avishai, Orit, Afshan Jafar, and Rachel Rinaldo. 2015. "A Gender Lens on Religion." *Gender & Society* 29(1): 5–25.

Barnett, Bernice McNair. 1993. "Invisible Southern Black Women Leaders in the Civil Rights Movement: The Triple Constraints of Gender, Race and Class." *Gender & Society* 7(2): 162–182.

Bartkowski, John P. 1997. "Debating Patriarchy: Discursive Disputes over Spousal Authority among Evangelical Family Commentators." *Journal for the Scientific Study of Religion* 36(3): 393–410.

Bartkowski, John P. 2001. *Remaking the Godly Marriage: Gender Negotiation in Evangelical Families*. New Brunswick, NJ: Rutgers University Press.

Basu, Amrita, ed. 1995. *The Challenge of Local Feminisms: Women's Movements in Global Perspective*. New York: Routledge.

Baxen, Jean, and Anders Breidlid. 2009. *HIV/AIDS in Sub-Saharan Africa: Understanding the Implications of Culture and Context*. Cape Town: UCT Press.

Berg, Julie, and Wilfried Scharf. 2004. "Crime Statistics in South Africa 1994–2003." *South African Journal of Criminal Justice* 17(1): 57–78.

Beyerhaus, Peter. 1987. *The Kairos Document: Challenge or Danger to the Church? A Critical Theological Assessment of South African People's Theology*. Cape Town: Gospel Defense League.

Biko, Steve. 1978/2002. *I Write What I Like: Selected Writings*. Chicago: University of Chicago Press.
Bjork-James, Sophie. 2021. *The Divine Institution: White Evangelicalism's Politics of the Family*. New Brunswick, NJ: Rutgers University Press.
Block, Sharon. 2006. *Rape and Sexual Power in Early America*. Chapel Hill: University of North Carolina Press.
Boff, Leonardo, and Clodovis Boff. 1987. *Introducing Liberation Theology*. Maryknoll, NY: Orbis Books.
Borer, Tristan Anne. 1998. *Challenging the State: Churches as Political Actors in South Africa, 1980–1994*. Notre Dame, IN: University of Notre Dame Press.
Borer, Tristan Anne. 2009. "Gendered War and Gendered Peace: Truth Commissions and Post-conflict Gender Violence: Lessons from South Africa." *Violence Against Women* 15(10): 1169–1193.
Bourke, Joanna. 2022. *Disgrace: Global Reflections on Sexual Violence*. Chicago: University of Chicago Press.
Branche, Raphaelle, and Fabrice Virgili, eds. 2012. *Rape in Wartime*. New York: Palgrave Macmillan.
Briscoe, Forrest, and Katherine C. Kellogg. 2011. "The Initial Assignment Effect: Local Employer Practices and Positive Career Outcomes for Work-Family Program Users." *American Sociological Review* 76(2): 291–319.
Britton, Hannah. 2020. *Ending Gender-Based Violence: Justice and Community in South Africa*. Champaign: University of Illinois Press.
Browne, Stephen. 1999. *Angelina Grimké: Rhetoric, Identity, and the Radical Imagination*. East Lansing: Michigan State University Press.
Brusco, Elizabeth E. 1995. *The Reformation of Machismo: Evangelical Conversion and Gender in Colombia*. Austin: University of Texas Press.
Buckenham, Karen, ed. 1999. *Violence against Women: A Resource Manual for the Church in South Africa*. Pietermaritzburg, South Africa: PACSA.
Bullough, Kathy M. 2000. "Serpents, Angels and Virgins: The Virgin Mary as 'Second Eve' in the Art of Edward Burne-Jones." *Religion and the Arts* 4(4): 463–490.
Burke, Tarana. 2021. *Unbound: My Story of Liberation and the Birth of the Me Too Movement*. New York: Macmillan.
Butler, Anthea. 2021. *White Evangelical Racism: The Politics of Morality in America*. Chapel Hill: University of North Carolina Press.
Campbell, Catherine. 1997. "Migrancy, Masculine Identities and AIDS: The Psychosocial Context of HIV Transmission on the South African Gold Mines." *Social Science and Medicine* 45(2): 273–281.
Cassidy, Michael. 1989. *The Passing Summer: A South African's Response to White Fear, Black Anger and the Politics of Love*. Ventura, CA: Regal Books and African Enterprise.
Cassidy, Michael. 1995. *A Witness Forever*. London: Hodder and Stoughton Religious Division.
Charlton, Joy. 2015. "Revisiting Gender and Religion." *Review of Religious Research* 57(3): 331–339.
Chikane, Frank. 1988/2010. *No Life of My Own: An Autobiography*. Eugene, OR: Wipf and Stock.
Chipkin, Ivor, and Mark Swilling, eds. 2018. *Shadow State: The Politics of State Capture*. Johannesburg: Wits University Press.
Chong, Kelly. 2008. *Deliverance and Submission: Evangelical Women and the Negotiation of Patriarchy in South Korea*. Cambridge, MA: Harvard University Press.
Choo, Hae Yeon, and Myra Marx Ferree. 2010. "Practicing Intersectionality in Sociological Research: A Critical Analysis of Inclusions, Intersections, and Institutions in the Study of Inequalities." *Sociological Theory* 28(1): 129–149.

Cock, Jacklyn. 1989. *Maids and Madams: Domestic Workers under Apartheid*. London: Women's Press.
Collins, Patricia Hill. 1990. *Black Feminist Thought: Knowledge, Consciousness, and the Politics of Empowerment*. New York: Routledge.
Collins, Patricia Hill. 1998. "The Tie That Binds: Race, Gender and US Violence." *Ethnic and Racial Studies* 21(5): 917–938.
Collins, Patricia Hill. 2015. "Intersectionality's Definitional Dilemmas." *Annual Review of Sociology* 41(1): 1–20.
Collins, Patricia Hill. 2017. "On Violence, Intersectionality and Transversal Politics." *Ethnic and Racial Studies* 40(9): 1460–1473.
Comaroff, Jean, and John L. Comaroff. 1991. *Of Revelation and Revolution*. Vol. 1, *Christianity, Colonialism, and Consciousness in South Africa*. Chicago: University of Chicago Press.
Concerned Evangelicals. 1986. "Evangelical Witness in South Africa: Evangelicals Critique Their Own Theology and Practice." *Transformation* 4(1): 17–30.
Cone, James H. 1970. *A Black Theology of Liberation*. Maryknoll, NY: Orbis Books.
Cooke, Lynn Prince, and Jennifer L. Hook. 2018. "Productivity or Gender? The Impact of Domestic Tasks across the Wage Distribution." *Journal of Marriage and Family* 80(3): 721–736.
Coomes, Anne. 2002. *African Harvest: The Captivating Story of Michael Cassidy and African Enterprise*. London: Monarch Books.
Cornell, Drucilla. 2014. *Law and Revolution in South Africa: uBuntu, Dignity, and the Struggle for Constitutional Transformation*. New York: Fordham University Press.
Costas, Orlando E. 1990. "Evangelical Theology in the Two-Thirds World." In *Earthen Vessels: American Evangelicals and Foreign Missions, 1880–1980*, edited by Joel A. Carpenter and Wilbert R. Shenk, 235–250. Grand Rapids, MI: Eerdmans Publishing.
Cott, Nancy. 1987. *The Making of Modern Feminism*. New Haven, CT: Yale University Press.
Crenshaw, Kimberlé. 1991. "Mapping the Margins: Intersectionality, Identity Politics, and Violence against Women of Color." *Stanford Law Review* 43(6): 1241–1299.
Crenshaw, Kimberlé. 2010. "The Curious Resurrection of First Wave Feminism in the U.S. Elections: An Intersectional Critique of the Rhetoric of Solidarity and Betrayal." In *Sexuality, Gender and Power*, edited by Anna G. Jonasdottir, Valerie Bryson, and Kathleen B. Jones, 242–260. New York: Routledge.
Cunradi, Carol B., Raul Caetano, and John Schafer. 2002. "Religious Affiliation, Denominational Homogamy, and Intimate Partner Violence among U.S. Couples." *Journal for the Scientific Study of Religion* 41(1): 139–151.
Dahl, Robert A. 1998. *On Democracy*. New Haven, CT: Yale University Press.
Darwin, Helana. 2018. "Redoing Gender, Redoing Religion." *Gender & Society* 32(3): 348–370.
Davidman, Lynn. 1991. *Tradition in a Rootless World: Women Turn to Orthodox Judaism*. Berkeley: University of California Press.
Decoteau, Claire L. 2013. *Ancestors and Antiretrovirals: The Biopolitics of HIV/AIDS in Post-Apartheid South Africa*. Chicago: University of Chicago Press.
DeGruchy, John W., and Steve DeGruchy. 2004. *The Church Struggle in South Africa*, 25th anniversary ed. Minneapolis, MN: Fortress Press.
Doan, Long, and Natasha Quadlin. 2019. "Partner Characteristics and Perceptions of Responsibility for Housework and Child Care." *Journal of Marriage and Family* 81(1): 145–163.
Donley, Sarah, and Chardie L. Baird. 2017. "The Overtaking of Undertaking?: Gender Beliefs in a Feminizing Occupation." *Sex Roles* 77: 97–112.
Dube, Siphiwe. 2016. "Race, Whiteness and Transformation in the Promise Keepers America and the Mighty Men Conference: A Comparative Analysis." *HTS: Theological Studies* 72(1): 1–8.

Dubow, Saul. 2012. *South Africa's Struggle for Human Rights*. Athens: Ohio University Press.
Dubow, Saul. 2014. *Apartheid, 1948–1994*. New York: Oxford University Press.
DuMez, Kristin. 2020. *Jesus and John Wayne: How White Evangelicals Corrupted a Faith and Fractured a Nation*. New York: Liveright Publishing.
Duncan, Sheena. 1991. "Some Reflections on Rustenburg." In *Women Hold Up Half the Sky: Women in the Church in Southern Africa*, edited by Denise Ackermann, Jonathan A. Draper, and Emma Machining, 386–390. Pietermaritzburg, South Africa: Cluster Publications.
DuToit, Louise. 2014. "Shifting Meanings of Postconflict Sexual Violence in South Africa." *Signs* 40(1): 101–123.
Ebrahim, Hassen. 1999. *The Soul of a Nation: Constitution-Making in South Africa*. Cape Town: Oxford University Press.
Edwards, Korie L. 2008. *The Elusive Dream: The Power of Race in Interracial Churches*. New York: Oxford University Press.
Edwards, Korie L. 2019. "Presidential Address: Religion and Power: A Return to the Roots of Social Scientific Scholarship." *Journal for the Scientific Study of Religion* 58: 5–19.
Ellison, Christopher G., and Kristin L. Anderson. 2001. "Religious Involvement and Domestic Violence among U.S. Couples." *Journal for the Scientific Study of Religion* 40(2): 269–286.
Ellison, Christopher G., John. P Bartkowski, and Kristin. L Anderson. 1999. "Are There Religious Variations in Domestic Violence?" *Journal of Family Issues* 20(1): 87–113.
Elphick, Richard. 2012. *The Equality of Believers: Protestant Missionaries and the Racial Politics of South Africa*. Charlottesville: University of Virginia Press.
Elphick, Richard, and Thomas Rodney Hope Davenport. 1997. *Christianity in South Africa: A Political, Social, and Cultural History*. Berkeley: University of California Press.
Emerson, Michael O., Elizabeth Korver-Glenn, and Kiara W. Douds. 2015. "Studying Race and Religion: A Critical Assessment." *Sociology of Race and Ethnicity* 1(3): 349–359.
Emerson, Michael O., and Christian Smith. 2000. *Divided by Faith: Evangelical Religion and the Problem of Race in America*. New York: Oxford University Press.
England, Paula. 2010. "The Gender Revolution: Uneven and Stalled." *Gender & Society* 24(2): 149–166.
Evans, Sara Margaret. 1979. *Personal Politics: The Roots of Women's Liberation in the Civil Rights Movement and the New Left*. New York: Vintage Books.
Fatton, Robert. 1986. *Black Consciousness in South Africa: The Dialectics of Ideological Resistance to White Supremacy*. New York: SUNY Press.
Feinstein, Rachel A. 2018. *When Rape Was Legal: The Untold History of Sexual Violence during Slavery*. New York: Routledge.
Ferree, Myra Marx, and Silke Roth. 1998. "Gender, Class, and the Interaction between Social Movements: A Strike of West Berlin Day Care Workers." *Gender & Society* 12(6): 626–648.
Ferree, Myra Marx, and Aili Mari Tripp. 2006. *Global Feminism: Transnational Women's Activism, Organizing, and Human Rights*. New York: NYU Press.
Fiorenza, Elisabeth Schussler. 1983/1994. *In Memory of Her: A Feminist Theological Reconstruction of Christian Origins*. New York: Crossroads.
Fishman, Robert M. 2011. "Democratic Practice after the Revolution: The Case of Portugal and Beyond." *Politics & Society* 39(2): 233–267.
Fishman, Robert M. 2017. "How Civil Society Matters in Democratization: Setting the Boundaries of Post-Transition Political Inclusion." *Comparative Politics* 49(3): 391–409.
Fitzpatrick, Brenda. 2016. *Tactical Rape in War and Conflict: International Recognition and Response*. Chicago: Policy Press.
Fredrickson, George M. 2002. *Racism: A Short History*. Princeton, NJ: Princeton University Press.

Gaitskell, Deborah. 1979. "'Christian Compounds for Girls': Church Hostels for African Women in Johannesburg, 1907–1970." *Journal of Southern African Studies* 6(1): 44–69.
Gaitskell, Deborah. 1997. "Power in Prayer and Service: Women's Christian Organizations." *Perspectives on Southern Africa* 55: 253–267.
Gaitskell, Deborah. 2000. "Female Faith and the Politics of the Personal: Five Mission Encounters in Twentieth-Century South Africa." *Feminist Review* 65(1): 68–91.
Gaitskell, Deborah. 2002. "Whose Heartland and Which Periphery? Christian Women Crossing South Africa's Racial Divide in the Twentieth Century." *Women's History Review* 11(3): 375–394.
Gallagher, Sally. 2003. *Evangelical Identity and Gendered Family Life*. New Brunswick, NJ: Rutgers University Press.
Gerber, Lynne. 2015. "Grit, Guts, and Vanilla Beans: Godly Masculinity in the Ex-Gay Movement." *Gender & Society* 29(1): 26–50.
Gerhart, Gail M. 1978. *Black Power in South Africa: The Evolution of an Ideology*. Berkeley: University of California Press.
Gibson, James L. 2006. "The Contributions of Truth to Reconciliation Lessons from South Africa." *Journal of Conflict Resolution* 50(3): 409–432.
Gibson, James L., and Amanda Gouws. 2005. *Overcoming Intolerance in South Africa: Experiments in Democratic Persuasion*. New York: Cambridge University Press.
Gifford, Paul. 2004. "Persistence and Change in Contemporary African Religion." *Social Compass* 51(2): 169–176.
Gill, Athol. 1975. "Christian Social Responsibility." In *Let the Earth Hear His Voice: International Symposium on the Lausanne Covenant*, edited by J. D. Douglas, 89–102. Minneapolis, MN: World Wide Publications.
Ginwala, Frene. 1991. "Women and the African National Congress: 1912–1943." *Agenda* 6(8): 77–93.
Gloppen, Siri. 1997/2020. *South Africa: The Battle over the Constitution*. New York: Routledge.
Goldblatt, Beth. 2006. "Evaluating the Gender Content of Reparations: Lessons from South Africa." In *What Happened to the Women: Gender and Reparations for Human Rights Violations*, edited by R. Rubio-Marin, 48–91. New York: Social Science Research Council.
Göranzon, Anders Bengt Olof. 2010. "The Prophetic Voice of the South African Council of Churches after 1990: Searching for a Renewed Kairos." PhD thesis, University of the Free State.
Gorski, Philip, and Gulay Turkmen-Dervisoglu. 2013. "Religion, Nationalism, and Violence: An Integrated Approach." *Annual Review of Sociology* 39: 193–210.
Govender, Indiran. 2023. "Gender-Based Violence: An Increasing Epidemic in South Africa." *South African Family Practice* 65(1): Article 5729.
Griffith, R. Marie. 2000. *God's Daughters: Evangelical Women and the Power of Submission*. Berkeley: University of California Press.
Gutiérrez, Gustavo. 1973. *A Theology of Liberation: History, Politics, and Salvation*. Maryknoll, NY: Orbis Books.
Hadjar, Andreas. 2003. "Non-Violent Political Protest in East Germany in the 1980s: Protestant Church, Opposition Groups and the People." *German Politics* 12(3): 107–128.
Hassim, Shireen. 2006. *Women's Organizations and Democracy in South Africa: Contesting Authority*. Madison: University of Wisconsin Press.
Hassim, Shireen. 2009. "Democracy's Shadows: Sexual Rights and Gender Politics in the Rape Trial of Jacob Zuma." *African Studies* 68(1): 57–77.
Heath, Melanie. 2003. "Soft-Boiled Masculinity: Renegotiating Gender and Racial Ideologies in the Promise Keepers Movement." *Gender & Society* 17(3): 423–444.

Hefner, Robert W. 2013. *Global Pentecostalism in the 21st Century*. Bloomington: Indiana University Press.

Hirschmann, David. 1990. "The Black Consciousness Movement in South Africa." *Journal of Modern African Studies* 28(1):1–22.

Holland, J., and P. Henriot. 1983. *Social Analysis: Linking Faith and Justice*. Maryknoll, NY: Orbis Books.

hooks, bell. 1999/2018. *All about Love: New Visions*. New York: Harper Collins.

Huber, Evelyne, Dietrich Rueschemeyer, and John D. Stephens. 1997. "The Paradoxes of Contemporary Democracy: Formal, Participatory, and Social Dimensions." *Comparative Politics* 29(3): 323–342.

Huber, Evelyne, and John Stephens. 2012. *Democracy and the Left: Social Policy and Inequality in Latin America*. Chicago: University of Chicago Press.

Hunter, Mark. 2010. *Love in the Time of AIDS: Inequality, Gender, and Rights in South Africa*. Bloomington: Indiana University Press.

Hurwits, Heather McKee, and Alison Dahl Crossley. 2019. "Gender and Social Movements." In *The Wiley Blackwell Companion to Social Movements*, edited by David A. Snow, Sarah A. Soule, Hanspeter Kriesi, and Holly J. McCammon, 537–552. New York: Wiley Blackwell.

Hyslop, Jonathan. 2005. "Political Corruption before and after Apartheid." *Journal of Southern African Studies* 31(4): 773–789.

Iannaccone, Laurence R., and Eli Berman. 2006. "Religious Extremism: The Good, the Bad, and the Deadly." *Public Choice* 128(1–2): 109–129.

Ingersoll, Julie. 2003. *Evangelical Christian Women: War Stories in the Gender Battles*. New York: NYU Press.

Irby, Courtney. 2014. "Dating in Light of Christ: Young Evangelicals Negotiating Gender in the Context of Religious and Secular American Culture." *Sociology of Religion* 75(2): 260–283.

Jankowski, Peter J, Steven J. Sandage, Miriam Whitney Cornell, Cheryl Bissonette, Andy J. Johnson, Sarah A. Crabtree, and Mary L. Jensen. 2018. "Religious Beliefs and Domestic Violence Myths." *Psychology of Religion and Spirituality* 10(4): 386–397.

Jaquette, Jane S., ed. 1989. *The Women's Movement in Latin America: Feminism and the Transition to Democracy*. Boston: Unwin Hyman.

Jaquette, Jane S., ed. 1994. *The Women's Movement in Latin America: Participation and Democracy*. New York: Routledge.

Jeffery, Patricia, and Amrita Basu, eds. 1998. *Appropriating Gender: Women's Activism and Politicized Religion in South Asia*. New York: Routledge.

Jessee, Erin. 2017. *Negotiating Genocide in Rwanda: The Politics of History*. New York: Palgrave Macmillan.

Jewkes, Rachel. 2010. "Gender Inequities Must Be Addressed in HIV Prevention." *Science* 329(5988): 145–147.

Jewkes, Rachel, and Naeema Abrahams. 2002. "The Epidemiology of Rape and Sexual Coercion in South Africa: An Overview." *Social Science & Medicine* 55(7): 1231–1244.

Jewkes, Rachel, Jonathan Levin, and Loveday Penn-Kekana. 2002. "Risk Factors for Domestic Violence: Findings from a South African Cross-Sectional Study." *Social Science & Medicine* 55(9): 1603–1617.

Jubber, Ken. 1985. "The Prodigal Church: South Africa's Dutch Reformed Church and the Apartheid Policy." *Social Compass* 32(2–3): 273–285.

Juergensmeyer, Mark. 2008. *Global Rebellion: Religious Challenges to the Secular State, from Christian Militias to Al Qaeda*. Berkeley: University of California Press.

The Kairos Theologians. 1985. *The Kairos Document: Challenge to the Church; A Theological Comment on the Political Crisis in South Africa*. Johannesburg: Institute for Contextual Theology.

Kaplan, Temma. 1997. *Crazy for Democracy: Women in Grassroots Movements.* New York: Routledge.
Katongole, Emmanuel, and Chris Rice. 2008. *Reconciling All Things: A Christian Vision for Justice, Peace, and Healing.* Downers Grove, IL: InterVarsity Press.
Katongole, Emmanuel, with Jonathan Wilson-Hartgrove. 2009. *Mirror to the Church: Resurrecting Faith after Genocide in Rwanda.* Grand Rapids, MI: Zondervan.
Kaufman, Jason. 2004. "Endogenous Explanation in the Sociology of Culture." *Annual Review of Sociology*: 335–357.
Klug, Heinz. 2010. *The Constitution of South Africa: A Contextual Analysis.* Portland, OR: Hart Publishing.
Krog, Antjie. 1998. *Country of My Skull: Guilt, Sorrow, and the Limits of Forgiveness in the New South Africa.* New York: Broadway Books.
Kuperus, Tracy. 1999. "Building Democracy: An Examination of Religious Associations in South Africa and Zimbabwe." *Journal of Modern African Studies* 37(4): 643–688.
Kuumba, M. Bahati. 2002. "'You've Struck a Rock': Comparing Gender, Social Movements, and Transformation in the United States and South Africa." *Gender & Society* 16(4): 504–523.
Lambourne, Wendy. 2009. "Transitional Justice and Peacebuilding after Mass Violence." *International Journal of Transitional Justice* 3(1): 28–48.
Langa, Malose, Adele Kirsten, Brett Bowman, Gill Eagle, and Peace Kiguwa. 2018. "Black Masculinities on Trial *in Absentia*: The Case of Oscar Pistorius in South Africa." *Men and Masculinities* 23(3–4): 499–515.
Langford, Malcolm, Ben Cousins, Jackie Dugard, and Tshepo Madlingozi. 2013. *Socio-Economic Rights in South Africa: Symbols or Substance?* New York: Cambridge University Press.
Leamaster, Reid J., and Rachel L. Einwohner. 2018. "'I'm Not Your Stereotypical Mormon Girl': Mormon Women's Gendered Resistance." *Review of Religious Research* 60: 161–181.
Lemmond, Jon. 2009. "'The Greatest Disorder on the Earth': Domestic Abuse in Sixteenth-Century Nuremberg." PhD diss., University of California Santa Barbara.
Lerner, Gerda. 1998. *The Feminist Thought of Sarah Grimké.* New York: Oxford University Press.
Levine, Lou, ed. 2002. *Hope Beyond Apartheid: The Peter Kerchhoff Years of PACSA.* Pietermaritzburg, South Africa: PACSA.
Levitt, Heidi M., and Kimberly N. Ware. 2006. "Religious Leaders' Perspectives on Marriage, Divorce, and Intimate Partner Violence." *Psychology of Women Quarterly* 30(2): 212–222.
Lichterman, Paul. 2005. *Elusive Togetherness: Church Groups Trying to Bridge America's Divisions.* Princeton, NJ: Princeton University Press.
Linz, Juan J., and Alfred Stepan. 1995. *Problems of Democratic Transition and Consolidation: Southern Europe, South America, and Post-Communist Europe.* Baltimore: Johns Hopkins University Press.
Lodge, Tom. 1998. "Political Corruption in South Africa." *African Affairs* 97(387): 157–187.
Louw, Antoinette. 1997. "Surviving the Transition: Trends and Perceptions of Crime in South Africa. *Social Indicators Research* 41: 137–168.
Mabuza, Wesley Madonda. 2009. "Kairos Revisited: Investigating the Relevance of the Kairos Document for Church-State Relations within a Democratic South Africa." PhD thesis, University of Pretoria.
Magaziner, Daniel R. 2010. *The Law and the Prophets: Black Consciousness in South Africa, 1968–1977.* Johannesburg: Jacana Media.
Mahmood, Saba. 2005. *Politics of Piety: The Islamic Revival and the Feminist Subject.* Princeton, NJ: Princeton University Press.
Mahoney, James. 2000. "Path Dependence in Historical Sociology." *Theory and Society* 29(4): 507–548.

Mahoney, James, and Kathleen Thelen. 2009. *Explaining Institutional Change: Ambiguity, Agency, and Power*. New York: Cambridge University Press.

Mamdani, Mahmood. 2001. *When Victims Become Killers: Colonialism, Nativism, and the Genocide in Rwanda*. Princeton, NJ: Princeton University Press.

Mamdani, Mahmood. 2002. "Amnesty or Impunity? A Preliminary Critique of the Report of the Truth and Reconciliation Commission of South Africa (TRC)." *Diacritics* 32(3): 33–59.

Mandela, Nelson. 1995. *Long Walk to Freedom: The Autobiography of Nelson Mandela*. New York: Back Bay Books.

Marx, Karl. 1843/1978. *The Marx-Engels Reader*, edited by Robert C. Tucker, 2nd ed. New York: W. W. Norton.

Mathewes, Shanaaz, Naeemah Abrahams, Lorna J. Martin, Lisa Vetten, Lize van der Merwe, and Rachel Jewkes. 2004. "'Every Six Hours a Woman Is Killed by Her Intimate Partner': A National Study of Female Homicide in South Africa." Medical Research Council Policy Brief No. 5.

McAdam, Doug. 1992. "Gender as a Mediator of the Activist Experience: The Case of Freedom Summer." *American Journal of Sociology* 97(5): 1211–1240.

Meintjes, Sheila, Cathi Albertyn, Rohina Harillal, Ellen Kornegay, and Nomsa Ngqakayi. 1993. "Dilemmas of Difference." *Agenda* 9(19): 37–42.

Metz, Thaddeus. 2007. "Toward an African Moral Theory." *Journal of Political Philosophy* 15(3): 321–341.

Meyer, Birgit. 2004. "Christianity in Africa: From African Independent to Pentecostal-Charismatic Churches." *Annual Review of Anthropology* 33: 447–474.

Meyer, David, and Nancy Whittier. 1994. "Social Movement Spillover." *Social Problems* 41(2): 277–298.

Miller, Donald E., Kimon H. Sargeant, and Richard Flory. 2013. *Spirit and Power: The Growth and Global Impact of Pentecostalism*. New York: Oxford University Press.

Minow, Martha. 1998. "Between Vengeance and Forgiveness: South Africa's Truth and Reconciliation Commission." *Negotiation Journal* 14(4): 319–355.

Moffett, Hellen. 2006. "'These Women, They Force Us to Rape Them': Rape as Narrative of Social Control in Post-Apartheid South Africa." *Journal of Southern African Studies* 32(1): 129–144.

Mohanty, Chandra Talpade. 2003. *Feminism without Borders: Decolonizing Theory, Practicing Solidarity*. Durham, NC: Duke University Press.

Molyneux, Maxine. 1985. "Mobilization without Emancipation? Women's Interests, the State, and Revolution in Nicaragua." *Feminist Studies* 11(2): 227–254.

Molyneux, Maxine. 1998. "Analysing Women's Movements." *Development and Change* 29(2): 219–245.

Molyneux, Maxine. 2001. *Women's Movements in International Perspective: Latin America and Beyond*. New York: Palgrave Macmillan.

Moon, Claire. 2008. *Narrating Political Reconciliation: South Africa's Truth and Reconciliation Commission*. Lanham, MD: Lexington Books.

Moon, Dawne. 2004. *God, Sex, and Politics: Homosexuality and Everyday Theologies*. Chicago: University of Chicago Press.

Moore, Beth. 2023. *All My Knotted-Up Life: A Memoir*. Carol Stream, IL: Tyndale House.

Morris, Aldon D. 1984. *The Origins of the Civil Rights Movement: Black Communities Organizing for Change*. New York: Free Press.

Moxey, Keith. 1989. *Peasants, Warriors and Wives: Popular Imagery of the Reformation*. Chicago: University of Chicago Press.

Moynagh, Maureen, and Nancy Forestall. 2012. *Documenting First Wave Feminisms*. Toronto: University of Toronto Press.

Nadar, Sarojini. 2009. "Palatable Patriarchy and Violence against Wo/men in South Africa: Angus Buchan's Mighty Men's Conference as a Case Study of Masculinism." *Scriptura: Journal for Contextual Hermeneutics in Southern Africa* 102(1): 551–561.

Naidoo, Kammila, and Denise Buiten. 2022. "Tackling Gender-Based Violence in South Africa." In *#MeToo and Beyond: Perspectives on a Global Movement*, edited by M. Cristina Alcalde and Paula-Irene Villa, 46–66. Lexington: University Press of Kentucky.

Nason-Clark, Nancy. 1997. *The Battered Wife: How Christians Confront Family Violence*. Louisville, KY: Westminster John Knox Press.

Nason-Clark, Nancy, Barbara Fisher-Townsend, Catherine Holtmann, and Stephen McMullin. 2018. *Religion and Intimate Partner Violence: Understanding the Challenges and Proposing Solutions*. New York: Oxford University Press.

Nattrass, Nicoli, and Jeremy Seekings. 2001. "'Two Nations'? Race and Economic Inequality in South Africa Today." *Daedalus* 130(1): 45–70.

Nepstad, Sharon Erickson. 2004a. *Convictions of the Soul: Religion, Culture, and Agency in the Central America Solidarity Movement*. New York: Oxford University Press.

Nepstad, Sharon Erickson. 2004b. "Religion, Violence, and Peacemaking." *Journal for the Scientific Study of Religion* 43(3): 297–301.

Nepstad, Sharon Erickson. 2008. *Religion and War Resistance in the Plowshares Movement*. New York: Cambridge University Press.

Nicholson, Linda J., ed. 1997. *The Second Wave: A Reader in Feminist Theory*. New York: Routledge.

Ntlha, Moss. 1994. "Evangelical Witness in South Africa: The Story of Concerned Evangelicals." *International Review of Mission* 83(328): 139–141.

O'Donnell, Guillermo A. 1996. "Illusions about Consolidation." *Journal of Democracy* 7(2): 34–51.

Omi, Michael, and Howard Winant. 2015. *Racial Formation in the United States*. New York: Routledge.

PACSA. 2009. *Journeying for Justice: Stories of an Ongoing Faith-Based Struggle*. Pietermaritzburg, South Africa: Cluster Publications.

Padilla, Rene. 1975. "Evangelism and the World." In *Let the Earth Hear His Voice: International Symposium on the Lausanne Covenant*, edited by J. D. Douglas, 116–146. Minneapolis, MN: World Wide Publications.

Pagels, Elaine. 1989. *Adam, Eve, and the Serpent: Sex and Politics in Early Christianity*. New York: Vintage.

Patel, Leila. 1988. "South African Women's Struggles in the 1980's." *Agenda: Empowering Women for Gender Equity* (2): 28–35.

Pattillo-McCoy, Mary. 1998. "Church Culture as a Strategy of Action in the Black Community." *American Sociological Review* 63(6): 767–784.

Petrou, Ioannis. 2002. "The Question of Women in Church Tradition." *Anglican Theological Review* 84(3): 645–660.

Philpott, Daniel. 2012. *Just and Unjust Peace: An Ethic of Political Reconciliation*. New York: Oxford University Press.

Phiri, Isabel Apawo. 2002. "'Why Does God Allow Our Husbands to Hurt Us?': Overcoming Violence against Women." *Journal of Theology for Southern Africa* (114): 19–30.

Rakoczy, Susan, ed. 2000. *Silent No Longer: The Church Responds to Sexual Violence*. Pretoria: Southern African Catholic Bishops Conference.

Rakoczy, Susan. 2004. "Religion and Violence: The Suffering of Women." *Agenda* 18(61): 29–35.

Ramos, Marcos Antonio. 2008. "The New Eve: The Virgin Mary in Irenaeus of Lyon's *Adversus Haereses*." MA thesis, University of St. Michael's College and Toronto School of Theology.

Rao, Aliya Hamid. 2015. "Gender and Cultivating the Moral Self in Islam: Muslim Converts in an American Mosque." *Sociology of Religion* 76(4): 413–435.
Ray, Raka, and Anna C. Korteweg. 1999. "Women's Movements in the Third World: Identity, Mobilization, and Autonomy." *Annual Review of Sociology*: 47–71.
Reeder, Caryn A. 2022. *The Samaritan Woman's Story: Reconsidering John 4 after #ChurchToo*. Westmont, IL: InterVarsity Press.
Renick, Timothy M. 1991. "From Apartheid to Liberation: Calvinism and the Shaping of Ethical Belief in South Africa." *Sociological Focus* 24(2): 129–143.
Rhee, Helen. 2020. "Irenaeus and Paul: Sexuality, Virginity, and Women." In *Irenaeus and Paul*, edited by Todd D. Still and David E. Wilhite, 203–224. London: T&T Clark.
Ridgeway, Cecilia L. 2001. "Gender, Status, and Leadership." *Journal of Social Issues* 57(4): 637–655.
Ridgeway, Cecilia L. 2011. *Framed by Gender: How Gender Inequality Persists in the Modern World*. New York: Oxford University Press.
Ridgeway, Cecilia L., and James W. Balkwell. 1997. "Group Processes and the Diffusion of Status Beliefs." *Social Psychology Quarterly* 60(1): 14–31.
Ridgeway, Cecilia L., and Shelley J. Correll. 2004. "Unpacking the Gender System: A Theoretical Perspective on Gender and Social Relations." *Gender & Society* 18(4): 510–531.
Riesebrodt, Martin. 1993. *Pious Passion: The Emergence of Modern Fundamentalism in the United States and Iran*. Berkeley: University of California Press.
Riesebrodt, Martin. 2010. *The Promise of Salvation: A Theory of Religion*. Chicago: Chicago University Press.
Rinaldo, Rachel. 2019. "Obedience and Authority among Muslim Couples: Negotiating Gendered Religious Scripts in Contemporary Indonesia." *Sociology of Religion* 80(3): 323–349.
Risse-Kappen, Thomas, Stephen C. Ropp, and Kathryn Sikkink. 1999. *The Power of Human Rights: International Norms and Domestic Change*. New York: Cambridge University Press.
Robins, Steven. 2008. "Sexual Politics and the Zuma Rape Trial." *Journal of Southern African Studies* 34(2): 411–427.
Robnett, Belinda. 1997. *How Long, How Long? African American Women in the Struggle for Civil Rights*. New York: Oxford University Press.
Ross, Fiona C. 2003. *Bearing Witness: Women and the Truth and Reconciliation Commission in South Africa*. London: Pluto Press.
Ross, Fiona C. 2010. "An Acknowledged Failure: Women, Voice, Violence, and the South African Truth and Reconciliation Commission." In *Localizing Transitional Justice: Interventions and Priorities after Mass Violence*, edited by Rosalind Shaw and Lars Worden, 69–91. Stanford, CA: Stanford University Press.
Roth, Benita. 2004. *Separate Roads to Feminism: Black, Chicana, and White Feminist Movements in America's Second Wave*. New York: Cambridge University Press.
Rueschemeyer, Dietrich. 2004. "Addressing Inequality." *Journal of Democracy* 15(4): 76–90.
Schönteich, Martin, and Antoinette Louw. 2001. "Crime in South Africa: A Country and Cities Profile." Occasional Paper No. 49. Pretoria: Institute for Security Studies.
Schuld, Maria. 2013. "The Prevalence of Violence in Post Conflict Societies: A Case Study of Kwazulu-Natal, South Africa." *Journal of Peacebuilding and Development* 8(1): 60–73.
Schutte, Augustine. 2001. *Ubuntu: An Ethic for a New South Africa*. Pietermaritzburg, South Africa: Cluster Publications.
Seidman, Gay. 1993. "'No Freedom without the Women': Mobilization and Gender in South Africa 1970–1992." *Signs* 18(2): 291–320.
Seidman, Gay. 1999. "Gendered Citizenship: South Africa's Democratic Transition and the Construction of a Gendered State." *Gender & Society* 13(3): 287–307.
Sewell Jr., William H. 1996a. "Historical Events as Transformations of Structures: Inventing Revolution at the Bastille." *Theory and Society* 25(6): 841–881.

Sewell Jr., William H. 1996b. "Three Temporalities." In *The Historic Turn of the Human Sciences*, edited by Terrence J. McDonald, 245–280. Ann Arbor: University of Michigan Press.

Sharp, Shane. 2009. "Escaping Symbolic Entrapment, Maintaining Social Identities." *Social Problems* 56(2): 267–284.

Sistig, Jennifer Jane, and Sarojini Nadar. 2009. "Who's in Charge in a Genderless Marriage? A Feminist and Queer Analysis of the Opposition to Same-Sex Marriage as Articulated by the Marriage Alliance of South Africa." *Journal of Gender and Religion in Africa* 17(2): 77–92.

Smith, Charlene. 2001. *Proud of Me: Speaking Out against Sexual Violence and HIV*. New York: Penguin Books.

Smith, Christian. 1996a. "Correcting a Curious Neglect, or Bringing Religion Back In." In *Disruptive Religion: The Force of Faith in Social Movement Activism*, edited by Christian Smith, 1–25. New York: Routledge.

Smith, Christian. 1996b. *Resisting Reagan: The U.S. Central America Peace Movement*. Chicago: University of Chicago Press.

Smith, Christian. 2017. *Religion: What It Is, How It Works, and Why It Matters*. Princeton, NJ: Princeton University Press.

Somerville, Diane Miller. 2004. *Rape and Race in the Nineteenth-Century South*. Chapel Hill: University of North Carolina Press.

Swartz, David R. 2012. *Moral Minority: The Evangelical Left in an Age of Conservatism*. Philadelphia: University of Pennsylvania Press.

Taylor, Christopher C. 1999/2020. *Sacrifice as Terror: The Rwandan Genocide of 1994*. New York: Routledge.

Taylor, Verta. 1989. "Social Movement Continuity: The Women's Movement in Abeyance." *American Sociological Review* 54: 761–775.

Tizon, Al. 2008. *Transformation after Lausanne: Radical Evangelical Mission in Global-Local Perspective*. Minneapolis, MN: Fortress Press.

Tripp, Aili Mari, Joy Kwesiga, Isabel Casimiro, and Alice Mungwa. 2009. *African Women's Movements: Transforming Political Landscapes*. New York: Cambridge University Press.

Truth and Reconciliation Commission of South Africa. 1998. *Final Report*. 7 Vols. Cape Town: Juta Press.

Tshitereke, Clarence. 2006. *The Experience of Economic Redistribution: The Growth, Employment and Redistribution Strategy in South Africa*. New York: Routledge.

Tutu, Desmond. 1996. *The Rainbow People of God: The Making of a Peaceful Revolution*. New York: Random House.

Tutu, Desmond. 2000. *No Future without Forgiveness*. New York: Doubleday.

Tutu, Desmond. 2011. *God Is Not a Christian: And Other Provocations*. New York: HarperOne.

Tutu, Desmond, and Mpho Tutu. 2014. *The Book of Forgiving: The Fourfold Path for Healing Ourselves and Our World*. New York: HarperOne.

Vetten, Lisa. 2007. "Violence against Women in South Africa." In *State of the Nation: South Africa 2007*, edited by Sakhela Buhlungu, John Daniel, Roger Southall, and Jessica Lutchman, 425–447. Cape Town: Human Sciences Research Council.

Villa-Vicencio, Charles. 1992. *A Theology of Reconstruction: Nation-Building and Human Rights*. New York: Cambridge University Press.

Walker, Cherryl. 1982/1991. *Women and Resistance in South Africa*. London: Onyx.

Walker, Liz. 2005. "Men Behaving Differently: South African Men since 1994." *Culture, Health & Sexuality* 7(3): 225–238.

Walshe, Peter. 1983. *Church versus State in South Africa: The Case of the Christian Institute*. London: C. Hurst.

Walshe, Peter. 1991. "South Africa: Prophetic Christianity and the Liberation Movement." *Journal of Modern African Studies* 29(1): 27–60.

Walzer, Michael. 1965. *The Revolution of the Saints: A Study in the Origins of Radical Politics*. Cambridge, MA: Harvard University Press.

Weaver Swartz, Lisa. 2023. *Stained Glass Ceilings: How Evangelicals Do Gender and Practice Power*. New Brunswick, NJ: Rutgers University Press.

Weber, Max. 1904/1994. "'Objectivity' in Social Science." In *Sociological Writings*, edited by Wolf Heydebrand, 248–259. New York: Continuum.

Weber, Max. 1904/2002. *The Protestant Ethic and the Spirit of Capitalism*. Rev. ed. New York: Oxford University Press.

Weldon, S. Laurel. 2006. "Inclusion, Solidarity, and Social Movements: The Global Movement against Gender Violence." *Perspectives on Politics* 4(1): 55–74.

West, Traci C. 2019. *Solidarity and Defiant Spirituality: Africana Lessons on Religion, Racism, and Ending Gender Violence*. New York: NYU Press.

Weyermann, Maja. 2002. "The Typologies of Adam-Christ and Eve-Mary, and Their Relationship to One Another." *Anglican Theological Review* 84(3): 609–626.

Whitnah, Meredith. 2022. "Evangelical Organizations' Responses to Domestic Violence: How the Cultural Production of Religious Beliefs Challenges or Enshrines Patriarchy." *Review of Religious Research* 64(3): 427–450.

Whittier, Nancy. 2016. "Carceral and Intersectional Feminism in Congress: The Violence against Women Act, Discourse, and Policy." *Gender & Society* 30(5): 791–818.

Wilcox, W. Bradford. 2004. *Soft Patriarchs, New Men: How Christianity Shapes Fathers and Husbands*. Chicago: University of Chicago Press.

Wilde, Melissa J. 2018a. "Complex Religion: Interrogating Assumptions of Independence in the Study of Religion." *Sociology of Religion* 79(3): 287–298.

Wilde, Melissa J., ed. 2018b. "Complex Religion: Intersections of Religion and Inequality." Special issue. *Social Inclusion* 6(2).

Wilde, Melissa. 2019. *Birth Control Battles: How Race and Class Divided American Religion*. Berkeley: University of California Press.

Wilde, Melissa, and Sabrina Danielsen. 2014. "Fewer and Better Children: Race, Class, Religion, and Birth Control Reform in America." *American Journal of Sociology* 119(6): 1710–1760.

Wilde, Melissa, and Lindsay Glassman. 2016. "How Complex Religion Can Improve Our Understanding of American Politics." *Annual Review of Sociology* 42(1): 407–425.

Wilson, Richard A. 2001. *The Politics of Truth and Reconciliation in South Africa: Legitimizing the Post-Apartheid State*. New York: Cambridge University Press.

Wood, Elisabeth Jean. 2018. "Rape as a Practice of War: Toward a Typology of Political Violence." *Politics & Society* 46(4): 513–537.

Wood, Richard L. 2002. *Faith in Action: Religion, Race, and Democratic Organizing in America*. Chicago: University of Chicago Press.

Worden, Nigel. 2000. *The Making of Modern South Africa: Conquest, Apartheid, Democracy*, 3rd ed. Hoboken, NJ: Wiley-Blackwell.

Yadav, Sameer. 2021. Panel on "The Origins of Race: A Multi-Disciplinary Panel on the Construction of Race." White Students for Racial Justice, Westmont College, November 8, 2021.

Yates, Timothy. 1996. *Christian Mission in the Twentieth Century*. Cambridge: Cambridge University Press.

Yellin, Jean Fagan, and John C. Van Horne, eds. 1994. *The Abolitionist Sisterhood: Women's Political Culture in Antebellum America*. Ithaca, NY: Cornell University Press.

Zuma, Khangelani, Leickness Simbaya, Nompumelelo Zungu, Sizulu Moyo, Edmore Marinda, Sean Jooste, Alicia North, Patrick Nadol, Getahun Aynalem, Ehimario Igumbor, Cheryl Dietrich, Salome Sigida, Buyisile Chibi, Lehlogonolo Makola, Lwando Kondlo, Sarah Porter, and Shandir Ramlagan. 2022. "The HIV Epidemic in South Africa: Key Findings from

2017 National Population-Based Survey." *International Journal Environmental Research and Public Health* 19(13): Article 8125.

Zuma, Khangelani, Olive Shisana, Thomas M. Rehle, Leickness C. Simbaya, Sean Jooste, Nompumelelo Zungu, Demetre Labadarios, Dorina Onoya, Meredith Evans, Sizulu Moyo, and Fareed Abdullah. 2016. "New Insights into the HIV Epidemic in South Africa: Key Findings from the National HIV Prevalence, Incidence, and Behavior Survey, 2012." *African Journal of AIDS Research* 15(1): 67–75.

INDEX

abuse: alcohol and drug, 89, 96; child and wife, 82, 89, 93; frequency of, 90; public acknowledgment of, 82, 118, 190n9; and rape, 91, 94–99; and the responsibility of the church, 58, 85–86, 153, 187n24; spiritual conversion and, 92–93; workshops about, 137

AE Witness, 34

African Enterprise (AE): African Leadership Development Initiative, 60; Bonginkosi, 31, 139; Bridge Building Encounters, 31, 37, 92, 138; Conference Center, 31, 36–37, 47, 93, 159, 189n51; discourse about women, 117; founding, 13, 30, 36–37; Foxfires program, 60, 92, 138; geographic location, 60; implications for GBV, 4, 180n70; internal history, 31, 168n66, 170n55, 188n37; International Team, 13, 60, 62; Jesus Way, 61–62, 66, 74, 113, 120, 151; leadership board, 13, 139–141, 188n49; posture toward race or racial groups, 34, 37–38, 50, 61, 90; posture toward women and gender issues, 113–120, 138–140; Social Empowerment and Development certificate program, 60; social positioning, 60, 63–66, 70, 74, 88, 90, 94. *See also* reconciliation theological culture; theological conviction; theological culture

African Initiated Churches (AICs), 11

African National Congress, 9, 39

Afrikaans, 45, 176n79

Afrikaner: Christians, 29; clergyman, 12, 22, 24; nationalist identity, 9; supporters of apartheid, 65

Afrikaner Weerstandsbeweging (Afrikaner Resistance Movement), 65

Aitchison, John, 40, 42, 71

Amnesty International, 39

Anglican: archbishop, 1; bishop, 22, 188n37; church, 13, 120; minister, 72; priest, 86

apartheid: freedom from, 3; and gender, 169n13; opposition to, 11; support from Afrikaners, 65; system for, 8–9, 27, 33, 40, 54, 56; and Desmond Tutu, 1, 20, 22, 25, 173n14

Appleby, Scott, 7

Bam, Brigalia: on silence surrounding GBV, 78, 99–100, 174n25; TRC process, 54–56

Bhiman, Alex, 43

the Bible: Amos, 71; attention to women, 128, 140, 187n24; book of Acts, 134; Colossians, 62; gender injustice, 108, 115, 140; hope, 89; Jesus, 24, 41; leadership programs, 175n61; liberation, 52, 54, 128; love ethic, 59; the Magnificat, 126; Mary, 109, 126; Matthew, 110; mourning, 110; reading, 85; sexuality, 175n58, 183n51; social concern and action, 35, 54; story of Naomi and Ruth, 120; transformation, 71, 111; wilderness journey, 52

Biko, Steve, 169n15

black: Africans, 171n94; anti-black racism, 3, 21, 185n89; church leaders, 12–13, 19, 22, 172n1; Concerned Evangelicals, 20; enslavement, 6; intersectionality, 4, 168n10; liberation, 184n73; marked categories, 4; oppressed population, 23, 26; theology, 170n35, 171n88; women, 5

Black Consciousness Movement, 22, 169n15, 171n88

Black Sash, The, 133

Botha, P. W., 31, 171n94

Bowers, Esme, 141, 188n49

Buckenham, Karen, 67–69, 83–86, 107, 136–137, 186n17, 187n24

Butler, Anthea, 167n30

Butler, Mark, 45–46

Calvary, 42, 59

Cape Town, South Africa, 53, 57, 78–79

case selection, 11, 156–158

Cassidy, Carol, 139

Cassidy, Michael: books by, 59, 152; Christian principles, 34, 59; founding AE, 13, 30, 168n66; on gender, 114; on the *The Kairos Document*, 31; on marriage, 60, 141, 175n58, 188n47, 188n48; political activism, 30, 61–62; on reconciliation, 33, 35–36, 38, 61, 63–64, 88

Catholic, 12, 190n9; Bishops Conference, 45, 153, 169n14; priest, 108

Chikane, Frank, 22, 53, 96, 144, 159; poisoning, 23; speeches by, 26, 57–58, 145; succeeded by Brigalia Bam, 174n25
Choo, Hae Yeon, 4
Christian: mind, 35, 85; principles, 34, 59, 62, 95; teaching, 84; values, 34–35, 41, 51, 61–63, 74, 175n61
Christian Institute, 22
Christianity: and colonization, 8; gender equality, 187n30; and sexism, 167n55, 183n51; suffering, 25; whiteness and, 45
Christianity Today, 190n9
Church Women Concerned, 125
civil rights movement: black women and, 5, 166n12, 166n13
Cochrane, Renate, 72–73
Collins, Patricia Hill, 4, 6, 79, 158, 178n13
Communications Unit, 55
complex religion, 6–7, 168n8, 186n11
Concerned Evangelicals, 20
Coomes, Anne, 168n66, 170n50
Cormick, Dina, 179n16
Crenshaw, Kimberlé, 166n11, 178n13

Deeb, Mike, 108
de Klerk, President F. W., 50
democracy: AE's theological culture, 61, 63, 66, 88–89, 94, 140–141; early years, 10, 14, 48, 51–52, 54, 56; fragile, 51; nonracial, 22, 50, 57; PACSA's theological culture, 66, 68, 81; representative, 50; SACC's theological culture, 99–100, 102, 123; women's roles, 123, 131
democratic transition, 14, 172n7, 173n9, 184n78; and AE, 33, 60–61, 66, 94; elections, 50; and GBV, 10; and God's way, 62, 88; and PACSA, 66–70, 72–73, 136, 187n25; and SACC, 23, 52, 54–57, 124, 174n24
Diakonia Sweden, 67
dignity: and blackness, 22, 27–29, 55, 184n73; Christian affirmation of, 55, 59; liberation and, 24, 122–123, 132; Rustenburg Declaration, 134; SACC's theological culture, 99–100, 102, 121, 124, 130–131; and the voices of survivors, 154; women's equality and, 3, 5, 95, 99, 113, 128
Dlamini, Lihle, 84, 138, 186n19, 187n31, 188n33
Dube, Phineas, 60, 114–115, 188n36
Dubow, Saul, 50, 171n94, 173n10, 183n38, 185n89
Du Mez, Kristen Kobes, 167n30

Duncan, Sheena, 133–134, 145
Dutch Reformed Church, 8, 22, 35, 49, 169n16, 170n55, 176n79
Dwane, Bishop Sigqipo, 94–95, 130–131

Easter: celebration, 41–42; message, 66; narrative, 69, 81, 108–109, 111, 132; newsletter, 41–43, 68, 71, 73, 80
economic marginalization, 51–52, 56–59, 64, 74, 124
ecumenical: against apartheid, 11; Decade of Solidarity with Women, 94, 181n86, 189n67; social movement, 22, 55, 93, 110, 124; Women's Conference, 143
Ecumenical Monitoring Programme of South Africa, 110
Eloff Commission, 23, 26, 169n24
Elphick, Richard, 8
England, Paula, 105–106
equality: and dignity, 95, 102, 121–122, 128; and freedom, 34, 71, 95; gender, 83, 95, 106, 114, 131, 187n30; of need, 28, 35, 38, 47, 64; as a principle, 24; promise of, 98; and race, 47, 64
Evangelical Church, 20, 170n49. *See also* Concerned Evangelicals

Faith and Mission Unit, 99
Ferree, Myra Marx, 4
Forestell, Nancy, 165n10
freedom: from apartheid, 3; Christ's message, 85–86, 118, 128; and dignity, 24, 27, 59, 95; and equality, 71; from oppression, 30, 51, 54, 56, 80; political, 34, 37–38, 62; religious, 62; women's, 9

Gardner, Colin, 44
Garratt, Marit, 60, 175n61, 188n36
Gatu, John, 65
gender: and apartheid, 169n13; equality, 83; essentialist beliefs, 106, 114–115, 118–119, 124–125; groups, 150; ideology, 152, 178n10; inequities, 83, 102; injustice, 108, 110, 126, 128, 135; justice, 74, 79, 100, 103, 113, 144–146; oppression, 84–85, 111, 130, 142; PACSA programs, 67, 86; and power, 14, 79, 88, 93–94; reconciliation, 80, 116, 121; relations, 90–91; and religion, 182n10; roles, 115–116, 147; SACC programs, 105, 143, 157; scholarship about, 167n30; and sexuality, 141; WCC programs, 95

gender-based violence (GBV): Brigalia Bam, 78, 99–100, 174n25; defined, 1–2; and democratic transition, 10; and the Gospel, 89–90, 93–94; implications of, 4–7; influence of patriarchy, 83, 144, 152; Peter Kerchhoff, 83; lack of response to, 80, 94, 101, 138–139, 145–146; and liberation, 3, 10, 97, 100, 102; men's role in, 136; PACSA programs, 151; partial response to, 3, 135, 143, 145, 153; and spiritual reconciliation, 101, 142; strong response to, 3, 79, 81–87, 93, 101, 137–138; and transformation theological culture, 79, 84, 138, 150, 159
Gennrich, Daniela, 67, 136, 176n92
Global South, 30
Goba, Bonganjalo, 35
God's way, 51; AE's theological culture, 33–34, 51, 63, 74, 114; and democracy, 61–62, 88; reconciliation, 3, 32; self-sacrifice, 59
Gospel: AE's theological culture, 59, 63–66, 80, 88, 90, 116–119; and black people, 27, 37, 61; changing lives, 93; forgiveness, 61; and GBV, 89–90, 93–94; inclusion of rape and social ills, 90–91; PACSA's theological convictions, 66, 69–70, 73, 86; SACC's theological convictions, 74, 105; youth groups, 60
Guinness, Dawn, 117

Haddad, Beverley, 72, 86, 186n19
HIV/AIDS: AE work, 60, 93, 115; children with, 69; crisis, 53, 93, 97, 109; epidemic, 50, 100; PACSA work, 67, 69–70, 109, 136–137; research publications, 67, 136, 186n12, 187n24, 187n28; rise of, 10, 60, 175n59; SACC work, 53, 97; theological culture, 60, 70
Hlongwa, James, 46
Human Rights Watch, 77, 177n1
human sexuality, 93, 99, 102
Hutt, Robin, 68, 110

injustice: apartheid, 25, 32, 38, 126, 150; challenging, 20–22, 39, 46, 78; church response to, 101; economic, 55, 57–59, 97, 113, 150, 177n96; gendered, 10–11, 102, 107–108, 110, 115, 125–126; indifference to, 72; intersectional, 15; patriarchal, 83, 132; racial, 2–3, 11, 78–79, 94, 113; reconciled relationships, 34; social, 134–135; and violence, 78–79, 84, 87, 102, 108, 131. *See also* gender: injustice
Inter-Church Aid program, 23, 53

International Day of No Violence Against Women, 136
International Human Rights Day, 136, 180n53
intersectionality, 4, 6, 165n6, 168n10, 178n13
intimate partner homicide, 1

James, Marilee, 60, 188n36
Jesus Christ: conversion and liberation of followers, 23–24, 27, 36; death and resurrection, 27; Gospel of, 49; and liberation theological culture, 122, 124, 128; and the mission of the Church, 33, 52, 128; solidarity with the poor and oppressed, 43, 88, 122, 124
Jesus Way: AE's theological culture, 61–62, 66, 74, 120, 151; characterized by, 113; gendered social order, 120, 151
Johannesburg, South Africa, 1, 12, 23
justice: and the Bible, 108, 115, 140; and marginality, 128. *See also* gender: justice; injustice
Justice Ministries program, 58

Kairos Document, The, 19–20, 31, 104
Kerchhoff, Joan, 41, 107
Kerchhoff, Peter: addressing GBV, 83; death, 67; history, 14, 39; incarceration and punishment, 40; PACSA work, 67; writing, 44–45, 82, 179n31
Kigali, Rwanda, 87–88
Kisten, Kesavan, 86–87
Kistner, Dr. Wolfram, 126
Kneifel, Theo, 43–44
KwaZulu Natal, 14, 67, 72; church leaders, 60; Council of Churches, 186n19; violence in, 39, 63, 93, 175n59

Lausanne Congress, 30, 170n49
Lawler, Clive, 91
liberation: and the Bible, 52; and dignity, 28, 184n73; GBV, 3, 10, 97, 100, 102; political, 69; struggle, 26–29, 34, 43, 123
liberation movement: African National Congress, 9; inclusion of women, 5, 127–130, 182n5, 184n65, 184n78; *The Kairos Document*, 19–20; motherism, 184n82
liberation theological culture: and early democracy, 52; economic marginalization, 56, 59, 95; gender justice and, 142–143; and

liberation theological culture (cont.)
 the Gospel, 105; response to GBV, 97, 100, 102, 145, 182n5; tensions around gender and leadership, 146; and women's equal dignity, 121–128, 131–132
liberation theology, 170n35; PACSA, 142–146; SACC, 22–30, 32–33, 52–57, 121–126, 131–132, 145–146
Lichterman, Paul, 142
Linda, Mbulelo, 96
Lindegger, Graham, 41–42, 109
Lubbe, Gerrie, 24
Luckett, Sid, 70–71
Lungu, Steve, 65
lynching, 6

Mabiletsa, Deborah, 144
Magdalene, Mary, 81, 126, 140; and Africa, 109, 126; liberation movement, 127
Majiza, Charity, 97
Makue, Eddie, 58
Malan, D. F., 8
male privilege, 108, 113; relinquishing of, 130–131, 152
Malinga, Purity, 112
Mandela, Nelson, 50, 173n14
Manley, Mark, 62, 175n57, 188n49
manyanos, 138, 188n32
marginality: gender injustice and, 128; of Jesus, 24, 26; women's, 108–112, 120, 124–127
Maritzburg, South Africa, 44
marked categories, 4
Marriage Alliance of South Africa, 60, 141, 175n58, 188n47
Massey, James, 44
Mbatha, Sikhumbuzo, 66
Mbeki, President Thabo, 77, 179n15
Methodist Church of Southern Africa, 112
#MeToo movement, 154
Meyer, Venita, 129
Mkhatswa, Father Smangaliso, 45
Moffett, Helen, 79, 177n3, 179n15
Molyneux, Maxine, 166n14
Moon, Dawne, 182n12
Moynagh, Maureen, 165n10

National Executive Committee, 13
National Initiative for Reconciliation, 31–32, 35, 38
Naudé, Beyers, 12, 22, 25, 128

Ngewu, Reverend Livingstone, 69–70
nongovernmental organizations (NGOs), 2, 39, 156; increase of, 11, 77–78, 136–137
Norwegian Church Aid, 67, 176n93
Nunes, Mzwandili Rodrigo, 71
Nuttall, Tim, 69

Odell, Mike, 62
Oduyoye, Mercy, 149, 153

Pan-African Christian Leadership Assembly, 31
path dependency, 8; scholarship on, 174n19; of theological cultures, 51, 53, 68, 73
patriarchy: church's complicity in, 119, 129; critiques of, 87, 129–130, 144, 187n30; influence on GBV, 83, 144, 152; and racism, 167n30; and sexism, 106, 108, 113, 124, 131; socialization of, 112; transformation, 3, 111, 132, 146
Pentecostal, 11–14, 22, 170n55, 172n7
Pietermaritzburg, South Africa, 13, 36–37, 44–45, 67, 92
Pietermaritzburg Agency for Christian Social Awareness (PACSA): Detainees Support Committee, 39; founding, 3, 13–14; GBV programs, 151; Gender program, 86, 136–137, 141, 176n93, 186n12, 186n19; Human Rights program, 137; implications for GBV, 187n24; international funding, 53; leadership board; mission, 38; name change, 165n5; posture of relative privilege, 70, 72, 74; posture toward race or racial groups, 39–43, 46, 50–51, 90, 94; posture toward women and gender issues, 74, 79–88, 96, 102, 105–107, 137–138; 16 Days of Activism, 86–87, 136; social positioning, 81, 84–85, 87, 101, 107–108, 113, 150; theological convictions, 44–45; transformation theological culture, 66, 102, 111, 131, 135, 146. *See also* theological conviction; theological culture; transformation theological culture
Pillay, Sandra, 119
political sociology, 50, 173n9
political transition: and emphasis of religious organizations, 33, 70, 172n7; theological cultures, 50–51, 57
Port Elizabeth, South Africa, 36–37, 90
Presbyterian Church, 169n16
Protestant Christian, 2, 11

racial groups, 47, 50–51; theological convictions and, 14, 20–21, 23, 29, 37–38, 102; theological culture and, 21, 34–35, 40, 61, 73–74, 90
racialized: categories, 65; experience, 29, 35, 37–38, 47; groups, 47, 50–51; violence, 2. *See also* economic marginalization
Rajuili, Moshe, 71
Rakoczy, Sister Susan, 80–81, 87, 179n21
rape: AE's reconciliation theological culture, 80; and enslavement, 6, 96; narratives of forgiveness, 88; organizations research about, 186n12, 187n24; in South Africa, 1–2, 10, 77–79, 96; and war, 6
Rape Crisis Center, 10, 82; Rape Crisis Cape Town Trust, 156
reconciliation. *See* social reconciliation; spiritual reconciliation
reconciliation theological culture: assumptions of inherent gender difference, 3–4, 80, 118, 142, 147; and early democracy, 61; gender justice and, 120; and the Gospel, 88; lack of practical response to GBV, 94, 139, 101–102
relational alienation, 3
religious activism, 7
Richardson, Neville, 42, 66
Ridgeway, Cecilia, 105
Rustenburg, South Africa, 133, 135
Rustenburg Conference, 50
Rustenburg Declaration, 49, 133–134
Rwanda, 87, 180n60

Satan, 118
separate development, 8, 87
Sewell, William, 172n8
sexual violence, 166n18; factsheets, 186n12; and oppression, 83; silence and, 81; testimonies to the TRC, 10
Smerdon, Greg, 89
Smith, Charlene, 77, 179n15
Smyth, John, 32
social reconciliation, 21, 30, 37, 60–61, 88, 90, 92
Soh Chye Ann, 62
solidarity: with black suffering, 21, 46, 54; contradictions about, 58–59; critical, 51, 56, 58–59, 70, 143, 151; with the liberation movement, 19, 25, 33–34, 53; with the marginalized, 21–24, 28, 32, 34, 51, 56; with the oppressed, 3, 23–29, 46, 51, 57, 95; with the poor, 25, 27, 39, 43; SACC, 51, 56, 58–59, 70, 143, 151; with the state, 57–59, 70, 74, 143, 151; transformation theological culture, 85; and white people, 28–29, 34, 36–39, 46; with women, 79, 84–85, 87, 101, 130, 135
South African Christian Leadership Assembly (SACLA), 31, 63, 115–116, 141
South African Council of Churches (SACC): Annual General Meeting of Women's Ministries, 123; Central Committee, 13, 94, 130; Committee of Justice and Reconciliation, 125; "critical solidarity," 51, 56, 58–59, 70, 143, 151; Development Ministries program, 53, 144, 174n28; discourse about women, 126–127; Executive Committee, 13, 22, 26; Human Rights program, 97; implications for GBV, 182n5; Inter-Church Aid Division, 23; *The Kairos Document*, 104; Khotso House, 23; posture toward race or racial groups, 21, 23, 29, 50; posture toward women and gender issues, 121, 123–126, 128, 131, 143, 145; social positioning, 97, 151; theological convictions, 74, 105; theological culture, 99–100, 102, 121, 124, 130–131. *See also* liberation theological culture; theological conviction; theological culture
South African Council of Churches (SACC) National Conference: Frank Chikane, 57–58; national organization, 13; Beyers Naudé, 25; themes, 1, 52, 105, 144, 181n3; topics about women and social movements, 104–105, 121–122, 128, 145; Desmond Tutu, 23
South African Human Rights Commission, 143
South African Missiological Society, 84
Southern African Catholic Bishops' Conference, 45, 169n14
Southern Baptist Convention, 153, 190n9
spiritual healing, 90–91, 116
spiritual reconciliation: bitterness and, 65; and GBV, 101, 142; the Jesus Way, 113; and racial reconciliation, 35, 37; and sin, 32; and social reconciliation, 21, 30, 37, 60–61, 88, 90, 92; theological convictions and, 80
Spong, Bernard, 55

theological conviction: AE and the Gospel, 50, 63; PACSA and the Gospel, 46, 50–51, 66, 69–70, 73, 86; and racial groups, 14, 20–21, 23, 29, 37–38, 102; SACC and the Gospel, 50, 63, 74, 105; and spiritual reconciliation, 80 theological culture: AE and God's way, 33–34, 51, 63, 74, 114; AE and Jesus Way, 61–62, 66, 74, 120, 151; AE and the Gospel, 59, 63–66, 80, 88, 90, 116–119; HIV/AIDS, 60, 70; PACSA, 39–40, 151; path dependency, 51, 53, 68, 73; political transition, 50–51, 57; and racial groups, 21, 34–35, 40, 61, 73–74, 90; and rape, 80; SACC and dignity, 99–100, 102, 121, 124, 130–131

Thipanyane, Abiel, 89

transformation theological culture: complicity of the privileged, 51, 68, 71, 107, 113; and GBV, 79, 84, 138, 150, 159; and gender, 107–108; PACSA, 66–68, 102, 111, 131, 135, 146; solidarity with the suffering, 85

Treurnicht, Andries, 8–9, 176n79

Trisk, Janet, 111

Truth and Reconciliation Commission (TRC), 1, 10, 50, 54–56, 168n62

Tsele, Molefe, 58–59

Turner, Shirley, 125, 143, 184n83

Tutu, Desmond: activism against apartheid, 1, 20, 22, 25, 27, 173n14; black consciousness, 20, 28–29; as a church leader, 49, 57; and religious conversion, 23–24; role with TRC, 168n62; speeches, 127, 174n37

ubuntu, 54–55, 64, 99, 174n37

Ujaama, 186n19

Umtata, South Africa, 114, 116

United Democratic Front, 22, 67, 169n15, 171n94

University of KwaZulu Natal, 12, 72

University of the Western Cape, 118

University of the Witwatersrand, 12, 156

unmarked categories, 4

Walshe, Peter, 167n55

Wartenberg-Potter, Reverend Barbel, 112–113

Weaver Swartz, Lisa, 167n30

Weber, Max, 7, 158, 166n24, 168n7, 168n9

Weldon, S. Laurel, 166n17, 167n56

white people: and complicity, 3, 21, 42–49, 72, 152; forgiveness of, 64–65, 74, 88; and ignorance, 36, 47, 63; racial consciousness, 28; racial formation, 168n10; racialization, 47; relinquishing privilege, 43; and solidarity, 28–29, 34, 36–39, 46

white privilege, 5; and male, 108, 113; relinquishing of, 21, 43, 45, 72, 87, 112

Wilde, Melissa, 6–7, 168n8, 186n11

Wittenberg, Gunther, 45, 109–110

Women's Dialogue, 121–122, 128, 189n62

Women's Ecumenical Conference, 143

Women's Ministries, 129, 144–145; Annual General Meeting of, 123

A Women's Service, 143

World Council of Churches (WCC), 12, 54, 94

Xingwana, Lulama, 129, 144–145, 159, 189n67

Zuma, Jacob, 77

ABOUT THE AUTHOR

MEREDITH WHITNAH is a sociologist who examines the intersections of gender, race, and religion in organizations. Drawing on extensive historical and qualitative analyses, her work spans from evangelical organizations in the United States to anti-apartheid groups in South Africa.